THE DEVELOPER'S
HANDBOOK TO

Interactive

MULTIMEDIA

THE DEVELOPER'S HANDBOOK TO

Interactive

MULTIMEDIA

A Practical Guide for Educational Applications

Rob Phillips

**KOGAN
PAGE**

London • Stirling (USA)

First published in 1997

Kogan Page Limited
120 Pentonville Road
London N1 9JN
and
22883 Quicksilver Drive
Stirling, VA 20166, USA

British Library Cataloguing in Publication Data

A CIP record for this book is available from the British Library.

ISBN 0 7494 2121 5

Typeset by Kogan Page Ltd

Contents

Foreword

Interactive multimedia (IMM) is a new technology with the potential to change the way we learn, the way we acquire information, and the way we entertain ourselves. This new technology brings together a range of fields and requires the skills of professionals from those fields. However, to create a satisfactory interactive multimedia product, on time and on budget, requires that these skills be blended and adapted to suit the new medium. Producing interactive multimedia is a very creative endeavour, but in order to be successful, it must be well managed. For a project to be well managed, effective modes of communication must be established between team members from such diverse backgrounds as graphic design and computer programming.

This handbook offers practical advice on these issues and more. It is based on mistakes made and lessons learned in developing a number of projects over a number of years. It discusses the project management, team-building and communications issues described above. However, it also gives practical advice on all stages of project design, from the initial feasibility study, through design and development, to evaluation and implementation.

The points made and lessons learned are illustrated by case studies from projects worked on by the authors. While the case studies are of educational applications, the issues discussed are applicable to all areas of interactive multimedia and further enhance the practical nature of this book. In fact, this handbook was written with the specific aim of being valuable to the broader IMM development community, as well as its obvious market in teaching and learning innovations in academia.

It is also important that this book is as independent of IMM authoring software as possible. Discussion of some current packages is included, but it is kept to a minimum, because of the speed at which individual packages become obsolete. Instead, this handbook focuses on general issues of design and production, which are applicable no matter which software is used in the development.

Structure of the book

There are two parts to this handbook (Chapters 1 to 7 and 8 to 11). In the first part, Chapter 1 is an introduction, while some pedagogical issues essential to educational IMM are discussed in Chapter 2. Chapter 3 describes the development process we advocate, with subsequent chapters discussing specific parts of the process. Chapter 4 is concerned with the user interface, ie the navigation and graphic design. Chapter 5 considers development issues, such as resources and programming techniques. Chapter 6 discusses all aspects of evaluation, and Chapter 7 addresses implementation and maintenance, ie how to make a working program available to users.

The second part consists of a series of case studies of projects worked on by the authors. Each case study describes a complete project, offering an analysis of the perceived weaknesses and strengths from the viewpoint of several of the development team members. More importantly, however, components of the case studies illustrate points made throughout the first part, providing practical examples for the theoretical content.

While most of this document is written by staff from the Computing Centre at Curtin University of Technology in Perth, Western Australia, some parts of the case studies have been written by teaching academics from the various schools who have been involved in particular projects. The projects come from collaboration with teaching schools in many areas of the University.

How to read this handbook

A range of different readers may gain from this handbook, and not all readers will wish to proceed sequentially. The following tips may help you in deciding how to use the text.

- If it is difficult to see the relevance of the theoretical sections early in the work then first read the case studies in Chapters 8 to 11.
- If you are seeking funding to develop your own project, then you should certainly read Chapters 1, 3 and 8 to 11.
- If you are part of an IMM development team, then Chapters 3 to 7 are most relevant, although the case studies could also be of assistance.
- If you are an undergraduate or postgraduate student of interactive multimedia, then you should at least work through Chapters 1–7.

Projects mentioned

Following is a summary of the projects referred to in this handbook. The first four projects are the case studies discussed in Chapters 8 to 11. Unless otherwise specified, all projects were developed using *Allegiant SuperCard* ™ on an Apple Macintosh computer.

In the text, case study examples are boxed to distinguish them from the normal text.

Microbiology case studies
A set of eight tutorials on second-year Microbiology were produced in HyperCard. The keystone of this work is the use of interactive, multiple-choice question case studies to develop problem-solving skills, as described in Chapter 8.

Dosage calculations
This project was developed to assist Nursing students in the calculation of drug dosages, a skill difficult to individualize using conventional teaching techniques. As described in Chapter 9, the use of IMM has added to the realism of teaching this content without compromising the mastery performance of the students.

Mitochondria
This project focuses on the metabolism of energy in the cell for first year Nursing and Human Biology students. The topic is difficult to visualize using traditional methods, but appears to be well suited to IMM (see Chapter 10).

Carbohydrates
A novel user interface was used in this interactive tutorial on the process of carbohydrate metabolism in the body. This project is described in more detail in Chapter 11.

SarcoMotion
This project, currently being designed, is based on an animation of the process of muscle contraction, which is used as a lecture aid. The animation has now become the basis of an associated self-paced tutorial. This project is used to provide examples of the IMM design process.

SuperPhysics
Curtin has eight different first-year Physics courses, which are mainly service units for other faculties. Many cover basically the same material, with

examples specific to the particular faculty. Originally, this project attempted to reduce the number of courses, by providing IMM resources tailored for each unit. It has now been rationalized to the 'Foundations of Physics', covering background physics material usually found in the first chapter of most physics textbooks.

Osmosis
This project simulates an expensive and potentially hazardous experiment in Human Biology. Students tended not to consider the concepts behind the experiment, because they were too busy coping with the equipment.

Understanding technical drawings
This project aims to assist the user to read and understand technical drawings and to mentally convert two dimensions to three. It utilizes some novel digital video techniques to allow the user to rotate three-dimensional virtual objects as if on the palm of the user's hand.

Japanese Videodisc
The Computing Centre was contracted by the Western Australian Distance Education Consortium to produce a large videodisc-based CBL program to teach Japanese. When complete, it will form an entire year's study.

Hitchhiker's guide to the Australian taxation system
This was a relatively small project providing remedial instruction about the Australian Taxation System for non-Australian students. It was developed with Asymetrix Toolbook under Windows.

Recreation Perth
This is an IMM database of recreational activities around Perth which has been developed for, and partly by, Occupational Therapy students.

Physiotherapy
A dedicated staff member has converted an entire course in Anatomy into HyperCard stacks. This has evolved into a comprehensive computer-managed learning environment.

Information systems
This project consists of four interactive *Asymetrix Toolbook* tutorials for a new unit of 1000 students on the foundations of Information Systems.

The Computing Centre at Curtin University

The Computing Centre at Curtin University has been involved in the use of computers in education since 1980, and in 1986 developed the Software and Courseware Online Reviews database of educational software (Winship, 1986).

The Computing Centre was well placed when the onset of IMM technology offered new possibilities for the use of computers in education. Curtin had a solid knowledge base and, with the adoption of a five-year Information Technology (IT) Strategic Plan, extra resources were available to employ academic and support staff with an interest in IMM. At the beginning of 1992, the first of a series of grants enabled us to commence serious development. At the time of writing, the Computing Centre has been involved with over twenty computer-based learning projects involving IMM and other technologies.

Because of the historical interest in computer-based learning by the Computing Centre, the institutional structure for development of IMM is different at Curtin from that at many other universities, some of which have set up separate IMM development units, sometimes in association with distance learning centres or media centres. This institutional structure has facilitated the success of the projects described here.

Acknowledgements

Many people have had a hand in the writing and production of this book. Nick Jenkins had a major input in all respects, and I thank him for all his contributions and for the advice he gave when I ran into difficulties.

The other major authors of chapters are to be commended for their efforts: Des Thornton, Angela DiGiorgio, Martin Hill, Peta Edwards, Karen Glaister and Linda Slack-Smith. Part of the graphic design section was based on material from Susan Perry. Minor authors, Onno Benschop and Michelle Robert-Libia are also thanked for their contributions. Rosemary Barrett and Angela DiGiorgio provided the independent constructive criticism of graphic design in Chapter 4.

Special acknowledgement needs to be given to the following people for their critical reading and comments on draft versions: Ian Moncrieff, Linda Slack-Smith, Dr Dorit Maor, Vikki Pedalina, Leonie Ramondt, Rod Kevill, Des Thornton and Dr Robin Watts.

However, four people did most of the work of proofreading this manuscript. Nick Jenkins reviewed most versions of this manuscript over its 18-month gestation period. Jo Winship did a wonderful job of consistency proofing, identifying every extra space, as well as problems with section and figure numbers. I especially want to thank Dr Bob Loss for his extremely thorough proofreading of the manuscript on two occasions. With so many authors using different linguistic styles, it is very difficult to edit material into a consistent form, and Bob's contributions were invaluable in this regard.

I am also indebted to Dr Clark Quinn, Russell Pennell and Kerry Moore for their thorough vetting of the penultimate draft and for their suggestions for improvement.

Rob Phillips

Chapter 1

Interactive Multimedia Development

Rob Phillips and Nick Jenkins

1.1 Introduction

The term 'interactive multimedia' (IMM) is currently enjoying enormous popularity, not only in the computing and educational communities, but also among the general public. Despite the hyperbole in the marketplace, there seems to be little doubt that IMM technology will combine with the burgeoning electronic networks (the so-called information superhighway, or Infobahn) to deeply affect the way that humans learn, work, communicate and even relax into the next century.

This book is a guide for people who want to develop IMM computer programs. While we have a particular interest in the use of IMM in education, many of the considerations discussed here are valid in other applications. Our aim is to give a practical description of the procedures which we have developed since 1992, illustrated by many examples from projects with which we have been involved. We also seek to give beginning developers an overview of what is possible with this technology. Our intended audience includes both:

- university academics who want an appreciation of the issues involved in developing IMM for computer-based learning, and
- IMM developers and students who want guidance on development methodologies for IMM projects.

1.1.1   What interactive multimedia is

The term 'interactive multimedia' is a catch-all phrase to describe the new wave of computer software that primarily deals with the provision of information. The 'multimedia' component is characterized by the presence of text, pictures, sound, animation and video; some or all of which are organized into some coherent program. The 'interactive' component refers to the process of empowering the user to control the environment usually by a computer.

Interactive multimedia is sometimes abbreviated to simply 'multimedia', but this is not strictly accurate – any television advertisement has all the aspects of multimedia, but does not utilize a computer and is not yet interactive.

1.1.2   What interactive multimedia isn't

Hardly a day goes by without some mention of 'multimedia' in the print or broadcast media. Computer retailers proudly extol the virtues of their multimedia computers, and there is a widely-held belief that having a CD-ROM drive means that you have multimedia. It is true that IMM is often delivered on a CD-ROM, but so are reference databases and many other software packages. IMM may just as well be installed on the computer's hard drive, or be delivered via a computer network.

IMM is neither a delivery mechanism nor a hardware platform, but rather it is a technology implemented in a software package.

The popularity of IMM has led to a huge increase in the amount of IMM software on the market. However, the following quote from the *Wall Street Journal* shows that many products do not sell, and it is likely that this is due to the poor quality of the software.

'According to PC Data Inc., the number of CD-ROM titles burgeoned to 2,057 by the end of 1994 up from 197 two years earlier. But much of the multimedia hype has been nothing but hot air, with 20% of titles selling fewer than 11 copies last December. Ninety titles sold only one copy that month.' (*Wall Street Journal* 1 March 1995, A1)

The true measure of IMM software is the quality of the software itself. What is its purpose? How appropriate is the content? How effective is the user interface and the graphic design? Does it perform responsively, and without errors?

1.2   Applications of interactive multimedia

1.2.1   The range of applications

IMM may be used in information kiosks, reference works, games, entertainment and in education, and has potential for many other areas. Some applications may extend across more than one of these categories.

All of these categories are theoretically characterized by a potentially high level of user control, although this may not always be achieved in practice. The development methodology described in this book can be applied in whole or part to all of the categories.

Information kiosks
Information kiosks are stand-alone systems which provide unattended information about a location or attraction. For example, they might be used in a department store as a directory to locate different services, or they might provide information about the attractions of a tourist destination.

Kiosk applications may be attractive to the user, and they are generally less costly than employing personnel for the same purpose. They can provide users with more flexibility in finding out information, with a richer choice of media than notice boards and displays, and they may be useful for shy people.

Reference works
There is a valuable role for IMM in presenting information sources and reference material, such as encyclopaedias. A richer range of media, working on a wider range of senses, can be utilized than in paper-based versions. For example, a bird may be described and shown in flight, and you may be able to hear its call. As in a printed encyclopaedia, there are numerous ways the material can be accessed and cross-referenced. Encyclopaedia-based CD-ROMs are also less expensive to duplicate and distribute than paper-based versions.

However, in this type of multimedia, only information is presented. Understanding relies on the user, who decides which way the information will be utilized.

Games
Although not readily recognized, computer games were probably the first examples of IMM. Certainly they combine most of the elements of multimedia with a high degree of user control. Initially, the quality of the media elements was not high, colours were restricted, animations were jerky and audio frequencies limited. To attain usable speeds, much of the programming was

done in assembly language rather than in higher-level languages, which restricted the authoring process to a small band of highly technical individuals.

It was only after the relatively recent development of higher level authoring tools that the education and training sectors became involved in IMM. The development of educational applications through powerful tools has happened without the involvement of game designers. This is unfortunate, as game designers have much to offer other IMM practitioners in terms of developing simple, engaging interactions between user and system. Game designers specialize in making seductive interfaces and appealing products. The success of their game depends upon customers choosing their product over those of many competitors. Consequently, game designers pay a lot of attention not only to the content but to its presentation, a point which is lost on many multimedia developers. Games which are based on simulations, in particular, demand elegant solutions to complex presentations of information. For example, the *SimCity* series of computer games from Maxis Corporation succeed both as games and as learning environments because of the smoothness of the user interface.

Entertainment

IMM is widespread in leisure activities. Besides games, the terms 'infotainment' and 'edutainment' have been coined to describe the existence of information or educational resources which are also entertaining. Popular examples of these are Microsoft's *Dinosaurs*, and, for younger children, Brøderbund's *Just Grandma and Me* .

While these topics are quite appealing, and show a range of information in an integrated way, there is a danger in these kinds of titles because they may contain inaccurate information and can mix fact and fiction. The *Dinosaurs* package, for instance, sacrifices fact for entertainment by showing video of dinosaurs and playing sounds that dinosaurs are purported to have made.

Education

IMM has the potential to be used extensively throughout society. If used appropriately, it also has the potential to improve the quality of the education process. When designing educational material, the education sector has an ethical responsibility to ensure there is a clear distinction between fact and fiction. At the very least, it must be able to produce educationally sound IMM which can compete for attractiveness with the infotainment distributed by the entertainment industry.

Numerous educational issues need to be faced in this area; these are discussed in more detail in Chapter 2. However, IMM has a number of potentially powerful characteristics which can be used to improve the education process.

1.2.2   The strengths of IMM in education

Mixed media

By definition, multimedia has a mixture of media, including animations and digital video. This offers clear advantages in some teaching situations over mono-media resources, such as whiteboards and audio cassettes. A particular advantage is the possibility of using the most appropriate medium for the required message, eg text for thoughts, graphics for spatial relations and animation for dynamic information.

It should be emphasized that video and television also have mixed media capabilities, but they lack the degree of user control available in IMM.

User control

Most IMM has the ability to allow users to take their own path through the material, and the potential to build up their own knowledge. A student-centred learning approach is becoming increasingly important in the 1990s, because the rate of change in technology means that employees will continually need to reskill themselves, in a situation of lifelong learning (Candy, et al. 1994).

The potential of user control is not realized at present because little is understood about the nature of a user interface which provides the user with control while at the same time encouraging deep learning. The situation is analogous to the early days of the automobile, where there was no consensus about the functions of the pedals. For example, the Model T Ford used two foot pedals to work the transmission – the left pedal changed the two forward speeds and the centre pedal selected reverse (Twite, 1973).

Simulation and visualization

IMM is especially suited to simulation. Many tertiary curriculum areas require understanding of complex, abstract, dynamic and/or microscopic processes. Simulations allow students to visualize the process and construct mental models. Cognitive scientists use the term 'mental models' to describe the understanding of such systems and their use in explanation and prediction – important characteristics of understanding these processes. Complex processes are especially hard to visualize using typical educational technology, such as a whiteboard or an overhead transparency, which is two-dimensional and static.

There is a clear role for IMM to be used as a lecture aid, projecting simulations of the complex concept in a classroom situation. A further advantage to this approach is that these simulations can then be made available for students in a self-paced manner for use as reinforcement tools.

Different learning styles

IMM has the potential to accommodate people with different learning styles. A learning style can be defined as 'the individual's characteristic ways of processing information, feeling, and behaving in learning situations' (Smith, 1983).

Investigating learning styles can be of some value, no matter how the different styles are described, because it is important that we as learners and as teachers are able to extend our range of learning strategies. Adopting different strategies helps students to become more flexible in their mental processing rather than being limited to their so-called style.

Interactive multimedia has the potential to create a multisensory learning environment which supports specific learning styles and, at the same time, encourages students to move out of their particular style as much as possible. However, much more research needs to be done in this area before this potential is realized.

1.2.3   The uses of IMM in education

From the above discussion, it is clear that IMM has potential for use in teaching and learning in several ways, in particular as an instructional aid, in interactive tutorials and in reference works. In many cases, a specific IMM application will contain a number of aspects of each of these. However, beware that IMM is rarely the sole answer to a given educational problem.

Instructional aids

The mixed-media nature of IMM makes it very suitable for displaying complex processes. In a typical classroom situation, the IMM is the display medium, and the lecturer generally guides the instructional sequence.

Interactive tutorials

If designed according to the principles discussed in Chapter 2, IMM can be suitable for self-paced tutorials, particularly when they focus on moderately complex processes, which may be realized in simulations. This computer-based learning (CBL) may be supplemented by print-based materials, or used in a classroom tutorial session. In general, it should only attempt to treat material which cannot be treated more efficiently in other ways.

Reference works

There is scope for IMM to be used purely as a reference source. For example, it might be used to store a series of microscope slides or radiographs. The user can view the resources, but learning is directed by an external source, such as a print-based study guide or a laboratory demonstrator.

1.3   Applications of IMM in education

Given the general considerations discussed in the previous section, it is worth considering in more detail topics that will repay the time and effort of creating an IMM program. Our group has spoken to many academics about potential CBL projects over the last few years. While it is technically possible to implement almost any idea, not all are suitable for IMM, as other media may be more appropriate. There may be other valid reasons for seeking to use IMM: reducing lecture load; delivery to remote students; providing alternatives to lectures. However, the bottom line should be that if the proposed project does not improve student learning then it is a waste of effort.

Any new technology attracts early adopters, who pioneer the use of that technology, and IMM has been no exception. Early adopters break new ground for others to follow. They also make mistakes for others to learn from. This book has arisen from the blood, sweat and tears of a range of early adopters, and it attempts to distil the lessons learnt from these projects.

One of the principal lessons we have learnt is that it is wasteful of resources and educationally ineffective simply to convert existing educational material into an electronic book. It should be realized that it is time-consuming and ultimately expensive to develop IMM. This expense needs to be justified by the perception of a significant gain. The key question to ask yourself of a potential project is, *'Can I do this in another medium?'*

If there are significant reasons why the topic can't be done as well in other media, then it might be worth the effort of creating a CBL program. The following examples identify teaching problems where IMM may be a suitable technology to use:

- Material which is difficult to visualize, such as microscopic processes.
- Material which is three-dimensional, which is difficult to visualize using traditional two-dimensional media such as books and whiteboards.
- Dynamic processes, which require understanding of the relationships between moving objects.
- Material which covers broad contexts, where a number of ideas need to be linked to form an understanding of the whole, not just the parts.
- Simulations of expensive or complex processes, where understanding may be hindered by the mechanical details of performing the process, or where there is no possibility of using the real equipment.

Each of the following examples involves the understanding of concepts, rather than rote learning of facts or sequences of actions.

The Carbohydrates program discussed in Chapter 11 covered the digestion of carbohydrates, from food to its use in the cell. The aim was for the student to appreciate the broad context of this process, while aiding their visualization of microscopic processes.

The case study approach in the Microbiology project (Chapter 8) attempted to give students an application of their knowledge and an appreciation of the effects of their actions. It puts their learning in context.

The Osmosis program simulated an expensive laboratory experiment, which was also hazardous because it used blood. Preliminary analysis had shown that students were failing to understand the concepts involved because they were too involved in the physical manipulations required to perform the experiment. While experimental techniques are an important part of this course, there was no requirement to emphasize these when the Osmosis topic was scheduled, early in first year.

Once you have a suitable idea, there is a substantial challenge to design the program so that it doesn't end up like a book. The discussion in Chapter 2 illustrates how difficult this is. It is appropriate to review a range of other CBL programs over a suitable period, and note what you think are good ideas. Discussions with existing IMM developers are also a useful source of information.

1.3.1 Factors to consider

Review the entire course

Instead of thinking of creating a CBL program for a specific topic, it might be beneficial to critically review your entire unit or course. There are a number of innovative techniques which can be used, and CBL is only one of these. Some examples are: journal writing, guided self-study, the use of presentation tools, and replacing tutorials with a case study approach. By reviewing your unit to use different teaching approaches, you may find that your proposed use of CBL changes, and it can be used where it is best suited.

Linda Slack-Smith from the School of Biomedical Sciences developed the Mitochondria and Carbohydrates programs (Chapters 10 and 11) as part of ongoing development for the Nursing Biochemistry unit.

Previous developments in this introductory biochemistry unit included production of a study guide with the unit divided into modules with clear objectives, some notes and figures and review questions. Further developments included guided self-study modules and computerized multiple-choice assessment during the semester by Computer Managed Learning. Around 30% of lectures have been replaced by guided self-study modules, and tutorials and practicals have been combined as 'interactive sessions'. These developments have been designed to promote active learning and the responsibility of the individual student. The use of guided self-study modules and computerized testing have allowed more flexible time management for both students and the lecturer.

The IMM programs were developed specifically to fill a niche which could not be filled by other approaches.

Peta Edwards from the School of Biomedical Sciences has extensively re-engineered her Microbiology unit for nurses over the last four years. This was mainly due to the high number of external students who needed assistance in this highly visual subject.

First, she developed Australia's first telecourse, putting her lectures on a series of videos which were also broadcast on regional television. Next, she introduced a mainframe-based computer-managed learning system to automate marking of the rote-learning aspect of the course. Third, she moved from a lecture-style tutorial to a case-study, discussion mode of tutorial. Fourth, she developed a series of hypertext, case-study-based tutorials for self-paced learning (Chapter 8). These tutorials were specifically integrated into the structure of the unit rather than being simply 'tacked-on'.

Professor Jack Wilson and colleagues from Rensselaer Polytechnic Institute in the United States (Wilson, 1994) have pioneered the use of 'studio learning' in the sciences and engineering. Studios combine lectures, tutorials and practical classes into a single activity where students work in pairs in a computer-based environment, which has been shown to be more efficient and cost-effective than the traditional environment.

Keep it small and focused

In section 3.3.8, we will show that it will take between 300 and 500 hours of development for each hour of student use of a CBL program. This should be a good incentive to keep a project small, especially for people who haven't developed IMM before.

Each project gets bigger once you start designing. In a lecture, you can limit the scope of information you give, and students requiring more can approach you personally. In CBL you don't know who will be using it in which circumstances, so there is a tendency to add more detail. This is usually justified, but it increases the size of the project. It is therefore important to keep your initial idea tightly focused on the required topic from the very beginning of the project.

The SuperPhysics project commenced with the aim of re-engineering entire first-year physics units. Curtin provides eight first-year units, mainly service units for students who may have minimal physics knowledge. The initial aim was to provide:

(i)   a shell and navigation system into which future physics modules could be incorporated;
(ii) the initial content was to cover the first six hours of lectures for most of the first-year physics units;
(iii) material in support of (ii).

A secondary objective was to reduce the number of lecture streams and reduce the very high student contact hours that each lecturer had.

At the time development stopped, (i) was complete, (ii) was 50% complete and (iii) was 85% complete. The development ceased because Bob Loss and Mario Zadnik from the School of Applied Physics ran out of ideas for suitable and appropriate engagements through which students could interact with the material. Bob says:

'Our mistake was in not designing the engagements first. We spent 600 person hours on planning before we started, but we only planned parts (i) and (iii). The hard part for the physics content was the engagements... The engagements should have come first. Superphysics has spawned several useful things so all is not lost. The reason it is not finished is because we didn't plan it down to the individual screen engagement in the first place.'

Appeal

Simply presenting information in a clear and logical way is not enough. In order for a project to be a success you must present the information in an attractive way. Like a successful advertisement, the project should pique your user's curiosity and lure them into the content. Even the dullest information can be rejuvenated by *judicious* use of examples, interactivity and graphic design. Elements of graphic design are covered in Chapter 4.

As already mentioned, computer game designers have a lot to teach multimedia developers about making attractive software. Games epitomize the seductive computer interface, and people are drawn in by their attractiveness. Most computer games provide an aspect of challenge to the user. When designing CBL, you should consider ways of making the material challenging in a meaningful way.

The Physiotherapy project on human anatomy used a consistent stratagem when the student wanted to go on to the next screen: before progressing, the student was asked to identify a piece of anatomy which had been described on one of the previous screens.

Flexibility and portability

Most computer programs are written to solve a particular problem on a particular machine. Thus people are continuously 'reinventing the wheel' – writing a program which has already been written. Multimedia projects are no different. If a physics lecturer produces a project on fluid dynamics, it may be possible that an engineer could adapt the same project for their teaching. Even a human biology lecturer might be able to use parts of the same project to illustrate blood flow in the human body.

Currently, however, it is often not practical to 'mix and match' parts of courseware, because of the lack of standards and multitude of authoring environments. It is none the less useful to consider a wider audience while developing your own product. While it is unlikely that many educational developments will be profitable, they may have other uses.

Additional flexibility usually involves a trade-off. If you design a project to have a wide audience, it might not be quite as useful for your own particular use.

Modularity

Splitting a program into a set of independent parts can ease the development task greatly. Having a *modular* project means that once you have finished one part of the project you may not need to go back to it, but can concentrate on the other sections. Modularity also means that if you have a multimedia resource, such as a sound file, which is used in a number of different places, it can be stored centrally. Thus, when you update the project you only need update the central resource, and don't need to update all the 'instances' of the resource. This aspect will be discussed in more detail in Chapter 5.

Things to avoid

Diana Laurillard (1993, p.204) believes that the student should focus on the content of learning, not on how to operate the program. She identifies a series of computer activities which 'give birth to loathing' of an IMM program:

- Looking for the ON button.
- Wondering why nothing is happening.
- Discovering you are unable to get back to where you were.
- Being told you're wrong when you know you're right.
- Wondering how long this is going on for.
- Trying to guess the word the program is waiting for.
- Coming upon the same feeble joke for the fifteenth time.
- Trying to work out how to get to the point you want.

Another common example is having to listen to the full piece of introductory music every time you get to the main menu.

   Some of these problems are easy to avoid, but others can only be circumvented by thorough design and comprehensive evaluation of the project. The most important aspect of the design is its educational nature. That is, will students actually learn more effectively from the IMM material than from traditional material?

Chapter 2

Educational Considerations

Rob Phillips

2.1 History

Computers were used in education long before the emergence of IMM technology. Computers have been used for programmed instruction and computer-based training. They have been commonly used as a vehicle for assessment, either in a drill-and-practice mechanism, or for automatic test marking in a computer-managed learning environment. These applications were typically text-based, but later applications made some use of graphics.

Application packages, such as wordprocessors, spreadsheets and databases, have long been used as tools assist in learning tasks. Computers have also been used in education in a purely computational sense, calculating mathematical models and displaying numerical results. Teachers have often used the results of such computation to assist students to obtain a more concrete understanding of abstract concepts.

Curtin University (Winship, 1994) realizes large teaching efficiency gains by testing some 12,000 students annually using the LMS computer-managed learning (CML) system running on VAX mainframes. Queensland University of Technology (Ellis, 1994) annually services 100,000 student hours of drill-and-practice tutorials, where the computer is used as an agent for asking questions of the student.

Computers have been extensively used for training, especially in the corporate and military sector where identical information is required to be learnt by rote by a large number of staff, possibly at different locations. This sort of training can be costly if done in a classroom environment where each new staff intake needs a new training session. However, the computer can be used cost-effectively to automate this process. This application of computers is often referred to as computer-based training (CBT).

2.2   Theories of education

2.2.1   Objectivism and instructional design[1]

When Computer-based Training first became possible, the currently popular educational theory was *objectivism*. In this theory (Marra and Jonassen, 1993), knowledge is seen as existing independently of any human experience. That is, there is an objective reality external to the learner, which has a structure that can be modelled for the learner. Reeves (1992a) states that the epistemology underlying objectivism is founded on the following premises:

- knowledge exists separate from knowing
- reality exists regardless of the existence of sentient beings
- humans acquire knowledge in an objective manner through the senses
- learning consists of acquiring truth
- learning can be measured precisely with tests.

An objectivist pedagogy assumes that knowledge is constructed in a logical way based on small components, or *learning objectives*. Objectivism assumes that the learner is an empty vessel, which can be filled with knowledge.

A methodology, called *instructional systems design* (ISD), or simply *instructional design* (ID) developed around objectivist theory, based initially on the work of Gagné (1977). ID provides many techniques for analysing curriculum material. It places strict emphasis on analysing the learning task, defining performance objectives, developing a hierarchy for instruction, and student assessment. ID provides one of the primary standards used for training in industry, and for technical and further education. It has also been used extensively in print-based distance education material as well as for CBT, as discussed in the previous section.

The ID analysis results in a very logical, linear structure of information, which the student receives in the way the teacher decides it has to be.

When applied to computer-based learning a number of problems arise. A basic tenet of objectivism and ID is the dominance of the instructor through the learning objectives. When applied to the computer, this implies that the computer takes the role of the instructor. By its very nature, this notion minimizes learner control, and it will be shown subsequently that a balance between computer and learner control is very important in the use of IMM in education.

A further implication of the objectivist view that the computer becomes the instructor is that the computer can replace the teacher. This view is attractive to administrators seeking to process more and more students for less money. However, it is argued in this book that while computers can be used to augment and improve some aspects of a course, teachers will continue to be more effective in other aspects. The key point is to use each approach where it is most appropriate.

Despite these arguments, text-based objectivist CBT may be an appropriate technology to use in training a large number of people to remember a set of predefined procedures.

2.2.2   Training and interactive multimedia

The onset of IMM technology enabled other media elements (eg sound and moving images) to be added to CBT. This made CBT richer, but it still retained its basic restriction of presenting information only in the order specified by the designer.

It is interesting to note that the other categories in which IMM can be used (kiosks, reference, games, entertainment) all feature high levels of user control. CBT developed according to the ID model specifically takes many aspects of learner control away from the user.

A strength of objectivism is its ability to address novice learning and skill development situations. However, many contend that objectivism is not a suitable approach to use for general education. Critics of objectivism claim that there is little scope for dealing with individual learner differences (Marra and Jonassen, 1993). Marra and Jonassen also differ with 'the objectivist's long-standing presumption that instruction can externally control what individuals learn'. Laurillard (1993) identifies a further problem with this instructional design approach in that 'the analysis into components of the teaching-learning process is not followed by any synthesis'.

Increasingly, educators want students not only to develop knowledge and skills but also to know how to learn and how to think. In this age of rapid change, students also need to prepare themselves for lifelong learning (Candy et al., 1994). The constructivist approach attempts to resolve these issues.

2.2.3   Constructivism

The *constructivist* epistemology (Marra and Jonassen, 1993) is referred to frequently in the current literature. Constructivism claims that reality is more in the mind of the knower, and the knower constructs or interprets a reality from his or her perceptions. In this view, the student constructs his or her own knowledge from the environment they are in. The task of the teacher is to provide material, explain, support and facilitate, but to let the student synthesize as much of their own knowledge as possible.

Reeves (1992a) summarizes the constructivist epistemology as follows:

- knowledge does not exist outside the bodies and minds of human beings
- although reality exists independently, what we know of it is individually constructed
- humans construct knowledge subjectively based on prior experience and metacognitive processing or reflection
- learning consists of acquiring viable assertions or strategies that meet one's objectives
- at best, learning can be estimated through observations and dialogue.

IMM software designed from a constructivist viewpoint can take advantage of all aspects of IMM. Material is designed so the student can build their own knowledge instead of the instructor dictating it.

A constructivist approach emphasizes student learning and doing. It can be implemented in any of a number of ways using IMM to assist students in gaining higher level thinking skills.

One possibility is to design an n-dimensional network of information where the student can navigate almost at will, instead of a quasi-linear flow through the program. This is sometimes called hypermedia (Cotton and Oliver, 1993). It is important that the design of the hypermedia material gives the student guidance on where to go and reference points to know where they are. Otherwise, there is the danger that the student can become 'lost in hyperspace' (Smith and Hahn, 1989) and be unable to form any cognitive structure of the information through which they are navigating. Some other approaches are discussed in Chapter 4.

The guidance does not need to come from the system, however. Much of current theory emphasizes the importance of the role of communication between instructor and learners and between learners themselves. While the communication does not have to be mediated in the IMM environment, it is increasingly available as a component that can be supported electronically. Either way, the overall setting within which the IMM exists needs to be considered, and there must be recognition that learning does not happen just by browsing through hypermedia references.

2.2.4 The continuum between objectivism and constructivism

Any educational theory is, in its essence, a mental construct which describes some aspects of a real situation. There is, in reality, no absolute instance of either theory. In terms of the two theories discussed here, there is a continuum between objectivism and constructivism.

In an IMM program based on the constructivist philosophy, there may be occasions where explicit instruction is needed (an objectivist approach). In a program based on objectivism, on the other hand, there may be instances where the user has a greater degree of control, in interacting with an animation, for example. We have already used the term 'CBT' to refer to a computer program largely based on an objectivist approach. We will use the term 'computer-based learning' (CBL) to describe IMM computer programs which explicitly set out to improve student learning through constructivism.

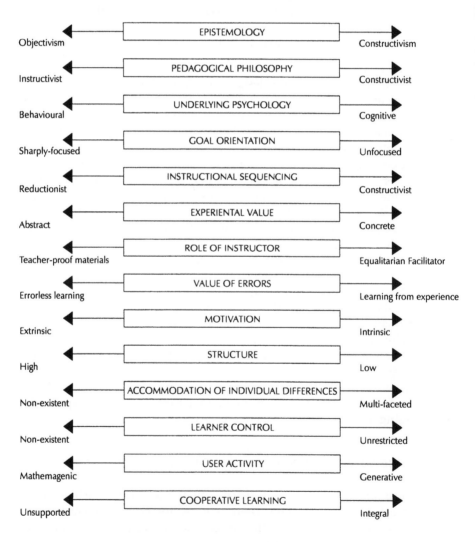

Figure 2.1   *Reeves' dimensions of interactive learning systems*

Reeves has attempted to quantify some of these ideas in his work on the effective dimensions of interactive learning systems (Reeves, 1992a). Essentially, he has identified a series of 14 pedagogical dimensions by which educational interactive multimedia programs may be analysed. Each dimension represents a different aspect of the objectivist/constructivist dichotomy. The 14 factors are shown in Figure 2.1, with the constructivist approach shown on the right hand side. The dimensions start at the philosophical or epistemological level, continuing into a more practical level, such as the ways in which users interact with a program.

The Reeves' dimensions may be helpful in analysing the educational 'style' of an existing package and for reflection about the design of a particular project.

2.3   Essential aspects of the teaching–learning process

It is informative to examine the ideal teaching–learning process, as proposed by Diana Laurillard, based on an analysis of different educational media (Laurillard, 1994, p.103). She argues that there are four main aspects of the teaching–learning process, with individual characteristics as shown in Table 2.1. The processes of interaction between these four characteristics is shown in Figure 2.2.

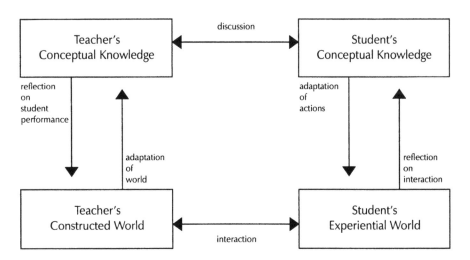

Figure 2.2   *Essential aspects of the ideal teaching–learning process (Laurillard, 1994)*

Table 2.1 *Characteristics of the ideal teaching–learning process (Laurillard, 1994)*

DISCUSSION
       between the teacher
       and learner at the
       level of descriptions
	• Teacher describes conception
	• Student describes conception
	• Teacher redescribes conception
	  in light of the student's
	  conception or action
	• Student redescribes conception
	  in light of teacher's redescription

INTERACTION
       between the learner
       and some aspect of
       the world defined by
       the teacher
	• Teacher sets task goal
	• Student acts to achieve task goal
	• Teacher gives feedback on action
	• Student modifies actions in light
	  of feedback

ADAPTATION
       of the world by the
       teacher and action by
       the learner
	• Teacher adapts task goal in light
	  of student's description or action
	• Student adapts action in light of
	  teacher's description

REFLECTION
       on the learner's
       performance by both
       teacher and learner
	• Teacher reflects on action to
	  modify description
	• Student reflects on interaction
	  to modify description

In a conference paper, Laurillard (1994) considers how different educational media and styles can be described in these terms.

Print material represents a one-way flow of knowledge from the teacher's conceptual knowledge to the student's conceptual knowledge (Figure 2.3a), which is only one aspect of *discussion*. A lecture or tutorial may be seen the same way, but there is a possibility of meaningful discussion between teacher and learner (Figure 2.3b), because students can query misconceptions and obtain feedback. IMM can easily support the one-way flow of information, but the discussion aspect is difficult to achieve. In practice, it is more likely that the two-way discussion will be achieved in a small class.

Figure 2.3a   *Representation of a textbook in Laurillard's model*

Figure 2.3b   *Representation of a lecture or tutorial in Laurillard's model*

A vital part of the learning process is *interaction* between the learner and the world. This gives a context to the knowledge, without which it remains abstract and lacking in meaningful interpretation. In an educational setting, the learner interacts with a teacher-constructed part of the world, which may be a field trip or a classroom experiment. A laboratory practical session assumes that the student already possesses conceptual knowledge, and experiential knowledge is obtained by interaction with the apparatus (the teacher-constructed world), as in Figure 2.4. IMM offers possibilities for interaction equivalent to, and in some cases more effective than, that possible in real life.

Figure 2.4   *Representation of a laboratory experiment in Laurillard's model*

The other two processes in Figure 2.2 are *adaptation* and *reflection*, which form links between discussion and interaction. The teacher evaluates the learner's performance (reflection) and adapts the material to improve understanding. The student uses the concepts provided by the teacher to make sense of their experience, and the experiential knowledge to make sense of the teacher's concepts. This reflection may lead to adaptation of mental constructs through further discussion with the teacher. CBL programs need to accommodate reflection and adaptation by the learner.

2.3.1   Weaknesses of IMM CBL

Given this theoretical framework, how well does educational IMM fare? While there are undoubtedly exceptions, the overwhelming majority of the hundred or so packages we have seen are very book-like, and can be described by Figure 2.3a. This may reflect the immaturity of the IMM market.

The normal, didactic style of lecturing attempts to transmit the lecturer's knowledge to the student. There is a natural tendency to take this transmissionist approach and try to implement it on the computer. After all, most other forms of imparting information (lectures, books, videos) follow this form. It is natural for the content expert to structure information in a linear form that is logical to them, and *impose* their structure of knowledge on the student. It is also natural for them to expect students to learn the information in that form, while giving the learner no *control*, because this is the traditional method of teaching. However, this mode of delivery is inconsistent with the tenets of constructivism, and does not address the other three aspects of the teaching–learning process identified by Laurillard.

Sequentially structured programs tend to have series of screens which contain text and images (sometimes sounds and animations), and the student is expected to read the screen, *observe* what happens, and go to the next screen by clicking on a button. There is very little learner-engagement, and students tend to click to the next screen before reading all the text on the current screen. Interactivity tends to be sprinkled on as an afterthought, rather than being an integral part of the design. That is, interaction is used as an attention-grabbing device, rather than with an educational purpose in mind.

The major drawback of IMM designed in this traditional way, is that a book or a lecture is probably more effective and certainly less expensive. For example, Nott (1995), in a report on the implementation of a large computer-based initiative in chemistry at the University of Melbourne, has estimated that the cost per student hour of a multimedia classroom is $Aus3.00, equivalent to that of a small group tutorial of 20. Traditional lectures to a group of 300, on the other hand, cost only $Aus0.50 per student hour.

A book is better than non-interactive linear IMM

Students understand the metaphor of a book. If the presentation of material raises a question in the mind of the reader, it is easy for them to leaf to another section to resolve the question. There are all sorts of visual cues (eg shapes of words on a page, headings), as well as formal mechanisms (such as the contents list and index) to allow the reader to easily find another piece of information. Some of these functions can be programmed into IMM, but they are not as intuitive or portable as a book.

A lecturer is better than non-interactive linear IMM

Students are familiar with lectures. If a student does not understand a topic, they can ask a question. The lecturer may also sense from the class when material has not been understood. The lecturer can adapt his or her response based on their experience and the needs expressed by the students. The lecturer can stimulate *discussion* and provide appropriate feedback, as well as some degree of *adaptation* and *reflection*, and can stimulate these reactions in students. These human responses can make even a mediocre lecturer more effective than a linear IMM program, if you only want to transmit information.

2.3.2   Strengths of IMM CBL

If IMM is not suited to transmission of information, which is better handled by books and lectures, then the question is raised, 'What is interactive multimedia good for?' Section 1.3 identified some appropriate uses of CBL:

- Material which is hard to visualize, such as microscopic processes.
- Material which is three-dimensional, which can't easily be conveyed with traditional two-dimensional media such as books and whiteboards.
- Dynamic processes, where it is important to understand the relationships of moving objects.
- Material which has a broad context, where a number of ideas need to be linked to form an understanding of the whole, not just the parts.
- Simulations of expensive, dangerous or complex processes, where understanding may be hindered by the mechanical details of performing the process, or where there is no possibility of using the real equipment.

Broadly, these are applications where either the content is hard to visualize, or where concepts need to be linked. If it does not fit one of these categories, then the subject matter can probably be better treated with some other instructional medium.

It is informative to analyse the above criteria in the light of Laurillard's ideas, shown in Figure 2.2 and Table 2.1.

Discussion between teacher and student

It should be clear from the above that it is relatively easy to create CBL which contains narrative information – too much of it in many cases. However, it is difficult to initiate a *two-way* discussion between student and teacher (or the computer acting as a teacher) in the absence of advances in artificial intelligence.

Nevertheless, the student should be able to make their own notes about the content of the program, and make these available to other students or to the teacher.

It is also important to recognize that not all aspects of the ideal teaching–learning process need to be implemented on the computer for effective learning to take place. There is a clear role in many cases for the computer-based materials to be used in conjunction with other modes of instruction, in an integrated educational process. It is perfectly appropriate, for example, for students to work with the computer program, and then to discuss their understanding with the teacher or with other students, particularly in front of the computer.

Reflection and adaptation by the teacher

The teacher-constructed world should be adaptable based on student feedback and performance and the teacher's own reflection on that. The left-hand side of Figure 2.2 can be interpreted as evaluation and modification of the program in the IMM sense. This aspect of IMM development has been ignored or given lip-service in most cases, but is an extremely important factor in producing educationally effective material. However, effective evaluation strategies, to be discussed in Chapter 6, are still being developed for IMM. It is also harder to subsequently modify IMM, because of the cost. This contrasts with the traditional teaching process, where it is relatively easy and natural to annually review lecture notes based on the teacher's perceptions of how the course went last year, and based on new advances in the field of study.

Laurillard's contention throughout her book (Laurillard, 1993) is that any teaching or learning strategy has to be firmly based on evaluation of its value to the *student*.

Interaction

It seems clear that the computer can be used in simulation to enable the student to visualize processes which are difficult to envisage, ie immerse the student in a teacher-constructed world. IMM is well suited to treating complex processes and structures, such as hydraulic design, carbohydrate metabolism, and any multidimensional process. It can also be used for visualizing microscopic processes, such as chemical reaction mechanisms, or processes which occur in a cell. It is also suited to dynamic processes, such as muscle contraction and wave motion.

Compared to the transmissionist approach (Figure 2.3a), it can be difficult to construct computer programs which encourage interaction, as in Figure 2.4, where the student has a large degree of control over the environment. However, such an exploratory environment is of little use if the student cannot view the interaction in a conceptual and contextual framework. Meaningful and effective engagements of the student with the educational content are much more difficult to achieve.

Reflection and adaptation by the student

A purely interactive environment needs to be complemented by opportunities for the student to reflect on their problems and discoveries and adapt their mental model accordingly, which we assume leads to learning. There is also some need for a range of narrative information with which to assist students in building their own concepts, as shown in Figure 2.5.

Laurillard characterizes this situation as 'discovery learning'. Discovery learning implies that the student has some skills as a researcher, and is able to make appropriate mental connections. However, while good students may have the skills to do this, weaker students may not. Laurillard (1994, p.23) makes the following point about discovery learning:

> 'The paradox of interactive media is that while in a user control medium the user expects to have and has to be given control, a learner is not in a position to know enough to be left in full control.'

In other words, the discovery learning environment needs to be supplemented by additional support to provide the feedback which may be needed. With the addition of a support environment and mechanisms for students to initiate discussion, the CBL becomes a Guided Discovery Learning environment, which encompasses the aspects of the teaching-learning process shown in Figure 2.2. Laurillard calls this a 'multimedia tutorial simulation'.

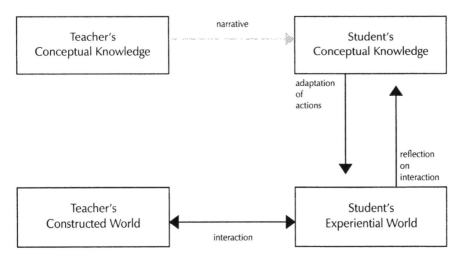

Figure 2.5   *Discovery learning in Laurillard's model*

2.3.3 Guided discovery learning

Laurillard (1993, pp.203–5) has identified a number of control features which should be available in the interface to support the four learning activities (Tables 2.2 and 2.3). Most of the student functions are not particularly difficult to program, but they may take up quite a lot of room on the screen and clutter the user interface. Many of the teacher functions, on the other hand, require a considerable amount of artificial intelligence to implement. In particular, the program needs to interpret student feedback and adapt its own actions based on this interpretation. This is very difficult to achieve at present on standard desktop computers. While Laurillard's recommendations should be considered in the educational design of a project, it may be better if they are not all implemented in software. Instead they could be achieved by other classroom activities, such as discussion with tutors or classmates.

In summary, considerable functionality can be added to the interface of a CBL program to assist the achievement of learning through a guided discovery approach. Programs should seek to provide the student with a *context* in which to place the knowledge they are discovering, for example, by providing a *map* and *glossary*, and a clear statement of the purpose of the program. It is important to allow the student to make links between ideas and build up their own knowledge. The user interface should be designed so as to encourage active student involvement and to provide a feeling of ownership to the student, perhaps by letting them record *notes* for themselves and comments for others. These comments could be available to other students as a form of social constructivism,[2] or as direct feedback to the teacher. David Jonassen (1994) calls these sorts of functions 'cognitive tools' which 'empower the learners to think more meaningfully and to assume ownership of their knowledge, rather than reproducing the teacher's.'

While cognitive tools may empower the student, they complicate the user interface. Each new function has to be accessible in some way, most commonly through a button, menu or icon. This can increase the visual complexity of the screen so that students may have difficulty in identifying the important information among the clutter of cognitive tools. The graphic design thus becomes extremely important.

> In the Carbohydrates program, we attempted to keep the user interface as simple and intuitive as possible, with minimal buttons. Because of this, the program lacked many of the support features outlined above. Some support was provided to students by printed handouts to work with, but this was minimal. The strength of the Carbohydrates program is that it has avoided a purely narrative style and has a novel, intuitive interface. The weakness is that it doesn't provide sufficient support and guidance to the learner. This raises an important dilemma. How can you implement a map or glossary without a button? If you do add buttons, then the interface is no longer simple, and you need extra functions to explain the interface, making it yet more complex.

Table 2.2 *Student perspectives of the control features to be available in an ideal interactive multimedia program*

	Student perspective	Comments and examples
Discursive	Allow access at any time to all aspects of the teacher's description of their conception	This is relatively easy to implement eg: a map of the content; a *backtrack facility*; a *find* function; ability to *print* material for later review
	Allow students to express their conception of the teacher's description	Laurillard suggests that this can be achieved through concealed multiple-choice questions (cmcq)* with keyword analysis Some less powerful, but easier to implement examples are: record student responses in a notebook for later review; publish their conceptions on the Worldwide Web for discussion with other students.
Adaptive	Enable students to generate the experiences they think they need	Laurillard suggests that this can be achieved by letting students sequence and select/construct their own task goal. Careful design is necessary to design the range of activities and entry points that any student may want to take, but it is straightforward to implement Some specific examples may be: allowing students to view media by criteria; providing a *glossary of terms*, or a *bibliography*; enabling the sound volume to be changed; allowing exit at any time
	Let students know what counts as achieving the task goal	This is necessary in some form, but not necessarily as the main mechanism by which one moves around Allow access to a statement of objectives of the program, and for sections of content
Interactive	Give clear task goals, so students know when they have achieved them	This can be easily implemented as a series of carefully designed open-ended questions, which the student works to answer Another option is to use a *story-telling* mechanism to guide the students in the program

Interactive	Give intrinsic feedback that is meaningful, accompanied by access to extrinsic feedback that interprets it†	A screen control which moves as the user manipulates it is intrinsic feedback. For example, instrument tools which investigate a simulated environment provide intrinsic feedback A *help* or *guide* option can provide extrinsic feedback
Reflective	Allow the student to plan for self-pacing	An example of this is to give an indication of the amount of material in each section. While this is straightforward to implement when the material is designed in terms of distinct sections, it is less clear in a less structured constructivist environment. However, this feature could be implemented in conjunction with a *map* function
	Require the student to test a new conception by offering a description of it for comment	Laurillard suggests that this be achieved by concealed multiple-choice questions. However, the keyword analysis is not currently feasible on desktop computers. Other options are to record student responses in a notebook, for later review, or to have students discuss it with colleagues, in person or over a network

*   Laurillard uses the term 'concealed multiple-choice question' for a technique where a multiple-choice question is rephrased so it can be answered in an open-ended fashion. A keyword identification algorithm is used to identify the correct answer (Laurillard, 1993, p.150).
†   Laurillard defines intrinsic feedback as that which is given as a natural consequence of the action. Extrinsic feedback does not occur within the situation, but is an external comment on it (Laurillard, 1993, p.62)

The ideal situation is to produce a simple user-friendly interface which also empowers the student in the ways described above. Two packages have been identified which incorporate some aspects of Laurillard's thinking. These are 'Investigating Lake Iluka' (Hedberg and Harper, 1995), 'Electrical Concepts' (Cosgrove and Alexander, 1993). However, the author is aware of only one effective implementation of all aspects of Laurillard's theoretical guidelines – the 'Discovering the Nardoo' project from the University of Wollongong in Australia (Hedberg and Harper, 1995).

Table 2.3 *Teacher perspectives of the control features to be available in an ideal interactive multimedia program*

	Teacher perspective	Comments and examples
Discursive	The program should give access to a range of media types	Interactive multimedia has this by definition, and the design should use appropriate media
	The program should contain a keyword analysis algorithm to interpret student descriptions, if the cmcq model is used	This is very difficult to do on current desktop computers
Adaptive	The program should have a matching algorithm to enable associative linking between the type of student description and the type of task goal, so the student can select an appropriate task	This is very difficult to do on current desktop computers, but it can be designed in a limited sense on paper
Interactive	There should be an algorithm to generate specific types of task	As above
	There should be a model to provide intrinsic feedback	This is quite easy in a comprehensive design
	There should be a matching algorithm to provide extrinsic feedback	Context-sensitive help is complex but not impossible with existing software
Reflective	The program should provide a questioning strategy to elicit student's descriptions	This is a difficult but not impossible part of the educational design process. The design should aim for higher level questions.
	The program should provide a means to interpret or categorize student's actions or descriptions to support the questioning strategy	This is also difficult to do, but it can be designed in a limited sense on paper
	Make a record of student's actions to enable interpretation/ categorisation	Recording the actions is easy. Interpreting them afterwards is more difficult

2.4   Summary

This book concerns itself mainly with the production of *learning* materials implemented using IMM technology. As discussed in Chapter 1, we do not cover the range of all applications of interactive multimedia, such as kiosks, games, infotainment or databases, although many of the techniques and ideas described can be adapted to suit a variety of purposes. This chapter has examined some of the issues involved in designing computer-based material from which the student can actually *learn*, rather than being *told*.

The discussion should make it clear that any learning material should be carefully designed and reflected upon. The cost of development of CBL is relatively high compared to traditional approaches, so it is even more important to base the design of courseware on sound educational principles and to evaluate the effectiveness of the approach.

In this chapter, we discussed two of the many underlying educational philosophies on which the pedagogical basis of IMM can be built. The *objectivist* assumes the learner is an empty vessel, which can be filled with knowledge. It leads directly to an *instructivist* or *transmissionist* pedagogical approach, where the teacher fills an empty vessel, which is the student.

The *constructivist* epistemology assumes that the learner can build their own knowledge based on an existing set of experiences, so the student is viewed as a researcher. A major goal of the constructivist approach is to ensure that the learning environment is as rich and interactive as possible. Interactive multimedia has clear possibilities for producing such learning environments which the student can explore at will. However, such discovery learning makes the often unfounded assumption that the student has research skills.

Gillespie (1995) recently contended that a well-designed piece of courseware should incorporate the most appropriate aspects of each learning theory:

> 'This is what we as instruction and learning environment designers ought to be striving for, using our expertise and knowledge of behaviorist, cognitive, and constructivist learning theory to combine with expertise in other disciplines (multimedia, human factors, systems engineering, telecommunications, etc.) to design and deliver the most appropriate solutions for our performance improvement and learning situations.'

The ideal piece of courseware incorporates the most appropriate parts of both theories, and the balance will be different for every application. However, current thinking indicates that the most effective environment for the use of IMM in education is guided discovery learning, based on a constructivist learning theory. This provides a rich environment in which the student has control in discovering knowledge, but the discovery is scaffolded by additional guidance functions (Laurillard 1993) to provide support and feedback.

The term 'instructional design' ID is often used to describe the process of designing the content and structure of learning systems. While ID offers many useful guidelines for analysing curriculum and designing content, it is largely based on an objectivist framework and, if applied too narrowly, can lead to transmissionist-style programs. In this book, we prefer to use the term 'educational design', because it reflects the tendency to constructivism and removes the implication that the computer is *instructing* the user.

The educational design is the most important part of the whole project! If you get it wrong, it doesn't matter how well the other parts of the package are done, it will not be an effective program.

Notes

1. The following discussion on educational theory is not meant to be comprehensive. It seeks merely to give an overview of current issues applicable to the educational use of IMM.
2. Social constructivism is an approach where students build knowledge by discussion and interaction with their colleagues (Maor and Taylor, 1995).

Chapter 3

A Model for IMM Production

Rob Phillips and Nick Jenkins

3.1   Developing interactive multimedia

The educational design issues raised in Chapter 2 need to be translated into electronic form to create an educational IMM program. This chapter discusses a particular incremental prototyping model which we have found useful in successfully producing IMM programs. IMM programs require considerable time and resources to create and, therefore, the development process needs to be as efficient as possible. We highlight some problems which may be encountered, and suggest that one method to achieve efficiency is to separate the design and production phases of the development as much as possible, while clearly documenting any decisions made.

The first part of this chapter discusses the general model of development, while subsequent sections discuss the range of skills required of the development team and the initial phases of the development, in particular the need for a thorough feasibility study.

Chapter 3 discusses the development model as a whole. Specific aspects of the model are discussed in detail in subsequent chapters: Chapter 4 design; Chapter 5 development and production; Chapter 6 evaluation; and Chapter 7 implementation and maintenance.

3.1.1   Incremental prototyping

In the early years of development of computer programs, programmers and their managers learnt some painful lessons about software development.

Many software projects were over-budget, late, full of bugs and failed to live up to expectations. The problem with most software is that, because of its intangible nature, it is often very difficult to specify in advance *exactly* what you want the software to do. Paradoxically, it is essential to make as much as possible of that specification in advance. IMM poses an even larger problem, due to its novel nature and because most people are unsure of what is possible with this medium.

It was essential for computer scientists to develop methodologies to manage the software development process. This required careful planning and a significant amount of experimentation before software designers came up with models that were effective.

A review of some different software development methodologies for hypermedia development is given in Howell (1992), many of which are loosely based on the Waterfall Model (Figure 3.1) (Sommerville, 1989), which offers a systematic, sequential approach to software development.

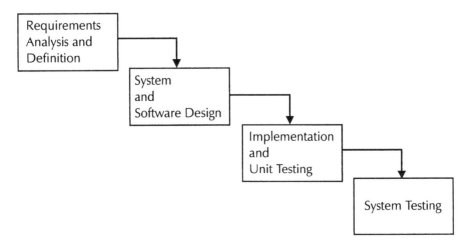

Figure 3.1   *The 'Waterfall Model' of software development*

The Waterfall Model assumes a perfect world where the design can be completed before the construction of the project can be started. If the project needs modifications, the development process starts again from the beginning. Research and practice indicate that an iterative, participatory approach is required. This is especially appropriate for IMM applications, where change is the norm. The resulting incremental prototyping model or rapid prototyping model can be illustrated in various ways, one of which is shown in Figure 3.2.

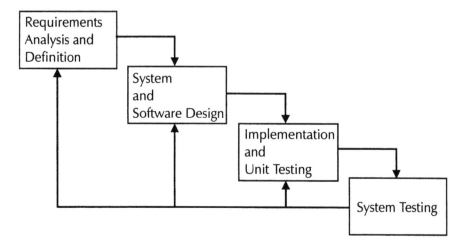

Figure 3.2 *The incremental prototyping model of software development*

Essentially, the process is gone through repeatedly, as many times as required (given the constraints of the budget). The project is designed and a prototype is constructed to test. Once the prototype is tested it can be discarded and a new prototype can be designed and built which incorporates the lessons learned. By discarding the prototype, the problems of the old prototype are not inherited by the new one.

In this way, the design can be continually refined and problems eliminated step by step. The alternative of constructing the whole project before trying to work out all the bugs is fraught with danger. The complexity of even the simplest multimedia project, and the lack of good support tools in this area, makes tracing bugs and correcting errors a very difficult process.

3.1.2 The IMM development model

An alternative view of the incremental prototyping development process, specific to IMM development, is shown in Figure 3.3. The process starts at the black triangle at the left and production proceeds through a cycle consisting of *design, develop, evaluate*, until the project is finished and *implemented* or installed.

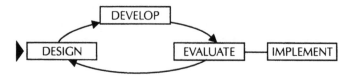

Figure 3.3 *The development process*

Experience has shown that the incremental prototyping model is an appropriate model for the production of quality educational IMM. Under this model all aspects of the project should be formatively evaluated and revised until the project team is satisfied with their effectiveness.

To make this process efficient, care should be taken not to waste time and resources on unnecessary production work on parts of the project which may change. Changes to the content and educational design will affect the graphic design. Changes to the graphic design will affect the user interface. Minimal effort should be spent on implementing these ideas until they have been well established.

There is an important role for making prototypes of some of the ideas of the design team, but the prototypes should remain just that: prototypes. A common pitfall is for team members to put too much effort into a prototype. The team may then be reluctant to revise so much work, and the project can become locked in to a sub-optimal design.

It cannot be emphasized enough how important it is to design the project as comprehensively as possible on paper, in order to produce a quality project within budget. After a comprehensive specification of the overall structure of the program has been produced, it is important to create a complete storyboard of all of the content of the program. Production should only commence after the storyboard has been agreed by the development team. This milestone in the process is formalized by the signing of a contractual agreement that this stage has been reached. The signing-off procedure is an important incentive to ensure that the design is complete, and that members of the team will not attempt to change some components of the design at a later stage.

3.1.3   Startup

A project usually commences with a content expert with a bright idea. The content expert needs to define what he or she requires the program to do in what computer scientists call a 'requirements definition' (Sommerville, 1989). The requirements definition is a simple, general description of the outcomes of the project.

The requirements definition usually forms the basis of a funding proposal, without which development can rarely proceed. As part of the funding proposal, the initial idea is discussed and refined. Discussions should be held with colleagues and other multimedia developers about the merits of the idea. The idea should be defined as clearly and comprehensively as possible. Not only can this save time and effort later, it will also increase the chances of being funded.

Any grant application should incorporate many aspects of a feasibility study (section 3.3). Funding agencies are unlikely to fund an 'idea', but will look more closely at a proposal which incorporates, say, 75% of a feasibility study. First of all, the educational effectiveness of the proposed project needs to be considered, including why it should be treated with IMM. Then, estimates of the technical merits of a project, and whether it can be implemented, should be made. Estimates also have to be made of the cost, the amount of labour involved, and a proposed timeline. Unfortunately, in too many academic projects, few of these are considered in detail and the grant application process involves only a cursory analysis of a poorly defined problem.

3.1.4   Development cycle

Once it has been decided that a project is feasible and funding has been obtained, development can start. Development occurs in the cycle shown in Figure 3.3: design, develop, evaluate. This is an iterative process, but different aspects have different weightings on each pass through the cycle.

An incremental prototyping model has the potential to be extremely wasteful of resources. There is a tendency to design and develop prototypes which include drafts of a substantial amount of content. This might include the entire navigational structure, and substantial amounts of content screens. The prototype is subsequently evaluated, and design deficiencies noted. Perhaps some topics in the hierarchy need to be moved and some navigation controls need to be altered. With a prototype of 50 or so screens, it can take significant time to make these modifications.

The 'Understanding technical drawings' package is a good example of this approach. Early designs identified the number and types of screens, and these were created, waiting for content to be prepared for them. The first prototype highlighted significant problems with the content structure and navigation, and substantial modifications were required. This process continued as more and more content was designed and prepared.

After three major revisions and countless minor ones, the project had grown to over 400 screens, and it was decided that some of the content had to be pruned. At this stage, however, it was very difficult to identify which parts to cut, because it was difficult to form an overview of the program as a whole.

Most of the design process was being implemented in full on the computer before being finalized. In essence, it was not prototypes that were being produced, but a series of supposedly finished products. Over 400 hours were spent in this cycle, and many of these could have been saved by finalizing the design before starting production.

The point of a prototype is that changing it requires little effort, unlike the full-blown program that had been produced here.

There is an understandable urge on the part of the development team, especially inexperienced members, to view what the finished product will look like. However, our experience is that this approach can be wasteful of resources. It is essential that the development team have a shared vision of the outlook of the finished product, but this should be achieved with as little production effort as possible. This is the key point of our development methodology: to separate the *design process* from the *production process*. Both of these processes follow the design, develop, evaluate model of Figure 3.3, but the design process has a higher weighting of the design component, while the production process is mainly concerned with development. Evaluation is important in both cycles.

Design process

The overall structure and content of the project is created in the design process. A technique we have found extremely useful is to conduct a brainstorming session with a large group of people with a range of experiences to start the production of a requirements specification. The purpose of the requirements specification is to clearly define the functionality and scope of the project. It is interlinked with some aspects of the feasibility study and evolves as the design process progresses.

After the initial design is produced, there is a focus on developing the requirements specification in finer and finer detail. Developments are reviewed by the team, and prototypes of the graphic design and of technically difficult programming areas may be developed.

As the requirements specification becomes more tightly defined, the group will start to develop a comprehensive description of the content of the project, called a 'storyboard'. Inevitably, work on the storyboard will expose deficiencies in the requirements specification. For example, certain decisions about the way that content will be presented may cause modifications to the user interface.

With each pass through the design process, there should be fewer and fewer changes to the design, until it is eventually complete. It is then appropriate to sign-off the design, after which the storyboard cannot be changed.

The development phase of the design process includes production of prototypes of technically difficult programming components and the creation of the graphic design, but it may also involve constructing physical models to visualize the structure of the project, or parts of it. For example, the project team may use index cards and string to map out the project on a wall or table.

Evaluation of the design usually consists of constructive criticism and reflection within the development team, and with other experts and end-users.

Production process

After the design has been completed, the production process commences. Some aspects of production may have already been completed as part of the prototyping, such as technically difficult programming issues. In the production process, the resources, such as graphics and sounds are prepared, and the major part of the programming work is done. Work is monitored while it is progressing, but the major part of the evaluation at this stage is in testing of the program, at first by members of the development team and subsequently by end-users.

The user-testing starts another pass through the development cycle, because programming bugs need to be fixed. If the process as a whole has been successful, few problems with the educational content or user interface will arise at this stage, because these will have been resolved during the design process. Bitter experience has taught us that navigational problems exposed at the end of a project can be very costly. Any changes of this type may affect any number of different screens (potentially thousands), and any of these may have unforeseen side-effects on other parts of the program.

3.1.5   Implementation and maintenance

When the user testing and other evaluation methods have determined that the project meets its requirements, the program is regarded as finished and can be made available to users; in other words, it is implemented. In the real world, a project is finished when the development money runs out! Hopefully, project management and design have been farsighted enough to ensure the project is complete and can be used.

At this stage, the program is installed on end-user computers, and can be maintained as a working product. This is where the project is completed. Any design changes after this point usually do not result in re-entering the development cycle, but lead to a new product.

Once the project is installed for use, it is appropriate to carry out a summative evaluation with the user population, details of which are described in Chapter 6.

An often forgotten part of a project is maintenance, that is, fixing any ongoing problems with the program. In an ideal project, maintenance takes up very little of the total time of the project, but in many cases, maintenance can take up half or more of the total time. In order to minimize this, it is important that the project is well designed and well managed. In particular, it should be designed to be easily modified. If a bug occurs or the project crashes, it is important to be able to locate the bug quickly and fix it. These issues are discussed in more detail in Chapter 7.

The Dosage Calculation program was mostly developed before we had adopted the current design methodology. The development was informal with no clearly defined timelines. It was also grossly underfunded. Inexperience on the part of all members of the team led to some aspects of the design not being thought through in sufficient detail. In particular, the testing modules should have been designed at the same time as the rest of the program, instead of being added at a later date. Consequently, more than 50% of the total development time was spent on unfunded maintenance and debugging of the program.

The Carbohydrates program, on the other hand, went through a comprehensive design process. In this case, debugging and maintenance comprised five hours out of approximately 300 hours total development time.

3.1.6   Why bother to design in such detail?

Readers will notice that this chapter describes the development model in considerable detail, and strongly recommends that the design phase be undertaken thoroughly. Our experience is that comprehensive design can significantly reduce the cost and time of development because mistakes, conflicts and oversights are discovered early and can be resolved with minimal effort.

Many content experts resist such a rigorous design process. They are used to working on their own ideas, or at the least communicating them to like-thinking colleagues or graduate students. Since they can communicate succinctly with colleagues in their own discipline, they may wonder: 'What is the point of wasting so much time writing it all down in detail?'

A potential problem of IMM is its multidisciplinary nature, where different team members may well not think like the content expert. Other team members have different skills and different ways of communicating, and/or interpreting the same statements. As well as this, the details which the content expert has glossed over in her or his head can be extremely important for the programmer or graphic designer. Without those details the other team members have to make assumptions, which lead to problems later.

In an IMM development, all team members need to fully understand what is required, because they all have an intellectual and creative contribution to make.

3.2   The development team

A team approach is essential for effective IMM development. In addition to content expertise, graphic design skills are essential to enable the project to be attractive and interesting. Programming skills are needed to produce an efficient system which is easy to update and modify. As well as this, a range of project design and management skills are necessary (Canale and Wills, 1993), as is an appreciation of the educational issues involved.

The ideal team would have a content expert, project manager, interaction designer, instructional designer, graphic designer, programmer, and experts from each of the media being utilized: video, audio, etc. Practically, few projects are funded to have such resources available. Pragmatically, the minimum team we recommend is a content expert, a graphic designer, a programmer, and a project manager. The project manager is primarily responsible for the educational design, and needs a relevant background.

Depending on your location, you may have access to media units with expertise in the various areas, or you may have to be quite creative in discovering the resources you have to use. For instance, at universities there are often media services units, or you may have to draw on students studying in relevant areas. In industry, your company may have some media production capabilities, or there may be existing material that has been developed for other training uses.

Care needs to be taken when using students on the production side of a project. The student's prime motivation is to meet all the expectations of their course, which may not be consistent with the need to meet project deadlines. Therefore, students need to be carefully supervised to ensure they gain appropriate skills and make use of them effectively.

With new projects, it can be useful to hold an introductory meeting of team members in an informal setting so they can get to know each other and share their world views.

3.2.1 Communication

One of the most challenging aspects of IMM project management is maintaining communication between members of the project team. The diverse skills of team members can lead to a whole range of management problems. Each member has a considerable creative investment in the work, and tends to claim intellectual ownership of the project. However, because each team member has a different set of skills, some aspects of the development are more important to them than to others. Different team members also have differing world views. During the design process each of the team members have distinct and important responsibilities which they must remember in addition to their contribution to the overall project design.

A continuing dialogue between content experts, designers, programmers and project managers, and reflection and evaluation of the successes and failures of a project are important to improve the processes by which projects are developed. The most important thing is *not to assume anything*. In our experience, when problems have occurred in projects, very often it has been that one team member has assumed that he or she knew what was required. Unfortunately, usually that assumption was proved to be false.

3.2.2   The content expert

Superficially, content experts are required primarily to generate the content, which probably already exists in other forms. The reality is not so simple. While it is quite easy to translate existing resources into an electronic book, this is unlikely to be educationally effective and is extremely wasteful of time and resources.

To create effective IMM content often involves a radical rethink of the content expert's conceptions of the topic and how to present it. This can be very difficult and time-consuming, especially for those content experts who are inexperienced with IMM.

However, the content expert is not just someone who can visualize how the content will appear in an IMM format and guarantee its accuracy. What is needed is someone who can put themselves in the role of the range of students who are likely to encounter the CBL product.

IMM challenges the content provider to think in a new way about their information. If they simply repackage their information to display it from a computer they are selling themselves and their customers short. IMM is about empowering the user to explore new realms by a variety of pathways. It should release the creativity of the user which is so often suppressed in rote learning.

Problems

One of the biggest difficulties for content experts is formulating the content so that it is suitable for a wide range of students. This problem is valid for all teaching, but is compounded in the case of IMM because of the multiple dimensions involved. The mental exercise of attempting to prepare material – not in the traditional, one-dimensional, linear form – but in two or even three dimensions is very difficult in many cases. One of the purposes of this book is to assist content experts in this process.

Another problem relating to many academics is in the clear definition of their ideas. Although they have good ideas in general terms, and can describe them in general terms, they sometimes have difficulty when pressed for more detail. This is particularly difficult for programmers to cope with, because they are trained to be extremely analytical. If the content is not defined in sufficient detail, programmers make assumptions about what is required, and these assumptions may not match the conceptions of the content expert.

Content experts should also be aware that development of IMM projects takes considerably more effort than the development of traditional educational material. It is unrealistic to expect that an entire first-year undergraduate programme encompassing several units can be produced in IMM form in one year of development!

3.2.3 The graphic designer

The graphic design of a project is very important because it determines the visual communication of the ideas contained within it. In addition to aesthetic value, it also affects the user interface of the project. A project's interface must be effective since it determines the way in which a user will interact with the program. By analogy, if a car had a poor user interface, people would be reluctant to drive it, not because of any inherent mechanical fault, but because the steering wheel was in the wrong place or the pedals didn't work the way expected. Conversely, a car with a good user interface would be a pleasure to drive. It would react smoothly and consistently, and wouldn't require you to use a foot pedal, for example, to activate the emergency brake.

This may seem self-evident, but it is surprising how often people violate the simplest rules of user interface design. A car whose pedals did different things at different times would be a positive danger to drive, and yet people are mystified when users complain that this is what their projects do. Consistency is the single most important factor in interface design.

The graphic designer often also undertakes the bulk of the work involved in generating the graphics to be used in the project, although specialist graphic artists may be used. In the design phase, the graphic designer will have to advise people on what is and is not possible in the way of graphics. eg, will you be able to reproduce an entire city map on a 13-inch monitor? How much text can you fit comfortably on a page? How do you make users *want* to use your program?[1]

Problems
One problem that can arise for graphic designers is that the search for the *right* design can be very time-consuming. Their motivation for this is to produce a vehicle which communicates more than just verbally. This aim may be difficult for other technically-oriented people to appreciate, because they often do not see the importance of visual communication. A drawback of this search for perfection is that, while the end-product may be exceptional, the budget suffers. It is necessary to strive for a balance between perfection and cost-effectiveness.

Another problem is that a graphic designer may select a look and feel for a project which the content expert may find inappropriate for the students using it. For example, aesthetically rendered graphics may be totally inappropriate for a scientific application, where unambiguous diagrammatic representation is indicated.

3.2.4   The programmer

The programmer has a considerable responsibility in all phases of the project. He or she will be responsible for translating the ideas and concepts of the design team into a working program. If there is something that will not work technically, then the rest of the team should be informed immediately, so that fresh ideas can be generated. The programmer also needs to keep in mind the long-term future requirements of the project, such as the need for maintenance and distribution, issues which may be overlooked by other members of the team.

Like the graphic designer, the programmer also has a primary role in the development of the user interface, as he or she will be the one who implements the navigation and interactive components. Programmers need to contribute to the discussion of how the user will navigate through the content of the project. Many programmers have a wide experience of different computer applications, and can contribute important insights to the design of the user interface. However, it is essential that the interface be designed with the user in mind, rather than simply with what is most easy to implement.

The programmer is also possibly the only one with a real understanding of the complexity of the project while it is being developed. To further the automobile analogy, the programmer is like the mechanic who builds a car out of the parts provided by other members of the team. Most people never see beyond the dashboard of the car, but the programmer knows in intimate detail what happens when you stamp your foot down on the accelerator.

At design time, the programmer needs to consider how the concepts of the team are actually going to be implemented. If concept A is implemented, is it going to mean three weeks' more work than if concept B is used? Is the complicated graphic design going to cause response times which frustrate the user? The programmer's experience in these areas is often critical in determining the overall effectiveness of the program.

Problems
Programmers sometimes may have less well-developed people-skills than other participants. They find it difficult to appreciate the other complexities of a project, especially why a content expert may decide to redevelop some aspects. Their outlook tends to be very black and white, and they may find it difficult to understand why a content expert or designer can't decide once and for all what functions will be included.

Care must be taken if a programmer takes on too much of a design role, because their view of a project may be narrowed by what is easily programmable, and not by what is educationally effective. It is necessary to achieve a balance between the two.

3.2.5   The project manager

The project manager must do his or her best to build and maintain the lines of communication within the project team and to keep the project on track. It is the project manager's responsibility to see that the members of the team know what is required of them, and what they must provide to other team members. Naturally, conflict resolution also falls to the project manager.

Each of the team members can have difficulty in appreciating the other's point of view. For example, programmers tend to be too unidirectional in their thinking, whereas graphic designers may be perceived as putting too much emphasis on the artistic aspects of the work. (This is the familiar right-brain, left-brain dichotomy.) Content experts can have difficulty in clearly expressing in detail what they want to achieve. One of the project manager's roles is to translate what the others mean and smooth things over, to keep the team working together.

Project managers also have the unenviable burden of being responsible for the project. If the project is late or over budget, it is the project manager who is responsible to superiors or outside authorities. This means that during the design phase they must plan and carefully monitor the progress of the project, deciding upon milestones and completion and delivery dates.

Like the other members of the team, project managers need to contribute their expertise and experience to the project. The project manager is likely to have been involved in a number of previous projects, which enables him or her to advise on what has worked in other settings and what is unlikely to work at all.

In our environment, the project manager has also had a significant role in the educational design and interface design of a project, working with the content expert and other team members to achieve a pedagogically sound product.

Problems

Project managers should plan to devote sufficient time to management. It is easy for managers to have extra responsibilities thrust upon them. It must be borne in mind that project management can take approximately 10% of the total effort of a project (see 3.3.8). This should not be taken lightly.

Because of other work responsibilities, there is a danger that the project manager can let a project 'look after itself' once production has commenced. This can lead to missed deadlines, breakdown in communications and conflict, as well as loss of money.

3.3   Feasibility studies

The main purpose of a feasibility study is to see if the project is worthwhile and what it will cost. As there is no clear line between specification of the problem and design of the material in IMM, aspects of the feasibility study are closely entwined with the design process.

Comprehensive feasibility studies are essential for traditional software development; feasibility studies for IMM development have a different emphasis. Initially, they are performed as part of the requirements definition, but not as extensively as would be the case in traditional software development. However, some aspects of the feasibility study, such as the choice of authoring language, may not be appropriate until the design phase has begun.

It is difficult to perform a full feasibility study of an IMM project, because clear definition of the project often does not occur until late in the development cycle. Instead, the feasibility study is often used to broadly define possibilities, without being overly specific. The feasibility study can establish some development boundaries, eg set guidelines for how long a user must wait for a response (the response time) from a system. In the creative phase of the design many ideas may be proposed, but can be rejected on subsequent testing against the responsiveness guidelines. It is very easy to forget implementation details when considering innovative educational ideas.

The following sections discuss various aspects of the feasibility study.

3.3.1   Find out what else has been done!

An important precursor to any project is to find out if anyone else has developed a similar program. At the very least, then, you should be aware of the competition. It may be that a product already exists which is adequate for your situation. Most likely, there will be a product which is similar to what you propose, but which does not appear to meet your educational needs.

If this is the case, beware the 'not invented here' syndrome. This is a common criticism of CBL software, where the academic chooses not to use software because he or she did not write it themselves and it does not exactly fit their course. Ask yourself if this is a considered opinion, or a reflection of professional envy? Perhaps it is easier to adapt aspects of your course than to develop a CBL program yourself. After all, many textbooks are inadequate, but are still used. It is often easier to evolve a course around an existing textbook than it is to write your own, and the same is true of CBL.

An important result of surveying existing products is that it gives you some idea of the potential market for your software. If a range of products exists, it might be better aiming specifically for your needs. If there is not much in this area, it may be worthwhile developing a more general product which can be adopted by other institutions. However, beware – the world is full of academics who have sought unsuccessfully to make their fortune by selling their software or texts! The purpose of educational IMM should not be to make money, but to meet an educational goal.

3.3.2   The audience

One of the key feasibility issues for any software development is knowing the users. How many are there? Are they all in one place? Are they all going to use the product in the same way? If not, how are they going to use it?

When you first begin, you are probably thinking about a particular solution to an existing teaching problem which affects *your* students in *your* environment. This is a sensible starting place. At the same time, though, it is worthwhile considering whether you can design for an even larger audience. The Carbohydrates program (Chapter 11) was intended for first-year Nursing students, but could very easily be adapted for more general use in secondary schools.

While it may seem evident that you are designing material appropriate to the user's educational and social background, this may not always be the case, and it is important to consider very carefully the design of the material from the user's perspective.

The computer-familiarity of your audience should be taken into account. There is no point designing a simulation requiring complex manipulation if users cannot use a mouse competently. If the interaction cannot be simplified, then the users must have the opportunity to gain appropriate skills. In the Osmosis project, students were advised to use the 'Meet the Macintosh' tutorial before using the program, if they thought they needed it.

A major question to ask when considering the audience, is: 'What type of hardware does the audience have access to?'

3.3.3   Hardware

The hardware, or delivery platform, is often ignored in IMM project design. Yet it is important to consider (without restricting your options) the software and hardware on which the project will be delivered. There is little point in designing a project to run on a colour graphics computer when the only machines end-users possess are black and white models. However, these considerations should not overly limit the project. The computing industry moves so fast that by the time the project is complete, the average platform will be considerably more powerful.

The Microbiology project (Chapter 8) was developed partly to assist external students studying second year Microbiology. Typically, these students were nurses studying at regional community centres, which have limited modern computer equipment. A decision was made to develop for very basic Macintosh models, with black and white screens. This decision was considered very carefully, because it had severe ramifications for the entire project since colour was considered to be an important design criterion. (The microscopic organisms being treated need to be viewed in colour for maximum effectiveness.) A choice had to be made between producing visually accurate material which could only be used by a few, or black and white material available to all. In hindsight, this decision appears to have been inappropriate, because the development took much longer than initially anticipated and more modern equipment is now available.

Consider making a *cross-platform* product, which is able to run on more than one type of machine and hence has a much greater potential audience than a product designed only to run on one type.

It is difficult to recommend specific hardware for development because of rapid changes in this area. However, a list of questions which need to be considered are presented below. One factor is certain: the mix of media in IMM programs requires significant amounts of memory and a fast computer to run effectively compared to most other software.

Hardware questions

- What platform is my audience using?
- Do I develop for Apple or IBM, or both?
- Do I consider other forthcoming platforms as well?
- What model computer does my audience have? Is it slow or relatively fast?
- How much memory does it have? How much free disk space?
- Are any extra peripheral devices needed? Do I need sound capability? Do I need a CD-ROM drive? Do I need to have a special video playback card?
- Are there sufficient machines available to cope with the extra student load that use of this program will put on resources?
- What machine will be used to develop the program?
- Will users need Internet access, and how fast must that connection be?

The answers to many of these questions will put constraints on your development. In some cases it even might preclude development. For example, if your target audience is farmers who only have access to older IBM XTs and 286s, then it is essentially impossible to produce interactive multimedia for your audience, because you need machines at least capable of running a graphical user interface environment.

A complicating factor in the choice of hardware is the distinction between development machines and delivery machines. Development machines are usually more powerful than those available to end-users. It is important to ensure that your package functions as designed on delivery machines. For example, a CBL package may perform well on the development platform, but have unacceptable response times on the delivery platform. In some cases, programs may not function at all on lower-end machines because of memory limitations. These issues must be resolved early in the development.

> When we started on the Osmosis Project, it was being developed on a Macintosh with 16 megabytes (Mb) of RAM. The chances of it performing satisfactorily on the expected delivery platform, which was a slow machine with only 4 Mb of RAM, were slim. Although the final platform was a much faster machine with 8 Mb of memory, this proved to be barely adequate. It was only after these machines were upgraded to 12 Mb that the program was able to run as intended.

The constraints imposed by the available delivery platforms may significantly affect the design of a project. Many good educational ideas may have to be abandoned or modified to meet performance standards. The ideas may be effective, and may be easy to implement, but they may slow the program down beyond expectation. Features like this should be identified and proto-typed early in the piece to assess their feasibility.

3.3.4   Software

As well as determining the audience and hardware, you will need to consider the software package or authoring environment to be used in developing the program. In some cases, the choice of authoring package will also determine the hardware. For example, if you choose to develop a cross-platform application with the *Apple Media Tool*, you will need to develop it on a Macintosh.

Most IMM programs are designed for Apple Macintosh or IBM-compatible PC computers, and a range of development environments is described in Appendix 1. The general characteristics of various types of authoring packages are discussed in section 5.3.1. The major authoring package used in our work has been the Macintosh program, *Allegiant SuperCard*. *Apple HyperCard* has also been used on the Macintosh, while *Asymetrix Toolbook* has been used for IBM PC development.

To a large extent, the authoring environment chosen will be influenced by the skills of the programmers available, or by a range of other subjective criteria about which package is 'good'. Some developers exclusively use *Authorware Professional*, others *HyperCard*, while others use *Macromedia Director*. It is often easier to cope with the quirks of the authoring package than to reskill the programmer, because most of the required IMM features can be achieved, with trade-offs, with most development packages.

The requirements for cross-platform products may impose other drawbacks. For example, while *Authorware Professional* has boasted dual-platform capability for several years, the flow chart metaphor on which it is based makes it very difficult to design material with greater levels of learner control.

Typical *Authorware* programs force the student to follow a predetermined path through the material, albeit with limited branches.

The second major software issue is speed, or responsiveness. While the inherent speed of the hardware also plays a part, some packages are appreciably slower than others operating on the same hardware. In general, most IMM programs are slow, because they are trying to cope with lots of large resources, such as graphics, sounds and video. An important issue is: 'How slow will it be on the chosen delivery platform?' This may force compromises on some interface ideas and on the use of some resources. Perhaps the graphic designer will have to modify their ideas, by using fewer colours or smaller bitmapped graphics, so that the program will achieve acceptable response times for the user.

The Information Systems 100 (IS 100) unit is a good example of the problems involved in choosing authoring software. This project was developed by the Business School, which had several labs of IBM compatibles, so the hardware choice was relatively fixed. Initially, it seemed preferable to develop in *Authorware* on the Macintosh for delivery under Windows, because of the recent acquisition of an *Authorware* site licence, and better graphics manipulation software (*Adobe Photoshop*) was available on the Macintosh at the time (1992).

An initial *Authorware* prototype was developed on the Macintosh. However, feasibility testing on the IBM exposed severe problems. High-resolution graphics developed on the Macintosh lost resolution on transfer to the IBM, while transitions between screens were taking over 20 seconds!

A second cross-platform tool, *Spinnaker Plus*, was then evaluated. Screen transitions were faster than *Authorware*, but still too slow for effective student use, and bugs in the program code caused continual system crashes. The next choice was the Windows-based *Asymetrix Toolbook*, which gave acceptable screen refresh rates and few bug problems. However, a Windows machine had to be acquired for development to proceed.

The other ongoing issue in the IS 100 project was the impact it would have on the existing delivery machines. Existing machines needed to be upgraded to handle 256 colours and the addition of an extra 1000 students for one hour a week to the already heavily utilized laboratories required intensive lobbying to purchase more machines.

The feasibility study period of the Microbiology project (Chapter 8) included a comparison of the *HyperCard* and *SuperCard* development environments. The example in Section 3.3.3 described the design aim of reaching an audience with access to black and white computers. Part of the feasibility study was to trial a colour version in *SuperCard* which could also be presented in black and white. This can be achieved by using appropriate foreground and background colours to make up patterns. Another consideration was to develop a black and white version containing coloured images for those with machines to view them. Eventually, the black and white version of *HyperCard* was chosen because the advantages of other possibilities were not perceived to be worth the effort.

3.3.5   Delivery

Another part of the feasibility study is to consider how you are going to distribute a program to users. Until recently, most programs could fit on one or two floppy disks, but this is generally not the case with IMM programs, which range in size from 2Mb to 500Mb (ie two to 357 floppy disks!) Floppy disks may be a solution for small projects, but someone has to be prepared to make copies manually every time a client requires the program.

These days it is quite feasible to distribute small to mid-sized projects over the Internet, but this also takes time. Another solution is to use removable hard disk cartridges, which range from 44Mb to 270Mb.

The most common delivery mechanism at present is CD-ROM. A CD-ROM holds up to 650Mb, and copies can be mastered on relatively cheap machines. Copies of the CD may be pressed in bulk (minimum 1000) from a master by CD distribution companies.

3.3.6   Infrastructure

One factor that is often forgotten in developing a multimedia system is the environment in which the project will be developed. It is relatively easy in the current university environment to gain funds to employ a programmer and graphic designer, but is the appropriate development hardware available for them to use? Many grants explicitly preclude the purchase of equipment, so alternative access to computers and other peripherals, such as scanners and video cameras should be sought. Some universities have development equipment associated with a resource centre which can be used for this purpose.

It is important that dedicated, high performance machines be available for the production team. If programmers and graphic designers have to use under-powered machines, their productivity decreases while development costs increase, because they may spend considerable time waiting for the computer to respond.

It is a good idea to investigate what services the university provides that might be of use. For example, if there is a media or graphics support group, it may be appropriate to use it rather than attempt to build up a complete infrastructure yourself.

Varying workloads of all team members can affect timelines and schedules. At exam times, academics are very busy; during semester, they are relatively busy (at least they say they are!), and during semester breaks they are often not on campus. There are only a few windows of opportunity, eg during semester breaks, when content experts can possibly devote quality time to a project, if they are not attending conferences. Other team members may be involved in several projects, and the project manager must take care to balance the workload to meet all timelines whenever possible.

Variations in team workload often make it difficult to develop academic projects in a short time frame. This lack of haste can be beneficial, because it gives all team members time to reflect on the design. On the other hand, it is essential to develop a clear timeline and firm deadlines to avoid projects dragging on forever.

Do you have institutional or departmental support? It is difficult for students to use your CBL program if the head of department or the university will not or cannot make funds available for a student computer laboratory. It is far easier for any teaching development project to be successful if it has a champion at a high level of management. The University of Melbourne, for example, has had financial and moral support from the very highest levels of management since 1992, and it is no surprise that IMM has had a large impact on the teaching environment at that university.

A key factor in any proposed development is to try to gain support from management. In Chapter 6 we discuss the collection of facts and figures that can support proposals in terms of cost savings, or improvements in learning outcomes, which may be of assistance in convincing the powers that be.

It will be helpful if your university and/or department has a policy to support innovations in teaching and learning. If not, an important first stage of the planning and development phase would be to market potential projects internally, highlighting outcomes and trying to stimulate interest and involvement amongst peers.

3.3.7 Installation

How is the program to be installed in the student computer laboratory? Is the lab serviced by a server and connected to a network? Or does it need to be installed on individual machines? The latter can entail considerable maintenance work to ensure that students or other laboratory users do not delete or corrupt the program.

A network installation, on the other hand, requires that the program be tested to ensure that it works in a read-only environment. We have struck this barrier with several projects, which ran perfectly in a testing environment, but which failed when 'protected' in a lab environment. Make sure this is tested early in the development cycle.

Storing files on a general access server can cause headaches during updating. Absolutely no one should be using the software while it is being changed. Having two parties changing the program at the same time could result in corrupting it. Some problems arising from these issues are discussed in Chapter 7.

3.3.8   Time and costing

By far the most difficult part of any feasibility study is estimating the cost. The major reason that the cost is difficult to estimate is that it is not always possible to determine all the content until the development process is substantially complete, and by that stage all the available funds may have been used up! One approach is to use general estimates when applying for funds, and once the funds are obtained, plan the project to fit the available funds.

The usual way of estimating the size of a project is to count the number of student contact hours for which it is intended. This figure is multiplied by a factor to determine the number of hours of development time required. The factor typically ranges between 50 and 500, but a realistic ratio is 300–500:1. That is, one hour of material takes between 300 and 500 hours to produce.

Brown (1991) disputed sources indicating the development time to run-time ratio to be 100:1 (ie 100 hours to produce one hour of courseware), suggesting that a factor of 217:1 was more realistic. As development teams increase in experience the multiplicative factor decreases, because of efficiency gains. The ratio also decreases with decreasing complexity. Two Curtin academics (Lee and Allison, 1992) produced black and white material in which they prepared only simple graphics. By the time they had produced 20 such tutorials, they were able to bring their development time down to 50 hours for each hour of student use.

To take a conservative perspective, a figure of 500:1 should be used for new projects. The Carbohydrates project took less than this, but the development drew on the experience of the earlier Mitochondria project, with essentially the same team. The Carbohydrates program took approximately 300 hours, not including the evaluation. This was broken up as shown in Table 3.1. Table 3.2 shows a more detailed breakdown of the development cycle of a typical project based on our experiences to date. These figures closely correspond to those estimated by Canale and Wills (1993), although some of their categories differ.

Table 3.1   *Development time breakdown for the Carbohydrates program*

Component	Time (hours)
Content	120
Programming	75
Design	75
Management	30

Table 3.2   *Breakdown of the development time for a typical project*

Curtin Estimate	% of time	Canale and Wills	% of time
Initial analysis	3	Research and analysis	12
Overall courseware design	35	Design	21
Software programming	20		
Media creation/sourcing	24	Development	46
Project management	10	Project management	16
Courseware evaluation	4	Documentation	4
Testing/revision	4	Testing	4

3.4   Funding

Most CBL projects are very expensive to produce, especially compared to other forms of educational technology. Because of the range of skills involved, it is almost impossible for a single person to develop a quality product alone and in their own time. It is therefore essential to obtain assistance and funding to develop a project.

Many of the common academic sources of funding (research grants) are generally closed to CBL developers, because CBL development is not considered a research activity *per se*. However, with appropriate structuring of the project, it may be possible to obtain research funding for a CBL project. Cognitive psychologists and educational theorists have legitimate reasons for studying user interfaces and the evaluation of IMM materials. Such research combined with a CBL need can be used to convince research funding bodies to provide funding.

In some countries, funds are specifically available for teaching developments, including IMM. In Australia, the Committee for the Advancement of University Teaching (CAUT) grants up to $Aus5 million each year. In the UK, the Teaching and Learning Technology Programme (TLTP) is funded to the tune of approximately £40 million. Other countries or individual institutions may also have similar funding schemes.

As in most research and development, it is always helpful to have attempted some of the development before applying for funds. In CBL development, this is more difficult because the multidisciplinary nature of IMM means that the individual may not have the required skills available in their department, and links have to be made to outside agencies, who may require immediate funding. It is recommended that informal, collaborative links should be established with other areas of the university, or possibly even externally.

Note

1.   This point is equally important for all members of the development team.

Chapter 4

Design

Rob Phillips and Angela DiGiorgio

4.1 Documenting the design

In discussing the incremental prototyping model of development in Chapter 3, we were concerned with general processes of IMM development. We made the point that it is essential to carefully carry out a thorough design process as part of the incremental prototyping model. The most important point made was to separate clearly the design and production processes. Essentially, no production should begin until the user interface design and all aspects of the content have been finalized. We suggest that most aspects of the design can most effectively be carried out on paper, with prototypes used to test ideas.

The first section of this chapter discusses the design process, in particular the way that design decisions are documented through the requirements specification and storyboard. Following this, more specific considerations of the design of the navigation structure of the program and the graphic design are discussed.

4.1.1 Requirements specifications

As described in Chapter 3, the requirements specification is the first phase of the design process. In traditional software development, such as database programs and defence systems, the requirements specification details all aspects of the program. In this environment, the requirements specification is completed well before design starts.

However, it is not practical to produce such a rigorous and complete description for IMM, because it is so much more difficult to finalize the form of the content and interactions. Typically, the structure does not become clear until the design process is partially complete. In many cases, it is not possible to determine whether a particular design strategy will be effective until after it has been developed to an advanced stage, implemented and evaluated.

The purpose of the requirements specification in an IMM development is to clearly define the functionality and scope of the project. The requirements specification is interlinked with the feasibility study and evolves as the design cycle progresses. Evaluation of prototypes will expose problems in the design, which in turn will lead to changes in the requirements specification. While it is difficult to arrive at a finalized requirements specification, the process of creating the requirements specification is absolutely essential because it documents the design decisions made.

The requirements specification provides the project team with as clear as possible an understanding of the structure of the project, including an overview of the content. It is essential that all team members are involved in the design of the content from the earliest stages, because even though other team members do not usually have content expertise, they generally have more experience in IMM and can provide important insights into how the content may best be structured to suit the IMM medium.

We have adopted the procedure of brainstorming at the beginning of a project with a group of all interested parties, which may be as many as ten to 15 people. The role of the brainstorming session is to give the team an idea of the scope of the project and to obtain a basic understanding of the content. The session starts with the content expert lecturing to the group and group members asking questions. When the group has basically understood the scope of the content, any and all ideas are advanced and discussed. After a general consensus has been reached about the basic structure of the project, the group contracts to form the project team and development proceeds.

The Carbohydrates program (Chapter 11) was the first in which we used a brainstorming session. The content expert gave her Carbohydrate lecture to a group of about 15 computing centre staff, who were involved, however tenuously, with IMM. The lecture was necessarily linear, following the progress of food through the digestive process, until it was utilized by the cell. The lecture was logical and well organized, and it would have been very easy to directly convert it into a book-like page-turning IMM application. There would have been some interactivity on individual screens, but there would have been very little learner control. It would have been a very teacher-centred project.

The brainstorming session that followed allowed the group to throw around different ideas about how the content could be presented, while trying to avoid imposing rigid structure at this stage.

The outcome of this meeting was to use a graphic of the body as the starting point, so that students could explore what happens to carbohydrates in different parts of the body by clicking on body parts. There is an implicit logical flow in this idea, in that food starts at the mouth, and there is a hint to start here, but this flow is not imposed on the student. Essentially the same information is accessed by using this interface as by using a series of menus, but the student has considerably more control.

Evaluation showed that some students chose to investigate the material according to the teacher's logic, while others chose different strategies.

When the requirements specification has been completed to the satisfaction of all parties involved, it should be signed off. At this stage the design of the program is complete and the signing off serves to set the design in concrete. After signing off, no further changes should be contemplated to the general design.

4.1.2   What should a requirements specification contain?

It is important to write down what team meetings decide should be in the project. In many of our earlier projects, the requirements specification was mainly described orally at meetings. The danger of this approach is that different team members have a different understanding of what is agreed. This can lead to substantial content changes late in the project, or to complaints that various team members added features that were not agreed on. The written approach is especially important in IMM development, because team members come from different professional backgrounds with different world-views, and it is common for what one has said to be interpreted very differently by another.

Ongoing team meetings investigate ways of structuring the content to meet educational and project goals. Essentially, they seek to develop *navigational strategies* for moving through the content. Inevitably, this leads to discussion of the user interface and graphic design. Typically, early meetings agree on navigational strategies at the highest level, with subsequent meetings examining how navigation may be achieved through specific content, while remaining consistent with the overall navigational strategy.

The requirements specification also defines the scope of the project and how each aspect of the project will be treated. It describes details of the user-interface, and it may contain some guidelines about the graphic design. It does not contain any content, other than perhaps the headings of the topics, or other details required to define the navigation. The requirements specification specifies the *functionality* required of the project. For example, if there is a 'glossary' function required, this functionality is fully described in the requirements specification. In an incremental prototyping model, the requirements specification will evolve from that originally agreed upon as its details are analysed and evaluated.

The Sarcomotion project, currently under development, is the first in which we have used a formal requirements specification. Extracts of a draft version are given in Appendix 2 to provide an idea of what a requirements specification may contain. While it takes time to prepare such a detailed document, it is generally cost-effective, because it saves considerable wasted development work later, when misunderstandings and oversights have to be overcome. It also keeps the team focused on the task at hand.

4.1.3   The storyboard

Once the requirements specification has been completed, work can begin on the content of the program, ie what is actually going to be on each screen. The requirements specification may have specified that there will be a screen about topic X, but would not have specified anything about the actual content of the screens. The storyboard defines all the resources required for each screen. Obviously, this means the text, but also includes graphics, video, sound and other elements. Some storyboards are less formal than others, depending usually on the size of the project. The content expert is usually responsible for the preparation of the majority of the storyboard.

In current development, we develop storyboards on a wordprocessor. Text is then copied and pasted into the authoring package. The use of a wordprocessor simplifies revision of the storyboard, and minimizes spelling errors.

The development process requires that the storyboard be comprehensively reviewed several times by other team members. Production work should not start until the content is agreed to be final, and signed off so it cannot be changed. If a storyboard is accepted as complete, but requires subsequent revision, then the resultant changes to the programming can take hours to modify, and may even require redesign of much of the user interface.

In the Osmosis project it was common to insert a large amount of text to explain a complex process. The difficulty was that, although you could cram the text into the A4 page of a storyboard, it was not possible to fit it onto a single screen. This meant that the topic might have to be split up onto several screens or redesigned completely.

Consider the effects of this on a storyboard which refers the user to the third screen of topic B. If the programmer subsequently has to insert another three screens at the beginning of the topic, then the reference to the third screen will be incorrect. If the reference is actually *coded* into the program, it is not only going to be misleading, by taking the user to the wrong place, but might also cause the program to crash!

Anything you modify *after the design phase* may have unpredictable repercussions.

The entire team should carefully read the storyboard from their point of view. It is very easy for inconsistencies and discrepancies to appear in the storyboard, and these may not be immediately obvious to the content expert who has written the material. Designers and programmers may discover things in the storyboard which don't match the requirements specification or which are simply not technically feasible. It is also difficult for all team members to appreciate all aspects of the project without thoroughly understanding the storyboard.

While the requirements specification and prototypes of the screen design are essential for team members to visualize the project, as little content as possible should be entered into the project until the storyboard is complete. If possible, content experts should try to visualize the project from the prototypes when writing the storyboard. This is difficult, but can save considerable effort and money later.

The original material of the Japanese Videodisc project used paper-based storyboards. These were essential for a project of such size. The storyboards were supplemented by other documents describing the Japanese script, the sound files, video frame numbers, etc. While this organization was suitable for the content experts and people who prepared the various resources, this system was not effective for the programmer, who had to refer to several sheets of paper for each screen.

Figure 4.1 shows a sample screen storyboard in Microsoft Word which is used for subsequent parts of this project. Here, all information is recorded in the same place.

Unit	11
Segment	1
Activity	Patterns
Date	27/10/94
Screen Name	Mr Tanaka's activity Answer Yes
Screen #	3 of 4
Background	
Sounds	7 items as correct response feedback Audioscript 11.patterns
Images	Mr Tanaka as used in Unit 3 Segment 1 Vocab-animated to wave Map of the world as used in Unit 2 Segment 3 Vocab
Video	Nil
Kanji	8 items 11.patterns. kanji

Figure 4.1   *An electronic storyboard template for use in the Japanese Videodisc project*

In this case, a very formal, comprehensive storyboard was required because of the size of the project (~2000 screens), and the range of resources needed for each screen. In other cases, a less formal approach is sufficient, as shown in an example from the Sarcomotion project (Figure 4.2). Here, the titles are shown in **bold**, hot text is underlined and instructions or queries are shown in [square brackets].

Thin Myofilament

Why do you need it?

Thin myofilaments contain attachment sites so that the swivelling myosin head moves the thin myofilament closer to the centre of the sarcomere.

[small animation showing the swivelling of the myosin head]

Figure 4.2 *An example of an electronic storyboard used in the Sarcomotion project*

4.2   Navigational design

There are a number of possible navigational schemes in IMM, as well as different techniques to implement them. Each has its advantages and disadvantages. In practice, several of these schemes may be mixed in a single project.

4.2.1   Linear

The linear structure of information (Figure 4.3) is the easiest conceptually and in some ways the most natural, given that this is the structure in which most other types of presentations, such as lectures, books and videos are prepared and used. One advantage of the linear structure is that the content provider can build up an argument piece by piece; while a disadvantage is that the user cannot easily return to a piece of information, except by reversing through the material. In some cases this limited control over navigation may be desirable, but material which has to be presented linearly like this is probably better treated in a medium to which it is suited, such as a book or video. The linear structure is most commonly implemented through a page-turning metaphor.

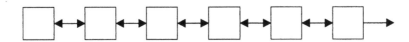

Figure 4.3   *A linear structure of information*

4.2.2   Hierarchical

One of the most significant advantages of using computers to present information is that it is relatively easy to set up a structure to access rapidly any piece of available information at will. This is usually achieved through a hierarchical structure, with topics, sub-topics and sub-sub-topics, etc (see Figure 4.4).

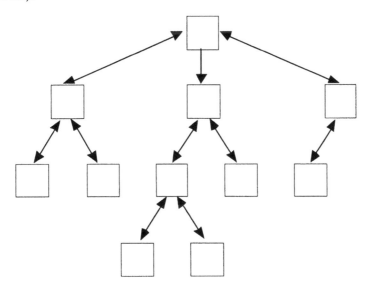

Figure 4.4   *A purely hierarchichal structure of information*

The hierarchical structure is relatively easy for content providers to conceptualize, because it is something regularly done in organizing content for presentation. It is common to divide the subject matter into sub-topics (or objectives), to reduce the complexity of the content into digestible chunks. A hierarchical structure is often implemented through menus and sub-menus. An advantage of the hierarchical structure is that it is relatively easy to come back to a specific piece of information.

The hierarchical structure paradoxically encourages a linear progression through the content, because the user tends to start at the top menu, and follows each branch of the hierarchy sequentially.

> The Hitchhiker's Guide to the Australian Taxation system, developed in 1992, follows a rigidly hierarchical structure. Each screen of information lies at the end of a series of menus. Having absorbed this information, the only way to get to the next, related piece of information is to go up to a menu, and then down again. The use of a rigidly hierarchical structure here may actually hinder learning, because there are too many steps between each piece of content. These extra steps make it difficult to make mental connections between sub-topics. Users found this going up and down frustrating. Because there were many levels of menus, it was difficult to remember where each chunk of content was located.

4.2.3   Mixed-hierarchical

By far the most common navigational scheme mixes the linear and hierarchical modes. In this way, the user can quickly get to a given topic, and then linearly move through the topic as shown in Figure 4.5. This structure mimics that of a book, with chapters and sections which are read sequentially.

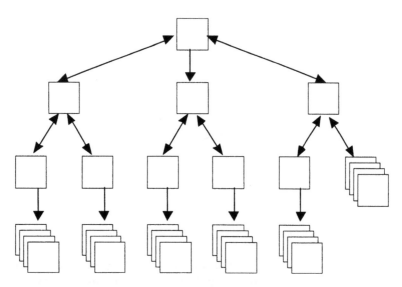

Figure 4.5   *A mixed-hierarchical structure of information*

The mixed-hierarchical structure has some of the advantages of its component structures. The content provider can build up an argument and the user can readily access the information. However, there is little user control, other than being able to go to different topics at will. The user still has to view the material as the designer dictates, and the usual menu structure encourages the user to start at the beginning and keep going. Another problem is that if the hierarchy has too many levels, it becomes difficult to know where you are within the program, which can hinder understanding.

The linear, hierarchical and mixed-hierarchical schemes follow naturally from an objectivist approach to educational design. The book-like structure has serious shortcomings when analysed in terms of Laurillard's (1994) ideal teaching learning process. There have to be other mitigating factors before the mixed-hierarchical structure can be viewed as more effective than a print-based mode of delivery of the same material.

> The Dosage Calculations project discussed in Chapter 9 is based on a mixed-hierarchical structure and an objectivist approach. It is desirable that this structure be based on an objectivist base, because it is important that the nurses get this skill absolutely right every time! Most constructivists would not like to be the recipient of a drug overdose because the nurse constructed his or her own knowledge of how to solve simple proportions.
>
> The mitigating factor for the Dosage Calculations program was that it provided a *context* for the learning in a simulation of the real world environment. Understanding was improved because the learning was *situated*, not abstract.
>
> The Mitochondria project described in Chapter 10 is a specialized example of the mixed-hierarchical structure in that the hierarchy is very flat, as shown in Figure 4.6. Basically, the program consists of a linear sequence of screens, but there are five 'entry points' at different points on the sequence.

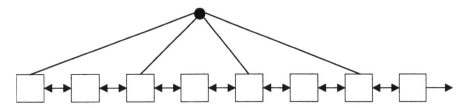

Figure 4.6   *The structure of the Mitochondria program*

4.2.4   Concentric

In the case of information resources or knowledge databases (knowledgebases), the navigational structure can be quite different. A knowledgebase may contain a number of reference topics, the information about which can be separated into well-defined, common categories. One example of this structure is shown conceptually in Figure 4.7.

Each topic is represented by a wheel. The user moves between topics along the axis of Figure 4.7, investigating the various categories of information at the rim of the wheels.

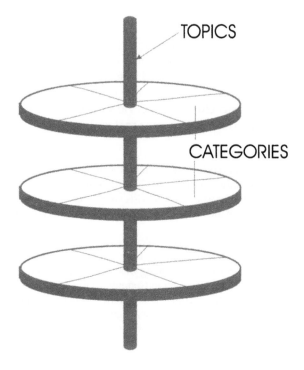

Figure 4.7   *The concentric structure of information*

> The Recreation Perth project (Figure 4.8) is an example of this type of structure. This project contains information about a hundred or so recreational activities around the city which Occupational Therapists can recommend to their clients. Each recreational activity is analysed according to a series of criteria: Description, Location, Task Analysis, Skills, and Special Needs. These form the outside of the wheel.

The concentric navigational structure is certainly useful for content which has the appropriate intrinsic structure, especially knowledgebases like Recreation Perth. It gives the user relatively quick access to appropriate information (without too many steps along the way), and the user has control over what information to look at. Because the knowledgebase only contains information, the student receives no guidance on how to make links between pieces of information.

Kennedy and Taylor (1994) have proposed that the concentric model can be used to foster a constructivist environment, because it avoids the implicit

Figure 4.8 *The navigational structure of the Recreation Perth project*

One screen like this provides access to all relevant information for each of the hundred or so activities. A colour version may be viewed at http://www.curtin.edu.au/curtin/multimedia/devhandbook/toc.html

directionality of the various linear and hierarchical structures. The concentric model need not necessarily imply a starting point: the user can start anywhere. In a hierarchy, on the other hand, there is a tendency to start at the beginning and work sequentially through to the end.

> The Sarcomotion project has a concentric structure. There are eight key parts of the microscopic structure of skeletal muscle, with a series of questions asked about each of the parts. It does not matter which part the student starts with, or which question. Student learning is assisted by the provision of hypermedia links between topics, which are intended to assist the construction of knowledge.

4.2.5 Hypermedia

Hierarchical structures enable the content expert to impose a two-dimensional structure on the content of an IMM program. This is desirable because the instructional design analysis required to derive the hierarchy demands that sub-topics can be logically identified and related to other sub-topics. However, the hierarchy requires that sub-topics be linked according to the purposes of the content expert. There may be other links between sub-topics which have to be discarded in forcing the content into the two-dimensional hierarchy.

Computers are not restricted by the two-dimensionality required by traditional media. The computer can easily keep track of any link between pieces of content, forming an n-dimensional network between nodes of information, as shown in Figure 4.9. It is equally possible to make links between nodes on a concentric structure.

The links on the information network are known as 'hyperlinks', and the general structure is known as 'hypermedia'. The hypermedia structure may be based on a hierarchical structure, with hyperlinks moving sideways between arms of the hierarchy (Figure 4.9a), or it may be truly n-dimensional as is shown in two-dimensional representation in Figure 4.9b.

The hypermedia structure offers important educational advantages over the other navigational structures, because it facilitates a constructivist approach. It is difficult to implement a constructivist approach in the linear, hierarchical and mixed structures, because they impose the content expert's view on the material. A purely hypermedia structure, on the other hand, enables the student to build their own knowledge in any way they wish. However, there are difficulties in allowing students unstructured access to all information within some programs.

First, the user can easily be sidetracked to follow an interesting thread of information to its end. In the absence of adequate navigation tools, the user may then have no idea where he or she is in the overall scheme of things. Being 'lost in hyperspace' (Smith and Hahn, 1989) in this way is a real concern

a. Structured

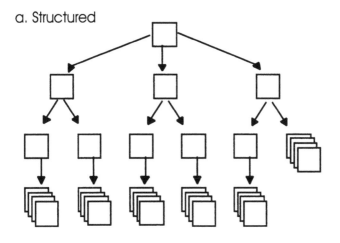

b. Unstructured

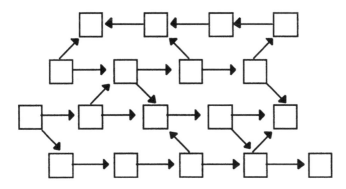

Figure 4.9   *Two forms of the hypermedia structure of information*

in the design of IMM. Second, the student may not have the requisite research skills to be able to construct knowledge from the knowledge network. As discussed in Chapter 2, it is necessary to give the students guidance in their discovery of knowledge, otherwise they may simply not investigate or make sense of the hyperlinks.

The dilemma facing developers of IMM is that the hypermedia structure has the potential for encouraging a constructivist learning environment, but this same structure may fail unless students are given the research skills and computer-based cognitive tools to enable them to make sense of the environment.

The World-Wide Web is a good example of a hypermedia structure. It is a truly n-dimensional network of information. However, in its current form, it is not being used particularly well educationally. Simply having resources available is not enough to guarantee learning. Students need guidance in building pieces of information into a mental structure. Furthermore, individual pages, once located, usually follow a highly transmissionist approach.

Many CBL projects are a mixture of the hierarchical and hypermedia structures.

The Microbiology project discussed in Chapter 8 has a mainly mixed-hierarchical structure, with topics and sub-topics leading to linear sequences of screens. However, the individual case study sections of each module have a hypermedia structure. The case studies are presented as multiple-choice questions, with different answers leading to new questions and different outcomes. Some threads lead literally to 'dead' ends, while others result in healthy patients.

4.2.6   Explicit structure

While there should be some structure to the information, the user should be given the freedom to find alternative paths through it. The navigational structure shown in Figure 4.9a has some potential for guiding the user's construction of knowledge. A balance must be sought between the imposition of structure by the content expert and too little structure in which the user can get lost.

Typical navigation schemes as discussed above follow directly from a transmissionist approach. The traditional way of implementing them is by menus made up of buttons. This metaphor imposes an explicit structure on the content, because in the western world we are culturally conditioned to start at the top left and continue until we have finished. The menu implies a 'start here' linearity.

Examples of typical menus made up of textual buttons are shown in Figure 4.10. Menus typically lead to a linear sequence of screens, which are commonly accessed by navigation buttons called next, previous, continue, more, back, etc. The buttons may also have representative icons, typically arrows, as shown in Figure 4.11. For users to move back up the hierarchy, buttons called topics, main menu, contents, previous menu, etc are often used. Some examples are also shown in Figure 4.11. Sometimes graphics and icons are used.

4.2.7   Implicit structure

A problem with the reduction of the content into a linear or hierarchical structure is that it tends to result in many screens with small amounts of information on them. While this is in accord with graphic design guidelines

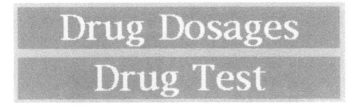

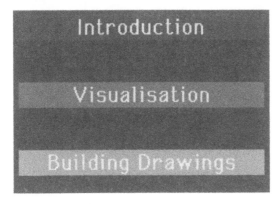

REFERENCE
TUTORIAL
CASE STUDIES
QUIZ

Figure 4.10   *A range of various menu structures*

A colour version may be viewed at http://www.curtin.edu.au/curtin/multimedia/
devhandbook/toc.html

that there should not be too much text on a screen, it is difficult for users to put this information in context to help synthesize their own knowledge; that is, it is difficult to make a mental picture of how screens link together. By contrast, it is relatively easy to obtain a contextual understanding of material in a book, by simply flicking through the pages until you recognize some element on the page.

Use the content to navigate

In typical linear and hierarchical navigation schemes implemented with menus and buttons the navigation is not always connected to the educational

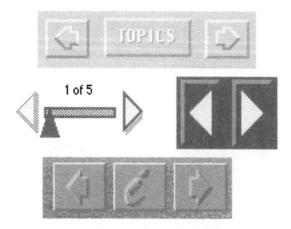

Figure 4.11   *Stereotypical ways of navigating between screens*

A colour version may be viewed at http://www.curtin.edu.au/curtin/multimedia/
devhandbook/toc.html

content. It is easy for the user to click on the next button without distinguishing the content of the current screen from any previous screens. There are no visual clues to put the content in context. Perhaps we should consider other metaphors to express the structure of the content which do not imply a starting point.

One possibility is to use parts of the subject material itself as the mechanism for navigation. In this way, the user interacts directly with the subject matter they are trying to learn. One approach is to directly interact with a graphical representation of the subject matter. A second method of direct interaction is to have the user click on 'hotwords' to navigate to other sections of content. Clicking on hotwords acts as an *aide mémoire* for the students, because they must interact directly with the *word*, instead of with an abstract navigation mechanism. Both of these mechanisms have been used in the Carbohydrates program.

The Carbohydrates program described in Chapter 11 actually has an implicit hierarchical structure, which is not initially apparent to the user. Here the menu is a stylized graphic of the human body (Figure 4.12) with no obvious starting point. While the title, 'Carbohydrates – from Food to Use by Cell' implies a progression from mouth to digestive track and thence to the cell, it is not necessary for students to approach it in this way.

The graphic of the human torso is explored by moving the mouse into objects on screen. It was thought that it is more intuitive for students to click on an image of the mouth than to click on a button labelled 'mouth'. Clicking leads to further information, which is explored by using hotwords instead of the usual arrows.

In this user interface, users are given full control over the order in which they explore the content and the depth to which they go.

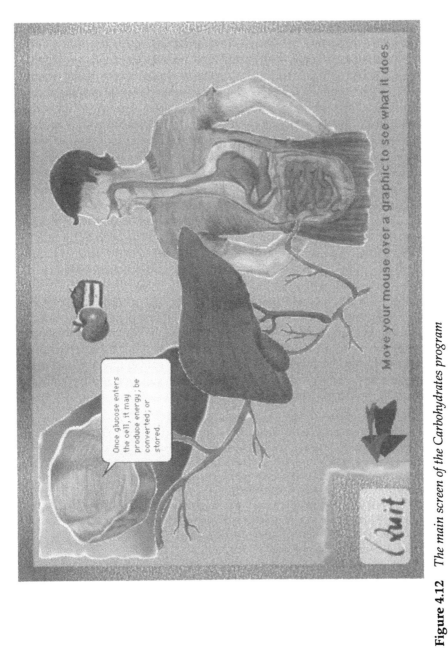

Figure 4.12   *The main screen of the Carbohydrates program*

A colour version may be viewed at http://www.curtin.edu.au/curtin/multimedia/ devhandbook/toc.html

Start from the end!

In several recent projects, attempts to analyse and design a project from a constructivist viewpoint have tended to result in programs which start from what was traditionally called 'the end'. This radical approach goes against the tenets of structured reasoning, a mental discipline which pervades all aspects of western society, especially academia. Structured reasoning involves constructing an argument by identifying a series of key points and forming them into a coherent argument, which has a logical conclusion. Structured reasoning is an important skill in tertiary environments, and indeed it is the method used to produce most lectures, textbooks, reports and research papers. However, structured reasoning leads directly to an objectivist/transmissionist approach to teaching and learning. This is natural, given that the purpose of each of these forms of communication is to *transmit* the author's knowledge to an audience.

However, as described in Chapter 2, educational IMM should be developed using a constructivist, guided discovery approach to learning, where the student is guided towards building their *own* structured argument (knowledge) of the topic. The multimedia developer must try to avoid imposing his or her own view of the topic on the student. This can require much mental discipline, because it is contrary to many years of experience in using structured reasoning. So many IMM products are transmissionist because it is much easier to design them in that way.

One approach we have used to achieve a constructivist IMM design is to start with the result of the structured argument, represented in some visual form. The student can then investigate any aspect of the content, to the depth and breadth they desire, essentially by tunnelling into it. The scope of this type of IMM design should be restricted to one key concept, which becomes the central starting point for the IMM project. Investigation of this concept leads to other information as required.

The Sarcomotion project uses this approach (Figure 4.13). The key learning issue is to understand the microscopic process of muscle contraction, shown by an animation which is used as a lecture aid. This animation is used as the focal point of the IMM program. Instead of providing knowledge of individual components leading ultimately to the complete process, we start with the process as a whole, and allow the student to investigate to the level they desire.

On the first level, the student simply observes and manipulates the animation, identifying the components and observing how they interact with each other. It is intended that this interaction will raise questions in the mind of the student, which they can answer at the second level.

On the second level, students can click to explore a particular part of the animation. This takes them to another layer which provides extra explanation or guides the student in their search for understanding. The detailed content is overlaid as a window on top of the animation, parts of which are still visible to maintain context. From here, highlighted words are linked either to a glossary or to other parts of the second-level information space.

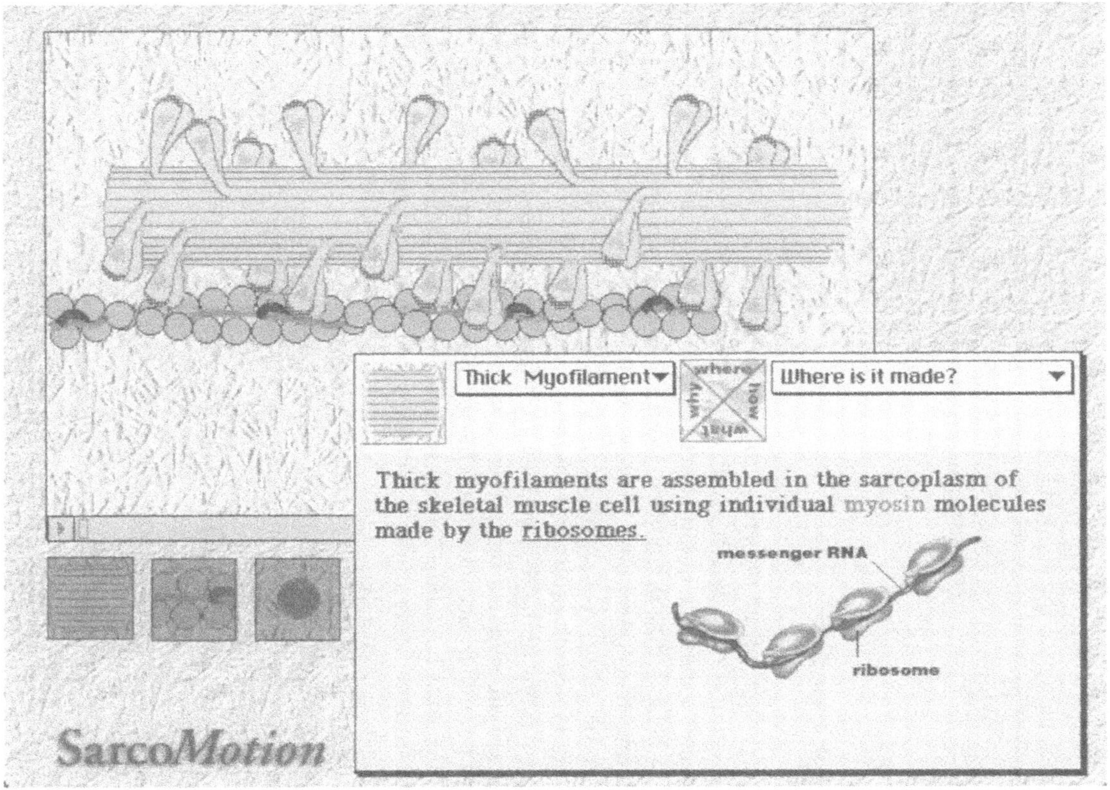

Figure 4.13   *The main screen of the Sarcomotion program. Users interact directly with the animation to tunnel in to the information they desire*

A colour version may be viewed at http://www.curtin.edu.au/curtin/multimedia/ devhandbook/toc.html

In this approach, the same domain of content exists as if it were structured, but the view of the knowledge space is radically different. Thus, many of the drawbacks of traditional navigation schemes are overcome. Users investigate the central visualization of the concept, and subsequent information appears in windows in front of the main visualization. With effective graphic design it can be much easier for the student to keep the information in context.

It is unclear at present how widely applicable this approach will be. The approach may be limited to concepts which have *simple* visualizations. Some abstract concepts, such as AC electricity, may be too complex to be treated in this way.

4.3   Graphic design

The graphic design[1] of the screen is crucial to educationally effective IMM. Graphic design or screen design provides the visual communication necessary to transmit a message in an attractive way. It is easy for academics in particular to believe that the written word is the only important factor in communicating the educational message to the student. This is because academics have learnt over many years to abstract information from the printed word. However, undergraduate students typically do not have this skill (gaining it is one of the reasons they are attending university). They also have a range of different learning styles, and one of the advantages of IMM is that it can potentially accommodate these different learning styles. Therefore, the IMM must have an effective screen design to communicate on all levels to the student. Some students will learn more from a picture or animation than they will from a description. No matter how learned the academic's words, they will not be understood if the student has trouble reading them, and it is well known that words on screen are harder to read than print in a book, because of the screen resolution and contrast. For all these reasons, *effective screen design is crucial.*

This section discusses the rudiments of screen design so that a developer can appreciate the issues involved. Special skills and talents are required to be able to produce good screen designs, and hence specialist assistance will be required in this area.

Designing for the computer screen differs from printed design in that light is transmitted, whereas with printed matter light is absorbed by pigments in the ink and by the paper. The screen resolution of 72 dots per inch is much less than that achievable in print. These factors introduce a new set of criteria of which to be aware when planning visual displays for use in screen design.

4.3.1   An overview of screen design

The term 'graphic design' describes the planning and thought process necessary to create effective visual communication. There are several issues to
consider when compiling a screen design and the following subsections
consider the various elements of the design.

It should be noted that there are no hard and fast rules associated with
screen design. All that can be provided is a series of guidelines which assist
the designer to construct ways and means of communicating visual metaphors. Many initial aspects of screen design can be done most effectively with
scissors and paper.

The brief
The brief is the description of the subject matter or concept. However you
choose to address it, the brief needs conscious planning. Each image must
have a meaning, as should each use of type, colour, line, space, plane, shape,
scale, balance and texture. All these combine to create a visual language which
communicates the concept to the viewer.

Layout
Once the concept has been decided upon, the next step is to determine a
layout which will communicate the intention of each screen. An effective
layout can make complex information easier to understand.

When planning a layout, keep in mind that, in the English-speaking world,
we are culturally conditioned to read a page from top left to bottom right. This
makes the top-left corner the primary focal point, or the place where the eye
will initially look when presented with a page or screen. Design decisions can
be made to allow for this tendency by placing the dominant element in this
position. Alternatively, emphasis can be placed on other areas of the screen
by implementing other design strategies. For example, the eye will generally
travel from the largest screen element to the smallest. Careful consideration
of colour can have the same effect; the eye being led to the strongest or darkest
colour first. The standard layouts shown in Figure 4.14 are examples of
well-balanced alternative ways of leading the eye to different parts of the
screen. Whichever one is chosen will be determined by the types of individual
screen elements which are involved, and their relative importance.

It is a good idea to work within the framework of the final screen size to
enable more precise positioning of each element. Paper cut-outs can be used
to represent text and graphics and can then be moved around to achieve the
best results, or the shapes and sizes required can just be pencilled in roughly.

Many computer hours will be saved by working out a rough sketch
beforehand. This will also allow other members of the design team to proceed
with their tasks.

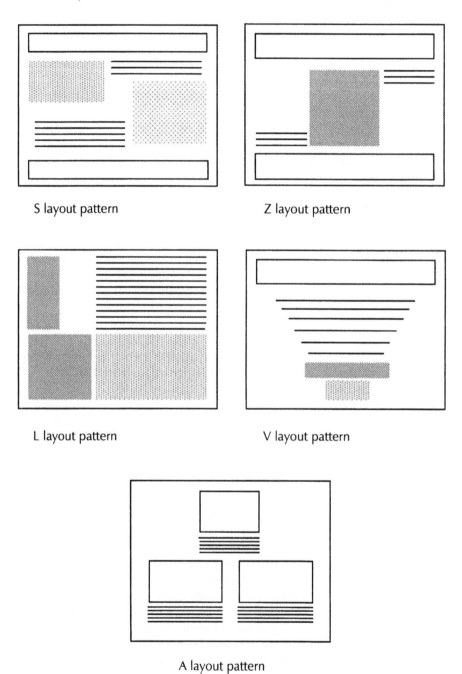

Figure 4.14 *Some standard screen layouts*

Direction

The direction of a layout is very important in determining the effectiveness of a graphic design. Elements must be balanced so that the eye of the user is drawn first to the most important element, and then to the next logical element, etc.

The examples in Figure 4.15 show how the eye is directed around the screen by the balance and weight of the elements. In the example on the left, the eye is directed first to the darker title area because of its prominence, then to the graphic at right, then to the content information on the left. In the second example, with the same layout but different balance, the eye is drawn first to the dark graphic, then to the title block, and finally to the text block.

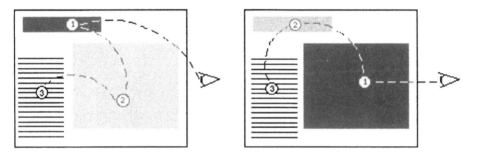

Figure 4.15 *Two examples of how the eye is led around the screen by the balance of the elements*

Format

If you decide on a specific screen format, try to be consistent and use the same format throughout. However, there are times when a change of format can be effective as in when a simulation is required, or an animation is used to illustrate a point. Be creative and imaginative but beware that too much variation can cause confusion.

Graphics

Interpretive drawings, diagrams and animations are all different types of graphics. It is essential to select graphics which work as part of the visual communication and not just as an addition because they look good. Choose images that relate to the subject matter. Avoid trying to fit readily available clipart into the design. Although clipart can be extremely useful it is not always applicable to the task at hand. Different sets of clipart are each likely to have a different graphic style which can cause difficulties with the consistency of the design.

4.3.2   The elements of design

Line, shape, texture, balance, space, colour and text all play an equally important part in creating a visual message. It is important to use these elements in context with the subject matter.

Line
When we think of the word 'line' it doesn't exactly bring to mind any innovative or fantastic ideas, but lines are not as trivial as you may think. The term 'line' can simply mean a drawn line, or it may refer to a series of screen elements which have the shape of a line. Although simplistic, the line is important in terms of the way in which a layout is looked at. Bad use of line will lead the eye off the screen, while good use of line will subtly guide the eye around the screen. Examples of the use of line are shown in Figure 4.16. In the upper example, the eye is drawn off the screen, while in the lower example, the eye is drawn to the centre of the screen.

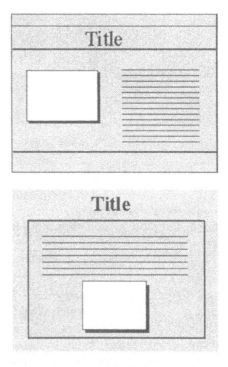

Figure 4.16   *An example of the use of 'line' in graphic design. In the upper example, the eye is drawn off the screen, while in the lower example, the eye is drawn to the centre of the screen*

Shape

Shapes, just like colours, have an aesthetic relationship to one another and therefore have to work together. When we say 'shapes', we are referring to the various elements which make up a screen. In order to place these together in an aesthetically pleasing manner we break down these elements into basic shapes. There are three basic shapes in design: the square, triangle and circle. For example, a block of body text could be represented as a square, a title could be an elongated rectangle, a graphic could be a circle while a logo may be represented as a triangle. When designing your layout, keep these shapes in mind when placing elements together.

Texture

Just as you would think of texture as being tactile, imagine it in a visual sense as well. For example, at first glance a block of text appears like a sequence of words strung together, but if you squint your eyes that text will appear to have a rough texture, while a flat colour will have a smooth texture. The same principle works for graphics and the overall layout of a screen. If too many rough textures are used together it can become very confusing for the viewer. However, a screen with no texture is very harsh on the eyes. The most pleasing appearance is obtained by using texture in moderation.

Balance

A completed screen should have an overall balance of the elements. This does not mean that we draw an imaginary line across our screen and place an equal amount of elements on either side of that line. The characteristics of all the elements need to be considered when balancing a design. Dark or vibrant coloured elements will have a heavier appearance than an element which is soft and subtle, while a larger object will catch your eye before a small object would (unless coloured vibrantly). Sometimes we can look at a design and it does not quite go together, yet we do not know why. The colours could have been especially put together and careful consideration has been given to the type and graphics, but why doesn't it hang together? Often, the reason for this is that not enough consideration was given when balancing the elements. For a quick indication of how to balance the elements, play around with cut-outs of the elements on a piece of paper which is the same size ratio as the working area on your screen.

Space

When we see an object, we should really take the time to look at it. As well as the space which the object occupies (the positive space), make a mental note of the negative space, which is the leftover area around the object. Negative space is just as important as the positive space and taking a different view of the object will hopefully give you a better perspective of it.

Colour

Never think that when you are using colour you have to make a statement with it and overuse it. This is a quick death for any design. Think carefully about colour schemes and they can be used to great effect. Things that need to be considered are: how does this colour relate to the topic? What psychological effects do these colours have? Do these colours work together or are they competing against one another? Warm colours give the psychological impression of heat, energy and sometimes aggression. Consider arcade games and the colours which are used: you will find that the majority use warm colours and the games themselves are very fast-paced. If we were to use this in a screen design for educational purposes, this could result in a tense feeling for the user. This is not to say that warm colours should be excluded from your palette all together, but they should be restricted to small areas.

Cool colours such as greens, blues and cool greys (ie greys containing a hint of blue or green rather than just black) are usually the best to use on screen as they create a calm feeling. Complementary colours, which sit opposite one another on the colour wheel (Figure 4.17) should not be used in conjunction with one another. Imagine if we had orange type on a blue

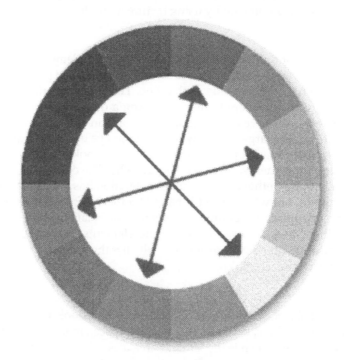

Figure 4.17   *The colour wheel*

background, the type would be hard to read and it would appear to be jumping around, which strains the eyes. If there are any obviously dark or bright colours on a screen, the eye will be drawn to that area automatically, and this can be used to your advantage. On the other hand, it could be a disadvantage if the eye is supposed to be drawn first to other screen elements.

Colours can be utilized as a cueing device. A user can become familiar with certain elements being in one colour which will make moving through a project easier. It is important to maintain colour consistency throughout a project.

Table 4.1 contains a list of colours which work well together. It is a guide only and should be considered as something to keep you on track with colour selections. It is a good idea to experiment with different combinations and see them side by side, and in that way get a better idea of which colours give off the most comfortable feeling. Table 4.2 is a list of colour associations taken from the August 1995 issue of *Desktop* magazine, which are likely to be valid in a western culture.

Table 4.1 *Appropriate use of colour*

BACKGROUND	SUGGESTED COLOURS	COLOURS TO AVOID
dark blue	yellow, pale orange, white, light blue	bright oranges and reds, black
dark green	soft pink, white	bright oranges and reds, black
pale yellow	medium to dark blue, medium to dark violet, black	white, warm colours, light shades of most colours
pale green	black, dark green	red, yellow, white, light shades of most colours
white	black, medium to dark shades of most colours	light shades of most colours, especially yellow

Table 4.2 *Emotions associated with various colours*

COLOUR	ASSOCIATION
pink	intimacy, softness, femininity
red	love, choleric, strength, virility

COLOUR	ASSOCIATION
purple	melancholia, madness
violet	mystics, meditative, jealousy, secrets
lilac	nostalgia, dreams, fantasies
green	hope, calmness, freshness, youth
yellow	sanguine, humour, extrovert
orange	dynamism, strength, stimulation
black	death, despair, sophistication (shiny black) rebelliousness
white	purity, life, innocence
grey	indecision, fear, indifference, calm
brown	compactness, honesty, nature
blue	depth, maturity, spirituality, infinity

Text

Reading text from a screen is difficult, so to get the best from our text we can separate it into two categories: body text and title text. Body text refers to information text, as opposed to titles or subtitles. The font should be small, clear and easy to read. Generally serif fonts are easier to read than sans serif fonts. Serif fonts are those, such as Times and Garamond, which have small strokes on the ascenders and descenders while sans serif fonts, such as Helvetica and Avant Garde, do not have these strokes.

Keep the number of fonts on any one screen to a maximum of two. If greater variety is required try enhancing the style of an existing font with the use of **bold**, *italic*, UPPER CASE or even a change of colour. Care should be taken not to overuse highlighting effects, and large amounts of body text should be written normally with minimal enhancing effects.

Table 4.3 *Factors to consider when selecting a typeface*

Appropriateness of type	Design for your subject matter. Think of the nature of your subject matter and what images it conjures in your mind. The examples in Figure 4.18 show some appropriate use of type.
The basic design of the typeface	Choose a balanced, well proportioned type. Consider whether you should use a light or heavy typeface for the purpose you have in mind. Light typefaces, such as Avant Garde and Times in Figure 4.19 are suitable for body text, while heavy typefaces, such as Helvetica Black and Garamond Bold (Figure 4.19) are better suited to headings and titles. Heavy typefaces used in body text are likely to be disturbing to the eyes and may distract attention from other important screen elements.
Is the typeface legible?	If not, it is either because of the font size or the design of the type itself.
Is it easy to read as a whole?	Long lines of text are harder to read than shorter lines of text as the eye has further to travel. Is the body text too close to any of the other elements.

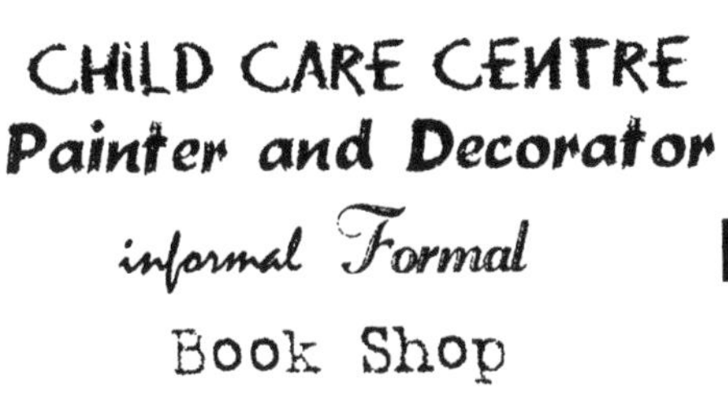

CHiLD CARE CENTRE

Painter and Decorator

informal *Formal*

Book Shop

Avant Garde

Times

Helvetica Black

Garamond Bold

Figure 4.18 *Appropriate use of type*    **Figure 4.19** *Heavy and light typefaces*

Use text sparingly and attempt to limit each screen to one idea with no more than 20–30 words with a maximum of seven to ten words per line. Keep text simple and clear and avoid unnecessary acronyms. The space between the lines of text (leading) should only be two to four point sizes larger than the actual size of the font. For example, 14 point type should have a leading size of 16–18 point. Leading which is too large will make the text difficult to read. As far as titles and subtitles are concerned, strong and simple fonts work best. If you are using titles over several screens ensure that they are placed in exactly the same position on each screen.

There are several factors which you should consider when selecting a typeface which is appropriate to your design, as outlined in Table 4.3 and Figures 4.18 and 4.19. When you have selected the typeface, consider how you should place it on your screen. It should ideally have a generous margin around it, because the overall appearance of a block of text is very textured.

4.3.3   Case studies of graphic design

The previous sections have discussed theoretical aspects of graphic design. However, graphic design is a visual topic, which is difficult to describe simply in words. In this section, we attempt to circumvent this difficulty by analysing the screen design of the four projects discussed in the case study section of this book. This was achieved by interviewing two graphic designers as they used the four programs. Neither had worked on the graphic design of the projects in question. Because of the subjective nature of this process, the language in this section is less formal than in others.

It should be noted that the value judgements made here refer only to the visual communication and graphic design aspects of the programs, and do not refer to their educational validity.

Microbiology
The title at the left in Figure 4.20 is very effective and clear. A nice feature is the way that fields of information pop up to describe the purpose of the buttons on the introduction screen. The consistent button bar at the bottom is easy to understand and users would never feel lost. An inconsistency is that the bottom left button changes from 'exit' to 'back' when you get into the content of the program. The icons on the button bar are a little large, but that would be ok for novice users. 'The black and white icons are adequate and do the job, but it is *only HyperCard*.'

Contents

The introduction section is designed to give you an overview of this program, how to use it and what we hope to teach you. We also advise first time users to go through the tour.

Introduction

| BUTTONS |
| REFERENCE |
| TUTORIAL |
| QUIZ |
| CASE STUDIES |
| TOUR |
| GOALS |

Reference Section :
Offers information on the anatomy of the urinary tract, collection procedures, processing of specimens and the diagnosis of urinary tract infection.

Urinary Tract

Figure 4.20 *Introduction screen to the Microbiology program*

In the reference section (Figure 4.21), a slider appears between the 'next' and 'previous' buttons. This is a good idea, because it lets you know where you are in a section, but it is not well implemented and it looks 'clunky'.

Figure 4.21   *The button bar in the reference section*

Within the case studies section (Figure 4.22), the multiple-choice questions work smoothly, and it is easy to navigate. There was a question about whether the word 'history' at the top left of Figure 4.22 was actually a button. 'Is there a reason for it to be separated from the other buttons? It feels like an add-on.' In fact, the reason for it being separate is that it was an afterthought of the design. The 'history' button only appears in the case studies section, and there was no space for it on the button bar. This function slipped through the cracks in the initial design.

There was also a confusion between the 'history' and 'backtrack' buttons. Experimentation resolved the issue, in that history takes one step-by-step back through the choices taken in the case study; while the backtrack button tracks back through the major topics in the program.

The stack map shown in Figure 4.23 is very effective. It looks good and works well, giving a good overview of the scope of the whole program.

A minor inconsistency is that sometimes page numbers appear in different parts of the screen. However, in general the design functions adequately, given that it is presented in black and white.

Dosage calculations

There are some problems with the main menu screen (Figure 4.24). It is hard to read because the menu items are centred and also numbered. It would be easier to read if the text were left-aligned. There was a question as to why IVT Test was highlighted, but this appears to have been the last option chosen the last time the program was used.

The introduction screen on 'How to get around' is good (Figure 4.25). In general, the navigation buttons are a little soft in colour and somewhat difficult to read, but this is not too bad. The overall soft green layout is a pleasant colour to look at.

Some elements on some screens are not well done. For example, in the drug label screen (Figure 4.26), the ovals used to highlight parts of the drug label are not well implemented. They overlap and generally do not fit well. The oval shapes waste space and the bright colours are too strong.'

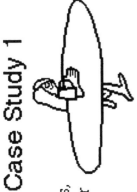

Figure 4.22   *A representative case study screen of the Microbiology program*

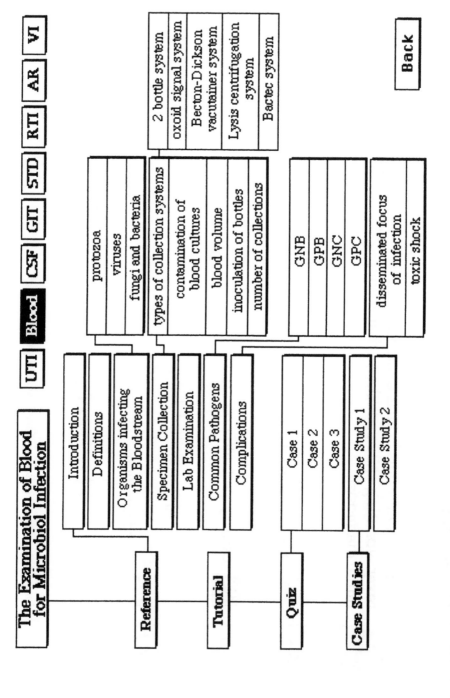

Figure 4.23   *A stack map screen of the Microbiology program*

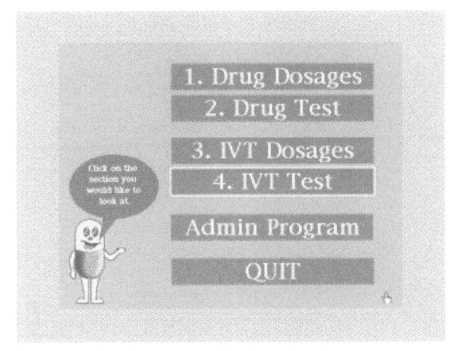

Figure 4.24   *The main menu screen of the Dosage Calculations program*

A colour version may be viewed at
http://www.curtin.edu.au/curtin/multimedia/devhandbook/toc.html

'Overall, the program is pretty smooth. It is interesting to use; there are lots of little things to look at and activities to do. The way that drug labels and prescription charts pop up as in Figure 4.27 is good.'

Mitochondria

The opening screen (main menu) of the Mitochondria program was thought to be particularly effective (Figure 4.28). 'I like it. It looks really good.'

The second screen (Figure 4.29) gives an introduction to the way the program works. The fact that help fields pop up as you move around this screen is very helpful.

The concept of the apple was liked. On some screens more information waits to be revealed. This is indicated by an apple, and each time information is revealed, a bite is taken from the apple. 'This works really well as a visual clue of how far you've gone.'

The topic icons at the left of each screen work well, and the use of the magnifying glass to indicate which section you are in is particularly effective.

The activities on some screens (like Figure 4.30) are good, as is the way

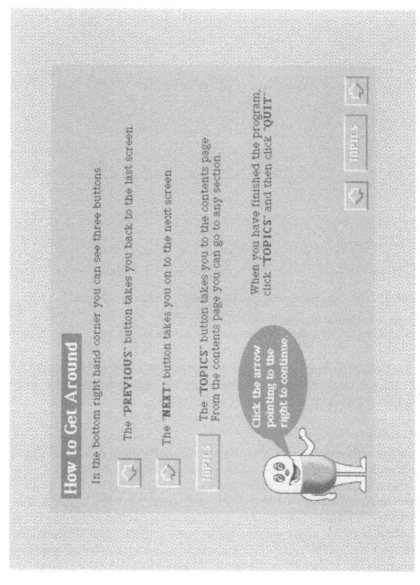

Figure 4.25   *The introduction screen of the Dosage Calculations program*

A colour version may be viewed at http://www.curtin.edu.au/curtin/multimedia/devhandbook/toc.html

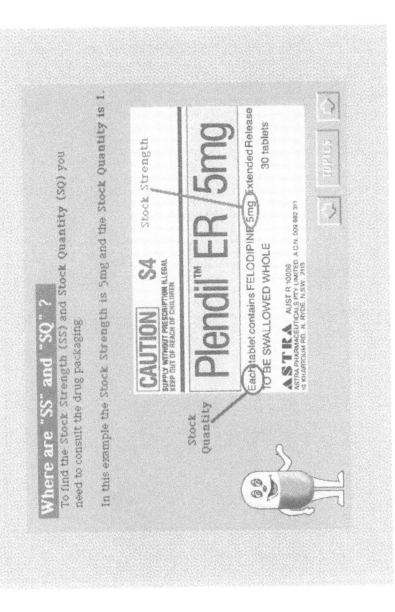

Figure 4.26   *The drug label screen of the Dosage Calculations program*

A colour version may be viewed at http://www.curtin.edu.au/curtin/multimedia/devhandbook/toc.html

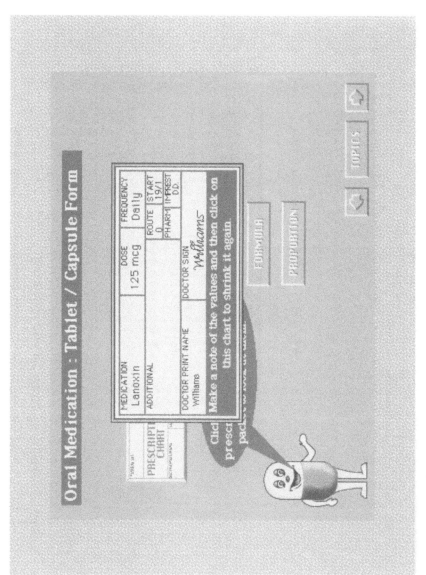

Figure 4.27   *A prescription chart popped up from a smaller background image*

A colour version may be viewed at http://www.curtin.edu.au/curtin/multimedia/devhandbook/toc.html

Figure 4.28   *The main menu of the Mitochondria program*

A colour version may be viewed at http://www.curtin.edu.au/curtin/multimedia/ devhandbook/toc.html

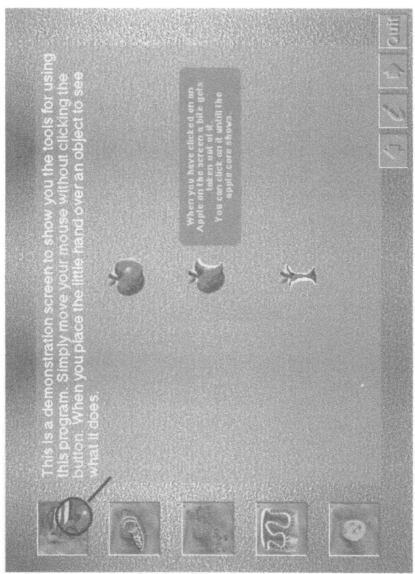

Figure 4.29   *The introductory screen of the Mitochondria program*

A colour version may be viewed at http://www.curtin.edu.au/curtin/multimedia/ devhandbook/toc.html

some diagrams build up. However, some elements on some screens use poor choices of colours.

One inconsistency is that some diagrams are active and can be clicked on, but the majority are not. There is a tendency to click on every graphic, but many of them don't react.

Overall, this program is attractive, it is consistent throughout and comfortable to look at. It is colourful without being gaudy, and it keeps the visual interest. 'At first sight some of the images look childish, but they grow on you… I like them now.'

Carbohydrates

The Carbohydrates program received the most criticism from a graphic design viewpoint. In the view of the two reviewers, several aspects of the graphic design of this program could have been improved to enable students to use the program more effectively. Despite these criticisms, the program was found to meet the required needs of its most important audience, the students.

Many of the criticisms described below stem from the tighter project management regime of this project. In a bid to rein in the graphic design budget and achieve deadlines, several compromises had to be made on the graphic design. The design team was aware of some of the problems, but made a conscious decision not to resolve them, in order to complete the project on time. This contrasts with earlier programs, where the graphic design was very good, but compromises had to be made in other aspects of the program.

It was felt that there were problems with the initial screen (Figure 4.31). 'The two background areas contrast in colour too much'. If there was less contrast, the title and instructions might have stood out more. The 'quit' and 'credits' buttons have different sizes and are not balanced. The instruction 'Click anywhere to continue' is in the same font and style as the subtitle 'From food to use by cell'. Because the latter is part of the title and the former an instruction, the instruction should be in a different type style. Otherwise the user receives the visual message that the instruction is part of the title.

The navigation and instruction functions of the rest of the screens, such as the main menu screen (Figure 4.12) also came in for criticism. The 'return' arrow was thought to be too red and important. The red instructional text at the bottom continually changes, adding to what is already an overly busy region. The flashing caused by changes in the text continually distracts the eye from the other things it is looking at. In general, the bottom strip of the screen takes too much importance, overpowering the other areas. The flashing text at the bottom was not actually part of the original design, but was added by the programmer. In the press of other development, this was not questioned by other members of the team.

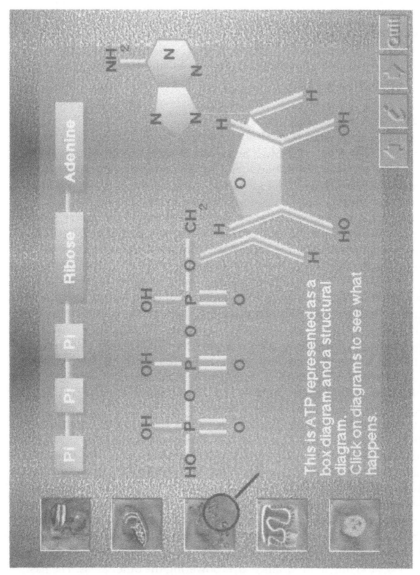

Figure 4.30 *A representative content screen in the Mitochondria program*

A colour version may be viewed at http://www.curtin.edu.au/curtin/multimedia/ devhandbook/toc.html

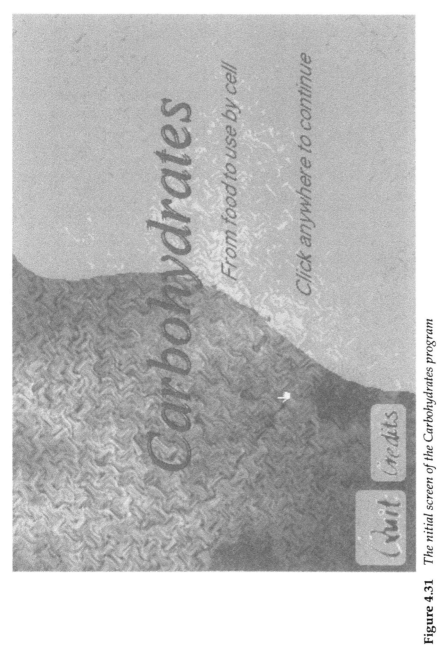

Figure 4.31 *The nitial screen of the Carbohydrates program*

A colour version may be viewed at http://www.curtin.edu.au/curtin/multimedia/ devhandbook/toc.html

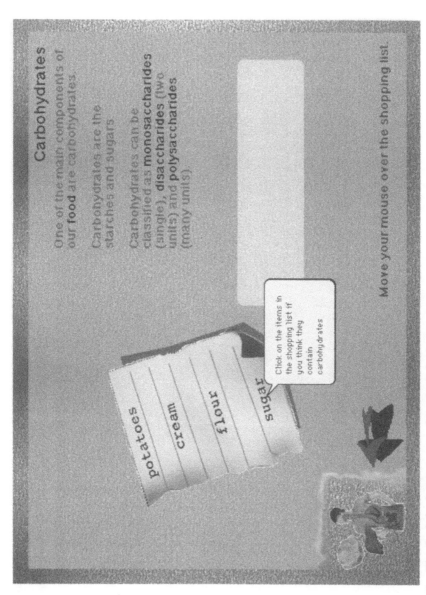

Figure 4.32 *The Carbohydrates screen of the Carbohydrates program*

A colour version may be viewed at http://www.curtin.edu.au/curtin/multimedia/ devhandbook/toc.html

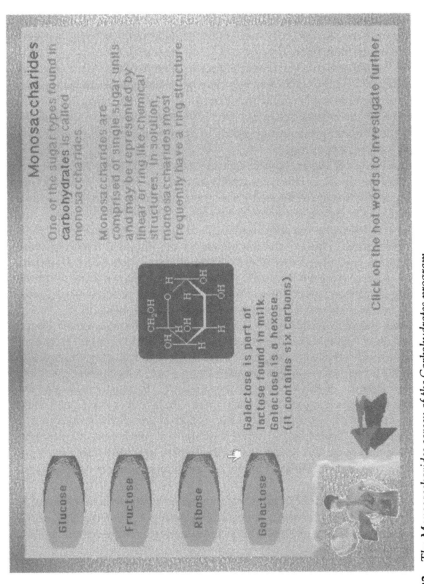

Figure 4.33   *The Monosaccharides screen of the Carbohydrates program*

A colour version may be viewed at http://www.curtin.edu.au/curtin/multimedia/ devhandbook/toc.html

The black and white pop up help balloons were felt to be not consistent with other labels on screen. This was another conscious design decision in order that the program performed as responsively as possible on the proposed delivery machines. Many discussions were held about whether to implement graphically-consistent help balloons, or whether to use the built-in help system of the Macintosh. It was finally decided that response times were more important than aesthetics.

Some content screens, like that in Figure 4.32, were felt to be unbalanced. It was thought that the text block may have been given more importance by being located at the left or on the top. The black hotwords were felt to be too strong against the orange body text. This leads to a tendency to click on the black without reading the orange words. A better choice of text colour may have been more appropriate.

The reviewers thought that the right alignment of the title meant that it was largely overlooked. This was actually a conscious decision of the design team, because it was felt that the title was not very important. In fact, the team discussed long and hard whether the title should be displayed at all.

Some activities, like the shopping list in Figure 4.32, were thought to be well implemented. However, some aspects of the implementation of these were suspect. The cream box underneath the text in Figure 4.32 was initially thought to be a program bug until it was realized that the answers to the shopping list quiz are given there. The decision to leave the cream box visible was also consciously made in order to speed response times.

Another example of poor balance was the Monosaccharides screen (Figure 4.33), where it was felt that the graphics compete with the text. The purple graphics on the left are too bright, and the black and orange in the centre is too vivid. The negative spaces around the objects are out of balance, and the separate elements of the screen just don't seem to fit together; instead the colours and shapes compete with each other. The layout of this screen could have been improved, except that some elements are used identically in a related screen on disaccharides, where the balance is much more harmonious. Had the graphics on this screen been relocated to provide better balance, it would have been more difficult to make mental links between monosaccharides and disaccharides.

In conclusion, while the graphic designers did not think that the Carbohydrates program had a consistent interface, most of the problems they identified arose either from conscious design decisions or from tighter management of costs and time.

Note

1.   A glossary of graphic design terms is given in Appendix 3.

Chapter 5

Development

Rob Phillips and Nick Jenkins

5.1 Introduction

This chapter discusses development – the actual process of sitting down and creating an IMM program. It does not cover any particular language or development environment: books already exist that do this admirably and some of these are referred to in Appendix 1. Instead this chapter concentrates on describing the use of different types of resources and some general techniques which can be used in any project.

The chapter also includes a description at a general level of the different types of development environments, the differences between them, and the strengths and weaknesses of each.

5.2 Resources

The heart of any multimedia application is its content, its resources. The text, graphics, video and sound which make up most multimedia applications are the factors which distinguish multimedia from previous generations of software.

However, simply including aspects of each of these types of media is not enough to make a multimedia application successful. There are many innovative and constructive techniques which can be used to make the most of each media type. This section discusses some of those techniques and how you can use them to their best advantage.

5.2.1   Text

Nearly all multimedia applications include text in some form. Text and the written language remain the most common way of communicating information in our society. The computer brings extra power to text, not only by allowing you to manipulate its size and shape (as described in section 4.3.2) but also by making it an interactive medium.

Digital text

One of the problems with many projects is that the development team fails to utilize the tools they have to hand. For example, a content expert will write out a storyboard in a wordprocessor, *print it* and send a copy to the programmer or graphic designer. The programmer will then re-type the text into a computer, possibly using the same wordprocessor. The programmer may thereby introduce typing errors into the content, as well as wasting time. A much better solution is to exchange the storyboard document using a medium like a floppy disk or e-mail.

If documents are exchanged electronically then simple processes like the 'search and replace' function available in most wordprocessors can be used to speed up the process even more. As another example, if the document exchanged between content expert and programmer contains comments which are formatted in a consistent way then the programmer can remove all the comments from the content in a single operation.

In a number of projects, we have also automated the process of entering text onto individual screens. A small program is used to read a specifically formatted text document and place the text on appropriate screens. This approach is discussed further in section 5.3.2.

Hypertext

Hypertext is the process of linking concepts within text documents through the use of 'hotwords'. A hotword is an active word within a document which the user can click on to navigate to another part of the project or to initiate some form of interaction. Hotwords are usually distinguished from their more mundane cousins by a graphical style, such as underlining or making them a different colour.

Hypertext can provide a very convenient method of navigating around a complex topic. Hotwords are particularly useful in the case of glossaries. It would be much more convenient to simply click on a word on this page to find out what it meant instead of having to thumb through the book and look it up in the glossary. However, navigation by hypertext can be confusing. As discussed in section 4.2.5, it is very easy for a user to become 'lost in hyperspace'. After a few clicks users can be so far from the original topic that they become hopelessly confused.

5.2.2   Graphics

In addition to the overall user interface (section 4.3), the style in which graphics are represented have a large bearing on the ability of an IMM program to communicate its message. The graphic designer should be able to develop a look and feel for the artwork, but it will be through his or her own interpretations of the subject matter. It is important that the content expert should inform the graphic designer of any ideas which concern the look and feel of the subject matter and how it should be presented. These ideas may include:

- a colour scheme they find appropriate
- the style of diagrams or illustrations; that is, whether they should be simple and representative or detailed and realistic
- ideas for animations.

The content expert may have preconceived ideas about the appearance of the content. Perhaps there are conventions about the way in which certain elements are represented. For example, in chemistry, chlorine atoms are usually represented as green. The graphic designer may not be familiar with these conventions and may adopt an entirely different perspective on how it should look. This is not necessarily a bad thing, because the new perspective may contribute additional richness to the design. However, it is essential that any style decisions made accurately reflect the educational outcomes desired.

In several projects, graphic designers began developing graphics in the manner in which they felt the subject should be represented. The content expert, in contrast, felt that this detracted from the content, and it was not consistent with what they had seen in their own mind. The solution to this problem is communication, and the content expert should precisely indicate what they require and the outlook they expect. Providing examples of illustration styles, colour schemes and typefaces gives the graphic designer a set of ground rules by which to develop an appropriate look and feel for the project.

Because graphic designers and content experts may interpret instructions and descriptions in different ways, it is essential that both parties agree on clear and precise ground rules for the graphic style at an early stage in the project, before any major production work is carried out. The look and feel of the project will also evolve as the project progresses. Changes in the educational and navigational design will affect graphic design decisions, and therefore it is essential for the graphic designer to be involved at all stages of design. The graphic design proceeds by the same incremental prototyping model as the project as a whole.

Production

Graphics can be produced in many ways. They can be scanned from photographs, slides, hand drawings or textbook images (given copyright permission). Sometimes graphics can be developed directly on screen, especially if special graphics tablets are used as the input device.

Every graphic designer has their own unique way of illustrating or representing images in a diagrammatic manner. However, a graphic designer must be able to adapt their style to one similar to that which may be required.

So long as the content expert provides a basic idea and discusses it with the graphic designer, a fully developed and detailed illustration can be developed, even from a quick hand-drawn sketch. The same applies to a detailed image as well, that can be simplified into a straightforward diagrammatic style.

5.2.3 Digital video

The ability to show moving images using digital video can greatly enhance IMM projects. However, digital movies in IMM have most often been used passively, in the same manner as a television set. Unfortunately, without special hardware accelerator boards, the image sizes and frame rates available on current computers cannot match that of television or video. Technical issues about digital video are discussed in Appendix 4.

For some time full-screen video has been considered the holy grail of the multimedia industry, but it actually has only limited IMM potential. A video recorder is still a more appropriate device than a computer to deliver an hour-long full-screen video. It is more portable, flexible and far less expensive. If high quality video is your major aim, then perhaps you should consider using a video recorder rather than investing time and money in developing an IMM program.

However, if there is a real need for digital video in a project, this should be kept succinct and address the point at hand. The reason for this is that linear video is a relatively passive medium, which we are accustomed to sit back and watch. IMM is, or should be, an active medium, where users want to interact with the material. Long video sequences can lose the attention of and sometimes even frustrate the learner.

Consider also the possibility of making computer-generated animations and displaying them as digital video. These can be much clearer in highlighting the key points of a process than a video of the real thing, where extraneous factors such as the background may detract from the process itself.

Digital video can become a very powerful communication medium, when coupled with the interactive control of a computer. In some cases it can form the basis of an entire project, as in the SarcoMotion project discussed below.

The two major digital video formats are Apple's *QuickTime* and Microsoft's *Video for Windows*. Both offer the ability to play back video movies, and let you manipulate that video and interact with it. *QuickTime* also offers the possibility of adding other time-based media to movies, like subtitles and sound tracks. The most recent version adds sprites, which are moving hotspots which can initiate other actions.

The remainder of this section discusses some innovative ways in which digital video can be used.[1]

Interactive movies

Video frames stored in *QuickTime* format can be accessed randomly. The movie can be played forwards, backwards or frame-by-frame. It can even be manipulated by a slider, so the user controls which part of the movie they want to see. In this latter case, there is more potential as a learning tool, because the user interacts with the movie instead of just looking at it.

> In the Sarcomotion project (Figure 4.13) an interactive movie is used as the centrepiece. The project demonstrates how muscle contraction happens and the processes involved. To illustrate this concept, the project uses an animated diagram of the muscle contraction as an interactive movie. The user can stop the movie at any point and step through it frame by frame (forwards or backwards) until they understand it. They can then click on the animation to explore deeper into the content.

Computer-based modelling

Computers can be used to model spaces or objects and to allow people to interact with them. This modelling usually requires large amounts of computing power and often requires an equally powerful computer to play back the images. The use of digital video offers a much better solution for distributing and playing these images.

A computer modelled environment can be output as a digital video using methods such as raytracing. Raytracing uses a computer to trace the path of light rays in a modelled scene to produce a very high quality, accurate picture of the scene. By outputting a series of these pictures and combining them into a digital movie it is possible to play back high quality animations on most desktop computers. These scenes could be used to model a virtual environment for use as a user interface.

Virtual reality

Building on the pioneering work of some early *QuickTime* users Apple released *QuickTime-Virtual Reality* (QTVR) in mid-1995. QTVR is a process by which people can quickly and easily represent objects and spaces on a computer.

There are two aspects to QTVR: panoramas and objects. A panorama is constructed by taking a series of still photographs in a 360 degree arc. The

Figure 5.1 *A raw QTVR panorama*

QTVR software then knits together these pictures to provide an interactive panorama of the space, as illustrated in Figure 5.1. People can 'stand' in the virtual space and look around it, examining objects and looking up and down. The panorama is stored at right angles to its normal orientation for efficiency reasons, because the viewer will normally pan sideways in the panorama.

The second aspect of QTVR – objects – are treated slightly differently. An object is modelled by taking a video camera and filming the object frame by frame from every angle. This is usually done by rotating the object rather than the camera. The sequence of film is then passed through special software which produces a *QuickTime* movie which, when played back, allows the user to 'pick up' the object and examine it from all sides, as shown in Figure 5.2.

The techniques of QTVR can be combined to offer a very immersive and accurate depiction of a room, building or area. The techniques can also be combined with other digital video techniques, like computer modelling, to produce virtual representations of places, phenomena or objects, some of which may not even physically exist.

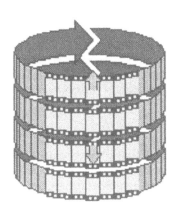
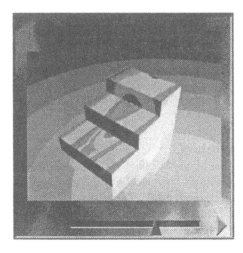

Figure 5.2 *The loops of film used to generate a QTVR object and the resulting object*

5.2.4 Sound

Just as video has a role in multimedia, sound also plays an important part in a project. As with video, however, there is a very fine balance between getting it right and overdoing it. A few carefully placed sounds can greatly enhance a project, but a continuous monologue can be highly distracting. Consider the context in which the program is to be used. On a single computer, sound can be very entertaining, but in a lab with 20 individual machines the cacophony from 20 different multimedia projects could be deafening. At the very least a program should offer the possibility of adjusting the sound volume. In essence, sound should be used in conjunction with other media (like text) to communicate to the user. A multimedia project is not likely to have a great penetration among the hearing-impaired community if it relies solely upon sound to convey information.

If speech is used in an IMM program as the exclusive method of transmitting a message it can become frustrating to the user. Human beings can read much more quickly than they can speak, and users may become frustrated at the delays in listening to a message when they want to progress to other parts of the program.

Atmosphere

Sound can be far more emotive than simple text and can be used effectively to change the atmosphere of a project. By choosing sound samples carefully you can influence the 'mood' of a project, making it that much more enticing for the user.

> The 'X' project from ULTRALAB at Anglia University in the UK uses sound very effectively. Designed by young children, the program is used to teach simple multiplication. One of the requests the children made was that the program include an element of tension – a challenge. As the user considers a question, the speed of the background music increases until, with only a few seconds to go, it reaches a frenetic tempo.

Text-to-speech

One of the problems with recorded sound files is that they take up a large amount of disk space and memory. One solution to this problem is to use the technologies of 'text-to-speech'. Normally, the human voice is 'digitized' as it is recorded so that it can be played back later in a multimedia program. With the text-to-speech technology, the computer interprets text and converts it into phonetic sounds in much the same way as a human would. Thus, the computer can read back any text within any program with reasonable fidelity. This feature can be very useful within an IMM program because large amounts of text can be converted to audio without large sound files. A particular use of this technology is to offer an alternative for vision-impaired people.

There are, however, some disadvantages to computer-generated speech. The speech can sound robotic compared to human speech, and it lacks the variable intonation that can make human speakers appealing. The quality of the robotic voices varies, and while some newer versions are of a high quality, this is offset by the disk space and Random Access Memory (RAM) taken up by text-to-speech software. For example, Apple's high quality voices use several megabytes of disk space each and consume another megabyte or so of RAM.

MIDI sound
Another sound technology which can reduce the size of sound files used in a project is the Musical Instrument Digital Interface (MIDI). MIDI can be combined with QuickTime to play back music while using very little disk space. MIDI records music as a series of notes and durations, and plays back the music by synthesizing it.

Sound digitizing
The technology exists to record sound from the user of a program and play it back later. This idea has particular application in linguistics packages. In designing a program to teach a language, the user can be asked to record their own speech of a given phrase. The phrase can then be reviewed and compared to the correct pronunciation, and the process can be repeated until mastery is achieved.

5.3   Programming

Media resources by themselves do not make an IMM title. The power of the computer to manipulate media resources and allow the user to interact with them is the key to IMM. How the computer manipulates the media, how the user interacts with the program, and ultimately how an IMM title works is determined by its programming. The programming is the 'glue' that binds the different elements together.

There are several styles of authoring languages, some of them enjoying particular popularity amongst multimedia developers. This section covers the types of programming languages and authoring environments that are typically used in a multimedia environment. This section also contains some useful hints for both novice and experienced multimedia programmers.

Readers should beware that this section is primarily intended for people with some computer programming experience, and some parts of this section are quite technical.

5.3.1   Authoring languages

Traditionally, programming was relegated to a small group of technical experts. Now, with more powerful computers, programming is becoming easier for the ordinary computer user. Most multimedia applications are now produced using visual programming languages which allow users to draw graphical objects directly on screen and control them quite simply. This type of authoring language considerably eases the process of developing IMM applications. All of the popular multimedia development environments like *Macromedia Director, Authorware Professional, Allegiant SuperCard* and *Asymetrix Toolbook* can be categorized as visual programming languages.

This section discusses the general *architecture* of different authoring languages, while specific details and advantages and disadvantages of various current languages are discussed in Appendix 1. However, regardless of whether you are using a text-based or a visual programming language, there are a number of approaches you can use to make programming simpler.

Standard programming languages

Standard languages, or third-generation languages, have traditionally been used to write all types of computer application programs. Although they have been supplanted to some extent by alternative methods, they remain the favourite choice for developing standard application packages, because they offer the best balance between ease-of-use, level of functionality and speed of operation. Standard languages have drawbacks for multimedia development because they often do not directly support elements of multimedia. Tools and graphics have to be explicitly created by program code rather than by simply drawing them. Standard languages also have steep learning curves, and initial development is slow, because elements have to be built from scratch. Furthermore, most multimedia programs simply do not need the power they offer.

Object-oriented languages

Object-oriented programming (OOP) languages offer some solutions to the problems of standard programming languages. In simple terms, OOP programs are designed in terms of component objects on which operations can be performed. Projects are built from libraries of these objects. OOP languages shorten development times compared to third-generation languages, and vastly increase the ease of maintaining and modifying the software. The drawback is again the learning curve which, if anything, is steeper than that for third-generation languages. Object-oriented languages are particularly suited to multimedia because different media types, like video or sound, can be easily represented as objects. The *ScriptX* language and the *Apple Media Tool Programming Environment* are both object-oriented languages designed specifically for IMM authoring. OOP languages are not recommended for development teams which do not include an experienced programmer.

Visual programming environments

Visual programming languages attempt to reduce development time for simple applications, like IMM, by integrating drawing tools and interaction elements with a programming language. This allows a programmer to create the visual 'face' of a program without recourse to code. A drawback of this approach is that these environments tend to lack the flexibility and speed of traditional environments.

Visual environments tend to be event-driven. Each event, such as a mouse click, is passed as a message through a hierarchy of objects, each of which can contain program code called a 'handler'. Because these languages are based on objects created by the programmer, there is a tendency for their various vendors to claim that their authoring environment is 'object-oriented'. For the majority of authoring environments this is simply not true. While they are 'object-based' almost all of these languages do not contain the essential elements of an object-oriented language.[2]

There are several styles of visual programming environments.

1.   Stack-based environments

The first stack-based program was *HyperCard* on the Macintosh. There are several successors to *HyperCard*, such as *Allegiant SuperCard*, *Oracle Media Objects* and *Asymetrix Toolbook*. All of these products use a similar programming metaphor, that of stacks of cards.[3] Each screen of information is called a 'card', and links can be established between cards. Cards have objects upon them, each of which has its own set of properties and can have an associated piece of program code, or 'script'. The essential element of stack-based languages is that they are based on the notion of a number of individual screens which are linked in some way.

A drawback of most stack-based environments is the difficulty in establishing and maintaining an holistic view of the project being developed. With other environments there is an intrinsic overview of the project and its *flow*. In a stack-based environment a project is split across dozens, if not hundreds, of cards, making it difficult to visualize the structure of the project. The use of many different cards can also make the project difficult to revise and maintain.

2.   Flowchart-based environments

This style of program is best exemplified by *Authorware*, and to a lesser extent, *ICON Author* and the *Apple Media Tool*. Multimedia and program elements are represented by graphical icons which are combined into a flowchart representation of the structure of the program. The flowchart approach implies a beginning and an end to the program. Flowchart-based programs tend to be linear, with occasional branches off to other sections before returning to the main thread.

Despite their limitations, flowchart-based programs are very simple for non-programmers to use. Screens can be created and linked together to form a multimedia title with very little use of scripting. The lack of emphasis on scripting, however, means that flowchart-type programs lack some of the flexibility of other programming environments.

3.   Time-based environments

Many IMM programs can be treated as complex animations which can be played back according to a time scale. *Macromedia Director* is an authoring environment which uses this approach. *Director* was originally an animation program, but it has been extended to become a fully-fledged IMM authoring environment. Development is founded on a time-based score, and a stage, on which multimedia objects (sprites) can perform. Each sprite can contain its own program code or script, which activates it or other sprites.

Director is particularly suited to developers with experience in media environments like video or audio. It is also well suited for highly graphical projects or kiosk-style applications. There are many commercial examples of impressive multimedia applications which have been constructed using *Director*, for example *Buried in Time* by Presto Studios, *Just Grandma and Me* by Brøderbund, and the *Star Trek Next Generation Interactive Technical Manual* by Warner New Media.

However, it can be difficult to translate projects which consist of discrete chunks or concepts into a continuous, time-based environment like *Director*. *Director* is also not as strong as other environments in handling text and user input of text. Despite these shortcomings, at the time of writing *Director* was, undeniably, the market leader in terms of multimedia development environments. One reason for this is that *Director* has an almost seamless cross-platform capability.

5.3.2 Programming techniques

Having briefly discussed aspects of programming environments, let us discuss some techniques for using them effectively.[4] Most of the projects discussed in this book have been developed in *Allegiant SuperCard*. Because of this, the examples in the following sections are based specifically upon *SuperCard*, but the techniques discussed can be applied to many languages and authoring environments.

Typical IMM programming involves placing text, graphic, video and sound objects on the screen, formatting these, and providing scripts to activate them. This can be a very time-consuming and repetitive task, especially when many screen objects have similar scripts and formatting. Authoring environments like *SuperCard* are very flexible but, because of this, they often take several steps to perform one function. For example, text fields have many attributes (font, fontsize, style, etc), which often have to be set individually for each such object. If the graphic designer decides to change the text font and colour throughout a project, this could result in many hours of tedious labour without productivity techniques such as those described below and elsewhere in this book. The same argument applies if it is necessary to make a small change to a script which appears in many objects.

There are various techniques which can be used to cope with the inevitable changes which occur in an IMM program, and these can be generally collected under the label 'elegant'.

Elegant programming

The highest commendation a programmer can bestow on a colleague is to describe their code as elegant. In the programming world there are two ways to do things: the brute force method and the elegant method. The brute force method typically solves the problem in the most direct manner, but this is often the worst way to do it. The definition of elegant code is a little more difficult. Elegant code is generally quicker in execution and more efficient than brute force code, but most importantly it is simpler to understand. Computer programs are complex enough without confusing people with complicated routines!

If you watch a group of programmers at work you will eventually see one of them turn to another and say something like 'Can you think of another way to do this?' They already know how to solve it one way, but would prefer a simpler solution – perhaps a more elegant method of solving the problem.

When you write programs you should be looking for simple solutions to problems. Spend some time planning, and analyse the task at hand from all sides. A little bit of lateral thinking would not go astray. Always try to look for the elegant solution, because it will save you lots of work later.

Make the code robust

Computer programs have a tendency to 'crash' or fail mysteriously. This can be avoided by writing robust code. Robust code fails less often and when it does, it fails gracefully, warning the user before it collapses.

When writing a function, do not assume that it will be passed the correct data. Validate the data passed to it in some way, and if it is incorrect then alert the user and abort the function. Handle errors in a coherent way. Do not just warn the user that an error has occurred, tell them *which* error occurred and *why*, if you can. This helps in debugging during development and during maintenance, and supports the user.

Make the code simple and understandable

One of the most difficult tasks faced by a programmer is to work on somebody else's code. In a team development environment, most projects will be handled at one time or another by several programmers. It is therefore essential that other programmers be able to understand the code. A complicating factor about trying to understand a piece of program code is that programmers are not only trying to understand the code itself, but the logic behind the code!

In the high level languages used in most multimedia scripting it is rarely worth cutting corners. One way of doing something is usually just as efficient as doing it another way. If this is the case then it should be done in the simplest but most transparent way, so that other programmers can understand what has been done.

Maintainability

Ideally, computer programs, once written, should run forever without needing to be altered. However, changing circumstances and changing user needs often require that programs be modified or even rewritten. In this case, some unfortunate soul, who might or might not be the original programmer, will have to do the work. They will have great difficulty in understanding the program unless it has been well documented and commented. The code might have been obvious to previous programmers, but the chance of following the same logic a year after it was written is slim; the chance of someone else following the same logic is less likely. For major projects, there may even be a case for full technical documentation to assist with maintenance.

At the very least, inline comments should be used liberally to explain how, and more importantly, why something is being programmed. An example of the use of comments is shown in Figure 5.9 (see page 124). In particular, it is important to describe all the global variables which are used.

Avoid global variables

A global variable is available to all parts of the program. It can be defined anywhere, at any time, by any object. In a traditional programming environment there is seldom a need to use global variables, since variables can simply be passed up and down throughout the scope of the project. In multimedia environments, global variables often need to be used to achieve the same end, with separate objects exchanging data through a common global variable.

A problem with global variables is that it is difficult to know exactly what state they are in. This is a particular problem if the global variable uses a common name which is (accidentally) used by another object. If you have to use a global variable, make the name as explicit and as unique as possible. The longer the variable name, the less chance there is that another programmer will pick exactly the same name for another global variable. This also reduces the likelihood that the program will mysteriously crash.

Avoid using explicit names

Using explicit names for resources in your project, such as files or objects, will severely restrict the ability to maintain them. If you hard-code the name of a video file, then when you want to change that file name you will have to change each and every occurrence of that name in the script.

Consider a simple children's reading program (Figure 5.3), which has a series of buttons containing the names of animals. When the buttons are clicked, a picture of the animal appears, and the sound of the animal is played. Figure 5.4 shows a sample *SuperCard* script for the dog button. Other similar

Figure 5.3 *An example of a children's reading program*

```
on mouseUp
        set cursor to watch

        - HideOtherAnimals is a routine which hides
other visible animals
        - from a previous use.
        HideOtherAnimals
        play sound file "dog"
        show card graphic "dog"
        pass mouseUp
end mouseUp
```

Figure 5.4 *A hard to maintain script*

scripts may differ only in the name of the animal. If we wanted to change this script from 'dog' to 'puppy', we would have to manually change every occurrence of 'dog' in the script.

```
on mouseUp
      ShowAnimal("dog")
      pass mouseUp
end mouseUp

on ShowAnimal Animal
      - play the animal sound and show a picture of
the animal passed
      - to this routine through the variable 'Animal'

      set cursor to watch
      - routine which hides other visible graphics
      HideOtherAnimals

      play sound file Animal
      show card graphic Animal
end ShowAnimal
```

Figure 5.5 *An easier to maintain script*

The script shown in Figure 5.5 is written in such a way that no matter how many times the animal is changed, the name has only to be changed in one place. This means that the script is quite easy to modify, no matter how often it is used throughout the program.

Use the same script in similar objects

The script shown in Figure 5.5 can be reused for other objects, for example 'cat', by duplicating the script and changing 'dog' to 'cat'. A more elegant solution is to use the name of the button to determine which animal to display. The script shown in Figure 5.6 enables the same piece of code to be used in any number of objects *without modification*. To create a button for a pig, simply duplicate the 'dog' button, and change its name. Of course, the programmer needs to beware that a graphic and a sound resource for the pig are in place.

Keep common code in one place

The script in Figure 5.6 can be used several times on one screen, and duplicated over any number of screens. However, what if it needs to be modified? Perhaps a modification of the design requires that the screen be locked before hiding and showing the graphics, so that transitions are smoother. This means

```
on mouseUp
        - use the name of the object clicked on to determine which
        - animal is chosen.
        ShowAnimal(the short name of me)
        pass mouseUp
end mouseUp

on ShowAnimal Animal
        - play the animal sound and show a picture of the animal passed
        - to this routine through the variable 'Animal'

        set cursor to watch
        - routine which hides other visible graphics
        HideOtherAnimals

        play sound file Animal
        show card graphic Animal
end ShowAnimal
```

Figure 5.6 *Using the name of an object to create reusable scripts*

that a 'lock screen' and 'unlock screen' message needs to be inserted in each of the perhaps hundreds of instances of the script in Figure 5.6. Programmers' time is too expensive to perform these tedious sorts of operations, and stack-based visual programming languages provide a mechanism to circumvent this through the message passing hierarchy, described briefly in section 5.3 under 'Visual programming environments'.

As a general principle, if a piece of code appears more than once in a program, it should be moved out of the object in which it is located to become a function or procedure further up the message-passing hierarchy, for example in a background script, or project script. In this way, code can be stored in a single location so that it is easy to find and only has to be changed in one place. This modularity makes programs much easier to maintain.

Figure 5.7 shows an example of this, where the button script calls the handler 'ShowAnimal'. The message hierarchy is searched until this handler is found and executed. In this case it is in the background script, accessible by all objects in the background. This script needs to be changed only once to change the behaviour of all buttons referring to it.

Reduce or automate repetitive tasks

There are certain tasks in any project which are repetitive and tedious, and these should be reduced or eliminated whenever possible. This allows developers to concentrate on innovative aspects of a project, using their time and abilities to the best effect. Having developers involved in copying, pasting

```
Button Script
on mouseUp
        - use the name of the object clicked on to determine which
        - animal is chosen.
        - ShowAnimal is stored in the Background script
        ShowAnimal(the short name of me)
        pass mouseUp
end mouseUp

Background Script
on ShowAnimal Animal
        - play the animal sound and show a picture of the animal passed
        - to this routine through the variable 'Animal'

        lock screen
        set cursor to watch
        - routine which hides other visible graphics
        HideOtherAnimals

        play sound file Animal
        show card graphic Animal
        unlock screen
end ShowAnimal
```

Figure 5.7 *A script with changeable code as far along the message-passing hierarchy as possible*

and formatting page after page of text in a project is wasteful of resources. In most cases, there is little reason why repetitive processes like formatting text cannot be automated.

There is also some scope for the use of tool palettes in large projects. If tasks are repeated often enough, there is a definite advantage to constructing a special tool to do the job for you. By grouping tools together in a palette, repetitive tasks can be 'factored-out', replacing complicated sequences with a single tool. Data entry, page layout and text formatting are all suitable candidates for automation. Figure 5.8 shows a sample tool palette which was developed for a particular application.

If you are planning to develop multiple titles then tool palettes are particularly useful. The tools developed in one project can almost certainly be modified to reduce or eliminate repetitive tasks in further developments.

This process can be taken even further by building a specialized tool which allows non-technical developers to build framework projects out of blocks of content. The 'IMM Toolkit' was designed to help multimedia developers quickly prototype their ideas and experiment with various designs. In its current form the compiler takes a design for an IMM project, in the form of a specifically formatted textual storyboard, and automatically compiles the design into a functional working prototype. The prototype can then be evaluated and the design modified, simplifying the process of developing CBL materials.

The use of the ToolKit provides a number of important benefits including:

- providing a clear and distinct blueprint for the multimedia project;
- allowing the content expert to concentrate on content and not implementation;
- potentially simplifying development of cross-platform multimedia.

Once the project document (textual description) has been created, it can be put into the Toolkit to compile the project into a prototype. The development team can then experiment with the prototype and see if it meets their requirements. If it does not, then the project document can be revised and another prototype compiled. When the prototype satisfies the development team, it can be handed over to the programmer with detailed instructions so that he or she can populate it with additional content and implement any of the complex interactions required.

While the toolkit is mainly suited for book-like, linear projects, it offers important advantages in some cases because it can dramatically reduce development time.

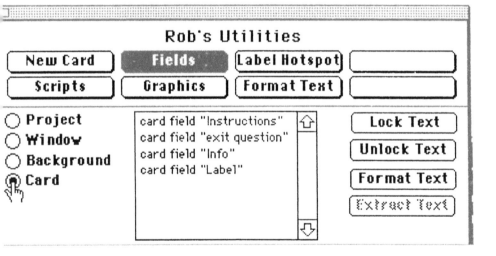

Figure 5.8   *Generic formatting tool palette*

5.3.3 Examples

An example of good programming
The script shown in Figure 5.9 is an example of good programming. It is well thought out and designed. It contains a header block, which is important in clarifying the purpose of the program code:

- it explains what the function is and how it works;
- it lists the variables and parameters of the function;
- it describes what parameters the function will accept and what it will return.

The function also uses meaningful variable names which help to explain the function's purpose.

```
—FUNCTION FINDSTRING
This function finds a string delimited by any two characters within another string.
The function accepts  a string and two character parameters specifying the
delimiting
characters for the substring.  The function also accepts an index into the string
telling
it at what point to start searching from.

VARIABLES : superString      the string to be searched by the function,
                afterCharacteran index into the string to specify the point at
                             which to start searching from (integer)
                firstCharacter the character delimiting the start of the substring,
                lastCharacter  the character delimiting the end of the substring,
                firstIndex     an index of the firstCharacter's position  in the string
                lastIndex      an index of the lastCharacter's position in the string
---------------------------------------
function findString superString,afterCharacter,firstCharacter,lastCharacter

        if afterCharacter>0 then delete character 1 to afterCharacter of superString

        put offset(firstCharacter,superString,0) into firstIndex
        add 1 to firstIndex
        put offset(lastCharacter,superString,firstIndex) into lastIndex
        add firstIndex to lastIndex
        subtract 1 from lastIndex

        if lastIndex>=firstIndex then return character firstIndex to lastIndex of
superString
        else return empty

end findString
```

Figure 5.9 *An example of elegant code written in* SuperCard

The formatting of the function is important. Although the function could be collapsed into a smaller number of lines, this could make it confusing (see Figure 5.10). The conventions used in Figure 5.9, eg indentation and capitalization of variable names, are reasonably standard and help to make the subroutine easier to read.

```
function findstring thestring,charA,charB,charC
    delete char 1 to charA of thestring
    put offset(charB,thestring,0)+1 into x1
    put offset(charC,thestring,x1)+x1-1 into x2
    return char x1 to x2 of thestring
end findstring
```

Figure 5.10 *A poor example from* SuperCard

The function also contains some error-checking capabilities. It does not assume that the variables 'afterCharacter' will be correct, but checks to see that it contains a valid value before it executes a script. The function also has an exit condition to resort to if the function fails. If the appropriate substring cannot be found, the function will return 'empty' or no value.

An example of poor programming

The piece of code shown in Figure 5.10, while fully functional, is difficult to understand. Trying to identify what this function does would be difficult, and it has only four lines! Some of the problems are:

- it has no comments and the variable names it uses have little to do with the values they contain;
- it has no formatting to visually separate logical parts. It flows continuously from one line into the next, which makes the flow of the function hard to follow;
- it contains no error checking and will crash if the wrong parameters are passed to it. For example if it were passed 'zebra' for the parameter 'charA', it would crash because the first line of the function expects 'charA' to be an integer.

It may be difficult to recognize, but the code in Figure 5.10 performs exactly the same functions as the code in Figure 5.9. Unfortunately, a lot of program code looks like that shown in Figure 5.10. There is a natural tendency for people to simply sit down and write the code they need to solve a given problem. They may think they will go back at some later time and add comments and modify variable names. However, in reality most people never get around to it, and the code remains just like it was written the first time. If code is commented as it is written and variables are given meaningful names to start with then overall development time can be significantly reduced.

Notes

1. Our experience has been mainly with Apple's *QuickTime* format, and the applications discussed in the rest of this section are specific to *QuickTime*.
2. Readers interested in further information about the principles of object-orientated programming are referred to Budd (1990).
3. Toolbook uses essentially the same metaphor, but calls the 'stack' a 'book' and the 'card' a 'page'.
4. Some aspects of this section may be too technical for non-programmers.

Chapter 6

Evaluation

Des Thornton and Rob Phillips

6.1   Introduction

In Chapter 3 we described an incremental prototyping model of IMM development consisting of a continuous cyclical process of design, develop, evaluate. In this model, the evaluation is an ongoing process where, at the end of each cycle, we critically examine what we have done before starting the next iteration of the cycle. The amount of effort put into the evaluation and the decisions made here determine the quality of the project, and hence its ultimate success or failure.

Ongoing evaluation is crucial in bringing a project in under budget, because design problems can be identified early enough to fix them, before they waste effort and money.

In the academic environment there are important added advantages of a thorough approach to evaluation, since the results can be used as a source of research output, as well as in funding applications.

6.1.1   What is evaluation?

The term 'evaluation' has a number of meanings depending upon the context in which it is being used. In its purest sense the term evaluation means a judgement of merit or worth against a predefined set of standards or expectations. The evaluation process is used to assign a value to the 'object' being evaluated so that its worth or intrinsic value can be conveyed to others. For example, one might evaluate the quality of the food at a restaurant or the workmanship of a tradesperson in order to recommend them to others.

The term 'evaluation', as applied to IMM and education in general, takes on a different emphasis and covers a much broader range of activities. The process of evaluating IMM material is not to assign some intrinsic value to it but to answer the many questions that arise during the development and implementation of the IMM software. The pitfall into which many IMM developers and users of multimedia fall when they begin evaluating multimedia is in attempting only to answer the question, 'Is this IMM package a better way of teaching than using the traditional approach X?' This is not such an unreasonable question, given that teachers are always looking for ways of improving the effectiveness of the learning process. There are, however, many other very important questions to which answers need to be found if multimedia is to improve and become an effective and efficient mainstream learning tool. For example:

- Do the students find it stimulating?
- Does learning take place?
- What was the long-term impact on student learning?
- How can the interactivity be improved?
- How could you have improved the IMM design process?
- How can we improve the IMM development process?
- Was the budget realistic and accurate?
- What improvements could be made to the resource allocation during development?

6.1.2   Some possible questions to ask

Reeves and Hedberg[1] (1997) suggests that there are four key areas on which to concentrate when framing questions about the interactive multimedia development and implementation cycle:

- Document evaluation (do the processes work?)
- Formative evaluation (can users use the program?)
- Summative evaluation (was learning effective in the short term?)
- Impact evaluation (was there long-term retention of knowledge?)

These points are discussed in the four following sections.

6.2   Document evaluation

Reeves calls the evaluation of the processes carried out during IMM development, 'documentation evaluation'. That is, evaluation of *what happened* or *is happening* during the development cycle shown in Figure 3.3 and how the resources allocated to the project are being utilized. This evaluation phase looks at answering questions about the processes and procedures followed during the development cycle. It addresses some of the critical issues of project management, such as:

- Is the project on schedule?
- *Who* has done *what* to date during development?
- Are the time estimates accurate?
- Is client communication adequate?
- What resources are still required?
- Is the project going as planned?
- What is the next critical stage?
- Have the project meetings been effective?
- Does the project development approach feel right?
- Did we learn to improve the development process?

The data required to answer these and many other project development questions are the type of information collected during the traditional project management cycle, for example, needs analysis, project proposal, project development plans, individual development timesheets, budget and financial records, developers' personal experiences, client correspondence and minutes of project development meetings.

6.2.1   Sources of information

Given that the sources of data for the 'documentation evaluation' are the people involved in the development cycle, it is important to implement *quality* data collection techniques as an integral part of the project management process. Diaries of activity should be kept by all persons involved as soon as the seed of a project is planted and the development process begins.

Collect data longitudinally over the timeframe of the project by monitoring things such as time, money, progress, resources used and the human story of the project development cycle. This information can be used to:

- tell team members if they are on task and going to see the end of the project;
- improve the overall design and development cycle;
- provide necessary data for costing and development of future projects;
- provide control over the development process;
- build cohesion between development team members;
- focus the development team on tasks and problems.

Some tools you might consider useful for collecting information are given in the following sections.

Minutes of meetings

Minutes of all formal project meetings should be kept by the project manager as a diary of project progress and as the foundation of the whole Project Diary. The minutes serve as an accurate history of progress, informing project participants of current status in a formal way and at the same time highlighting action items to be addressed. It also ensures a constant link and monitor between the planned project development cycle and actual project progress.

In all recent projects we have been keeping concise minutes of what has occurred, especially any action items and how they are resolved. A representative example is shown in Figure 6.1.

Minutes of Muscles CAUT meeting

2 pm, 22 November 1994
Present: RP, RK, NJ, GF, SF

1.   Minutes of last meeting

2.   Matters arising
ACTION: AD to continue to work on the interface.
ACTION: AD and RP to start implementing some ideas. Discussion is needed to do it efficiently.
RESOLUTION: RP demonstrated a prototype of the interface, based on work with AD. Some graphic design work remains, but it is generally satisfactory. Glossary needs to be less busy, as does the 'trailer' screen.
ACTION: GF to continue producing a storyboard for one key term for next meeting.
RESOLUTION: Intro screen contents produced. No time yet for other content.

3.   Discussion
Minor changes were made to the requirements specification to do with intro screens. See the documents: Fyfe Requirements 22/11.

SF and GF were very happy with the Actin formation animation. Some work needs to be done with all three together. It is getting quite urgent to finish the process and formation animations.
ACTION: AD to make a time with RP, GF and SF to discuss touchups to the Actin animation.
ACTION: AD to demonstrate the formation animation for the next meeting.

GF is having difficulty in working on the content (no time and higher priorities). She will not have time until her leave in January. SF has time and offered to start work on some aspects now.
ACTION: SF to work on content for ATP/ADP and CA^{++} for next meeting.

The map screen was thought to be useful.
ACTION: RP to print this for GF.

4.   Next meeting
2.00 pm 29 November. CC Boardroom

Figure 6.1   *A representative extract from the minutes of a project meeting*

Personal activity logs or time sheets

As the name suggests this instrument is used to record an individual's activities during the development cycle. The quality of the information provided is dependent upon the detail with which the instrument attempts to measure activity. For example, an instrument which contains only broad headings such as those shown below,

- analysis
- design
- production
- evaluation

will not be able to distinguish fine detail about the time spent during the development process and as a consequence cannot provide data to look for weaknesses in the process.

Figure 6.2 shows a timesheet used by a graphic designer to document the time spent on a number of projects.

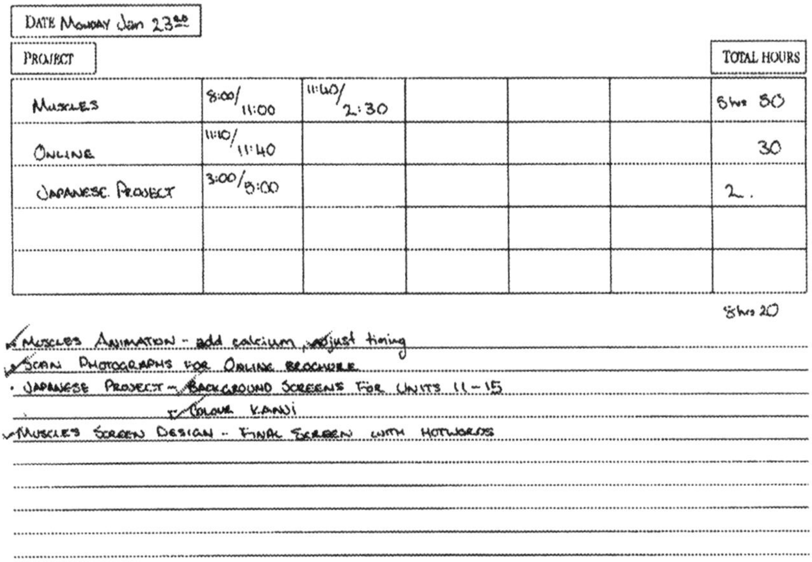
DATE Monday Jan 23rd

PROJECT						TOTAL HOURS
Muscles	8:00/11:00	11:40/2:30				8hrs 50
Online	11:10/11:40					30
Japanese Project	3:00/5:00					2.

8hrs 20

Muscles Animation - add calcium, adjust timing
Scan Photographs for Online brochure
· Japanese Project - Background Screens for Units 11-15
Colour Kanji
Muscles Screen Design - Final Screen with Hotwords

Figure 6.2 *A representative time sheet used in project development*

Status reports

These are the reports presented by developers at project meetings relating to issues such as progress to date, activities planned for the next period, problems requiring resolution, resources required or available and any other matters associated with the project that are felt to be important. Given that the whole development process depends critically upon human communication and cooperation, Reeves recommends that participants be encouraged to tell the human side of the story where appropriate. The comments at the end of the case studies (Chapters 8–11) seek to describe the human side of successes and problems experienced by team members at the coal face of IMM development.

Another aspect of status reports is shown in Figure 6.3. This report from the Microbiology project was e-mailed to all group members by the programmer, to inform them of the current debugging status of each module.

```
Here's the updated version of the Status Report.  Please let me know
about any inconsistencies:
```

	Content Sent/Rec'd	Prog Done	Bug Report Round 1 Sent/Rec'd	Debug	Bug Report Round 2 Sent/Rec'd	Debug
"MicroBiology"	**	*	**	*	–	–
"UTI Intro"	**	*	**	*	–	–
"UTI tutorial"	**	*	**	*	**	–
"UTI Reference"	**	*	**	*	**	–
"UTI Geriatrics"	**	*	**	*	–	–
"UTI Tests"	**	*	**	*	**	–
"UTI Paediatrics"	**	*	**	*	–	–
"RTI intro"	**	*	**	*	–	–
"RTI reference"	**	*	**	*	**	–
"RTI tutorial"	**	*	**	*	**	–
"RTI Case Study 1"	**	*	**	*	–	–
"RTI Case Study 2"	**	*	**	*	–	–
"RTI Case Study 3"	**	*	**	*	–	–
"RTI Case Study 4"	**	*	(odd report)	*	**	–
"RTI Case Study 5"	**	*	**	*	**	–
"RTI Tests"	**	*	**	*	–	–
"GIT intro"	**	*	–	–	–	–
"GIT reference"	**	*	–	–	–	–
"GIT tutorial"	**	*	–	–	–	–
"GIT Tests"	**	*	–	–	–	–
"GIT Case Study 1"	**	*	–	–	–	–
"GIT Case Study 2"	**	*	–	–	–	–
"STD intro"	**	*	–	–	–	–
"STD reference"	**	*	(no errors?)	–	–	–
"STD tutorial"	**	–	–	–	–	–
"STD Tests"	**	*	**	–	–	–
"STD Case Study 1"	**	*	(no errors?)	–	–	–

Figure 6.3 *Status report of the Microbiology project. Asterisks indicate whether the report has been sent or received, respectively*

Sign-off forms

Our experience has shown that *not* getting the client to sign off the content or agreed design as satisfactory can present real problems later in the development cycle. 'That's not what we agreed!' can be a very difficult phrase to deal with ten weeks into a project. The sign off signifies that both parties have an understanding of each other's expectations with respect to the project. As discussed in Chapter 4, the storyboard should be signed off before work proceeds further (ie into the production cycle described in section 3.1.4). This ensures that all fine points of detail are nailed down and agreed.

In the same way, completed modules should be signed off by the client when they have been tested to their satisfaction, or have been through an agreed number of user testing cycles.

The sign-off form covers both the developers and the client and affords a degree of protection to both. Reviews of content or design undertaken by people outside the group should also be signed off in order to add credibility to the development process and product.

Resource audit sheets

In a project involving three or four people with each being responsible for different resource components, the coordination of resource availability can be an issue. For example, if sounds must be recorded, video captured, graphics produced and text-based content provided it is important that these be staged to coincide with the development phases. An inventory of required resources should be developed during the design phase and then used to produce a schedule for resource production. It is very important to highlight critical resources upon which the whole development process depends and ensure that a close monitor is kept upon these.

> For example, in the Japanese Videodisc project, sound resources were particularly important. Work could not be carried out on programming interactive exercises involving these sounds until these resources had been recorded and digitized. Resource audit sheets, like that shown in Figure 6.4, listed details of spoken Japanese expressions needed for each segment of the program. The resource audit sheets were used in conjunction with the storyboard (shown in Figure 4.1) to provide a cross-reference of all resources needed in this large project.

Problem reports

In a perfect world everything should go according to plan and the customer will be totally satisfied! The reality is that a range of technical problems will arise during the development process and some of these may be of major significance. Normal problems can be handled during project meetings as a matter of course. However, in the case of major problems one course of action is to document the problems as accurately as possible and form an expert

---

JAPANESE INTERACTIVE VIDEODISC PROJECT

30 May 1994

Unit 11 Set Expressions - Answers for Audio Recording

Segment 1: Have you ever been to Japan?
1.   ... ga suki desu
Segment 2: Talking about Japanese food
1.   ... ga ichiban suki desu
Segment 3:Talking about cooking
1.   ... mashō ka
2.   li desu ne
Segment 4: Planning an outing
1.   ... wa dō deshō
2.   Hoka no yotei ga arun desu
Segment 5: Asking to use the phone
1.   ... hō ga ii desu
2.   ... te mo ii desu ka
3.   Dōzo
Segment 6: Borrowing things
1.   ... ni kanshin ga aru
2.   Yoroshiku onegai shimasu

Figure 6.4   *List of sound resources for one part of the Japanese Videodisc project*

group to address them. The information gathered during this phase can be used to identify weaknesses in the initial design phase.

Typically, many small problems are not documented. Instead they are resolved quite quickly by talking to colleagues. However, some problems are quite intractable, and the only way to solve them is to form a small group to focus specifically on them. It is very important to clearly define the problem before trying to solve it. The mental discipline involved can often lead to its solution; if not, then at least everyone in the group knows that they are talking about the same problem, or the same aspect of the problem.

During the Japanese Videodisc project we came up against many technical problems. In one case, we were not able to get video to display on a newer model of Macintosh. A staff member had half-developed a solution, but then he found another job, and we had to employ an independent programmer to develop a solution for us. The software requirements were written down and discussed with the programmer, but the end result did not function as it was supposed to. The root of the problem was that documentation was not comprehensive enough and consequently the programmer made assumptions different to those of the person who wrote the specification.

Was this the fault of the programmer who made assumptions without checking with the client? Or was it the fault of the problem report? The fact was that the communication failed, and the project was delayed by at least a month.

Budgets

It goes without saying that regular reviews of the planned budget against actual expenditure should be undertaken. Running out of money two-thirds of the way through the development cycle does not impress anyone and not knowing that you have run out of money is even less impressive to all involved!

A common characteristic of IMM development is that the number of hours spent increases as deadlines approach. The project manager may be making a linear extrapolation of the budget towards the deadline, only to be confounded as extra hours are put in the last-minute rush. In our experience, hours worked must be collated at least weekly to obtain an accurate overview of the current budget position.

One project management model uses the triangular form shown in Figure 6.5 to indicate the constraints experienced during project development. Of the three fundamental parameters in the model (cost, quantity and quality), it is most likely that cost and quantity will be fixed in most developments. A project usually has a fixed amount of funding available, and a comprehensive design process results in a fixed storyboard, thus defining the quantity. Therefore, the consequence of running out of money during development is that the most important factor in the model – the quality – is going to be compromised. (A specific example of this was discussed in Section 4.3.3 with regard to the Carbohydrates program.)

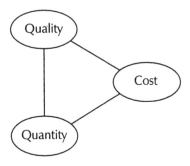

Figure 6.5 *The cost-quality-quantity triangle*

Summary

The above methods are just a few of those that you could use to gather information in order to evaluate the development process. The information collected is most useful if it is collated into a chronological Project Diary represented as a well-documented timeline. In this form it can be used as a basis for project reporting or a reference point for future project planning.

6.3   Formative evaluation

Having survived the battle of deciding on the most appropriate design strategy for the delivery of the IMM material and put in place mechanisms to collect as much information as possible the next question is – *will it work with students?*

There is no point in waiting until the final product leaves the bench before testing it with students or other staff to see if the design works. You want to see if:

- the navigation is effective,
- students enjoy using it,
- the approach used to deliver information is intuitive,
- the screen designs are effective,
- it works the way it was planned.

In the past, many developers have seen the evaluation process as something which occurs at the *end* of the development process. This is the narrowest view that could be taken in evaluating IMM, because it assumes that the initial design specifications are perfect and cannot be improved. Based on research and practice, a more appropriate (and broader) view is that evaluation pervades all aspects of the development process. It is imperative to use evaluation as a vehicle for obtaining valuable information about how improvements can be made to both process and product.

6.3.1   Formative vs summative evaluation

The spectrum of educational evaluation lies between the extremes of summative evaluation, where attempts are made to obtain absolute measures of the key underlying variables involved in the learning process, and formative evaluation, where as Flagg (1990) puts it 'systematic collection of information for the purpose of informing decisions and design and improving the product' is undertaken. Summative techniques are useful in an environment where traditional experimental designs, using treatment and control groups, are being employed in order to compare the effectiveness of two or more instructional approaches. Formative techniques, on the other hand, can be used to provide a rich source of data about what the students think and feel about the interface and design. It is these data that will answer the questions that arise during the design and prototype development phases.

Reeves (1992b) argues strongly that in the evaluation of IMM materials the three primary principles of contemporary cognitive learning theory should be addressed. He identifies these primary principles in relation to IMM:[2]

- learning is a process of knowledge construction as opposed to knowledge absorption,
- learning is knowledge-dependent and uses existing knowledge upon which to build new knowledge,
- learning is highly tuned to the situation in which it takes place.

Reeves and Hedberg (1997) suggests a model for the evaluation of IMM materials as consisting of the following components:

> The evaluator should establish a number of unobtrusive monitoring procedures before the experiment begins. First, the IMM should include automated response-capture routines so that paths and process through the IMM options are tracked. Second, measures of individual differences (such as demographics, previous experience) thought to be relevant to the interpretation of outcomes should be incorporated into the IMM. (Reeves and Hedberg, 1997)

Reeves stresses that a key factor in the evaluation of IMM materials is the learner's appreciation of the user interface and the way in which it integrates and complements his or her learning style.

A range of techniques is available, and we recommend that you use several of these to obtain converging evidence by triangulation.

6.3.2   Formative techniques

Some of the formative evaluation techniques that Reeves and others suggest one could use during the design and prototype development phase are described below:

Expert review

A range of both internal and external experts should be consulted to provide comment and feedback on issues such as the:

- accuracy and completeness of the content;
- motivational and instructional strategies used;
- screen designs, general aesthetics and user-friendliness;
- educational approach adopted;
- general effectiveness of the approach.

Information on the above topics can be collected using a number of tools such as:

- questionnaires;
- expert review sheets;
- interview schedules;
- video recordings.

The key point is to collect as much data as possible for review and reflection and to report them to others when presenting information about the history and development cycle of the product.

A further advantage of using expert review is that not only can experts identify problems, but they can also offer advice on how to resolve them.

Student observation and interviews

It is advisable to have students interacting with the prototype screens as early as possible, to compare their reactions and comments on the educational design strategy, navigation mechanisms, user interface design, degree of interactivity, clarity of objectives, ease of use, etc, with your expectations. What seemed clear and easy to use in the design phase may well not work at all with students. Those sounds which you included to give feedback and indicate errors made by the student may be a major disruption in the learning process; the aesthetic gains in screen design of pleasing bitmap graphic images may be outweighed by the resulting slow response which may be unacceptable to students; the help system you spent hours building may never be used; the text sizes and screen layout may not be easy to follow; students may miss major objectives because they were not easily identified or given sufficient emphasis.

While the students are interacting with the prototype you can gather useful data by observing and noting the sorts of problems and joys they experience, by utilizing video equipment which shows both their screen interactions and facial expressions, or by having teams of observers each monitoring different aspects of the prototype evaluation. In all cases it is important to record accurately your observations taking note of the specific data that will enable you to answer the design questions under review. All observers should use a standard template with appropriate headings and space for additional observations.

Interviewing the students and using a well-structured interview schedule after they have interacted with the prototype can provide valuable information and insight into student impressions. The interview can be undertaken on a one-to-one basis or in a group situation with a number of students being asked to reflect on the same question.

Automatic data collection

One valuable source of data is to collect information about student interactions, in the form of mouse clicks, topic visits and use of navigation tools, as the students use the package in a real learning environment. If the data are logged to a file with a date and time stamp they can be replayed to replicate the student's learning process or analysed via some other utility to show what actually occurred. Using this technique can give you valuable insights into how the students learn in the environment you have provided. For example, this might show that students never used the help facility, or that some key topic areas were never visited by students because the navigation environment was unclear, or that students repeatedly clicked the mouse because the system response was too slow and they were not sure if their first mouse click was recorded.

Clearly, it is important to identify what questions are being addressed when designing data collection. There is little point in collecting large volumes of data and then trying to decide what to do with them. Fishing for an answer is not an effective approach.

> The Carbohydrates program contained a novel, built-in auditing facility. Student progress was recorded as they moved from screen to screen. The navigation method they used and the time spent on the screen were recorded in a text file.
>
> A visual mechanism was developed for viewing the audit results. The diagram shown in Figure 6.6 shows a typical audit screen. The student progress and time on screen is superimposed over the main screen forming a map of nodes and links. Darker lines indicate paths or links chosen by the student. Lines became thicker each time the student used a given link. Nodes on the map are highlighted if they have been visited. The highlighting becomes progressively darker the longer the student stays on that screen, and the time in seconds is recorded to the right of each node.
>
> A series of student audits can be recorded into a *QuickTime* movie to obtain an overview of how the cohort of students has used the program.
>
> The auditing facility was used for two purposes. At the one level it was used to analyse the ways in which students navigated from place to place in the program, because several navigation methods were possible at any time. At a second level, it was used to triangulate student learning with the parts of the program visited. The contention was that if students had not visited a given part of the program, then they would not have a good understanding of that part of the content.

Verbal walkthroughs

Another useful technique is to have the students verbalize their thoughts and reactions to each screen as they work through them and then record their reactions for analysis using a video camera. The students will need to be coached in the technique of thinking out-loud rather than just saying what they are doing at this point in time. You are interested in reaction and feeling. Questions like:

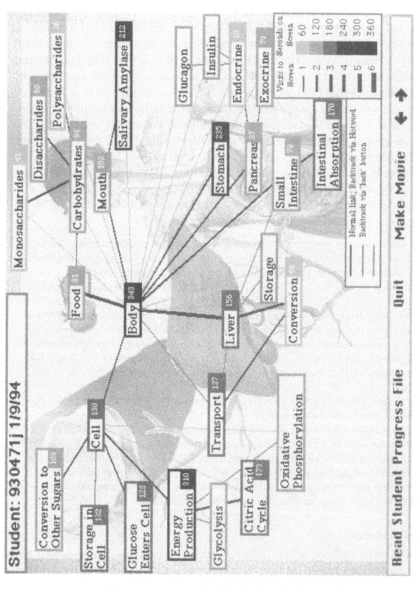

Figure 6.6   *The Carbohydrates program audit screen*

A colour version may be viewed at http://www.curtin.edu.au/curtin/multimedia/devhandbook/toc.html

- 'Why did you go that way?'
- 'Is it clear what you are supposed to do?'
- 'Do you know the reason why you are doing that?'
- 'What is your reaction to this material?'

are what the students should be answering as they work through the material. Once the skill is developed it will provide some very useful data about first reactions to your design.

Alpha and beta field tests

As the product develops, small alpha field trials should be undertaken with groups of prospective users who have not previously been involved with the instructional material. In observing the trials you are looking for evidence of learning/comprehension taking place, evidence of the fact that students are enjoying working with the material and evidence that the material is truly interactive. Information can be gathered by observation/recording, interviews with users after the event, or by well-structured focus groups.[3]

Beta field tests with larger and more diverse populations can be run much closer to the date of implementation. It is most likely that these tests will not greatly influence the design but they will highlight existing 'bugs' and allow fine tuning of the interface. In framing the beta tests it is important to take the following points into consideration:

- The beta tests should replicate as closely as possible the environment in which the final product will function. For example, if the product is to be run in a self-paced mode with little or no lecturer/tutor input then the test should be conducted in that mode. The aim is to look for real-world problems, so it is important to replicate the real-world environment.
- The population selected for the test should be as broad a cross-section of the intended audience as possible. It might be a good idea to undertake the trials at a number of different sites so that you minimize the possibility of trial population bias which might exist if you have undertaken all testing in one location.
- Consider bringing external evaluators into the process in order to broaden the evaluation and possibly to gain a different perspective which may provide data that can be used to triangulate your earlier observations.

In beta test mode it is important to monitor closely the version numbers of the software as 'bugs' are fixed and new releases are generated. Mechanisms for tracking fixes and updating all sites to the same version at one time must be put into place. Given that the time for delivery/implementation is probably approaching quickly, it is possible that you may still be undertaking beta tests and bug fixes in parallel with the first implementations of the product. Some of these issues are discussed in more detail in Chapter 7.

6.4   Evaluating the effectiveness of the implementation

Having designed, developed and implemented the IMM product, some core questions to ask are:

- Does it achieve the educational objectives for which it was developed?
- Is the student's knowledge or skill enhanced?
- Has the student's attitude to the subject matter been influenced in some way?

As Reeves and Hedberg (1997) point out, we are trying 'to determine the short-term effectiveness in meeting objectives' of the material and as a consequence deciding if it should be adopted for wider use, be promoted for use by others, be enhanced, or be discarded. This is also known as the summative evaluation.

A very useful technique recommended by Reeves and Hedberg (1997) is the use of a data collection matrix in which questions form one axis and possible data sources form the other axis, as in Figure 6.7. For each question, appropriate data sources are ticked in the matrix. It can then be verified that all data collection methods have been prepared and collected.

QUESTIONS	Anecdotal Records	Questionnaires	User Interviews	Lecturer Interviews	Observations	On-line data collection	Exam/Tests	In-basket Exercises	Performance Test
What skills were acquired?									
What knowledge was acquired by students?									
What attitudes were formed by students?									
What were the lecturer perceptions?									
What were the student reactions?									

Figure 6.7 *Data collection matrix for evaluating effectiveness*

One axis of the matrix looks at the questions we are attempting to answer and the other axis summarizes possible methods which could be used to gather the necessary data to answer these questions. This evaluation matrix is a very useful tool in that it neatly summarizes the evaluation methodology and at the same time forms the basis of the effectiveness evaluation plan. It is important to develop such an effectiveness evaluation plan for the project so that it can be reviewed by others, and because it will prompt you to investigate other outcomes of the learning process involving IMM not usually considered in traditional educational evaluation.

6.4.1   Measuring outcomes

The approaches that can be used in order to evaluate the short-term outcomes of the product are described below:

Traditional tests and examinations

Tests or examinations are the traditional means by which educational effectiveness is measured. 'The score on the test or examination is an *indicator of the effectiveness of the learning* which has taken place.' Don't forget that this statement is true only if the tests or examinations (instruments) which are being used are *valid* and *reliable*. That is, the items measure what they are supposed to measure (the instrument is valid), and that repeating the measurements with other groups of students will give consistently similar scores for high achievers and low achievers (the instrument is reliable). The data provided by using instruments that have not been shown to be valid and reliable are to all intents and purpose useless!

Computer-based tests or simulations

In certain situations it may be appropriate to incorporate a test or quiz, which is administered and marked via the computer, as part of your IMM educational material. This approach has a number of advantages in that,

- a longitudinal study can be undertaken if the data from each student's test are logged to a file;
- accurate and timely feedback can be given to the students on weaknesses in their knowledge or understanding of the subject matter;
- using the computer to mark the tests reduces the burden on the evaluators.

If the aim of the IMM material is to improve student skill in some technique, then rather than using a test to evaluate performance, it might be more appropriate to use a computer simulation which puts the student in a situation in which they have to use their newly acquired skill. If the simulation is designed in conjunction with the other material then close attention can be paid to ensuring that all aspects of the newly acquired skill are tested.

Other measures
There are a number of other techniques which can be used to monitor the effectiveness of the interactive multimedia material.

In-basket exercises
These are paper-based simulations of real problems that the student would be expected to be able to solve with their newly acquired knowledge or skill. Ideally, there will be a range of exercises covering a range of real-world problems that can be presented to students at random.

Performance tests
In situations where paper or computer-based tests are not a suitable evaluation tool, performance tests, which place the student in real situations where they have to apply their newly acquired knowledge or skill, can be used. This approach is particularly suited to situations where skill development is the aim of the IMM material.

Some other measures
Apart from the knowledge, skills and values (Posna and Rudnitski, 1994) measures commonly used in the traditional evaluation of the educational process in the classroom, there are a number of areas in which the use of IMM enhances, enriches and provides flexibility to the learning environment. For example, the use of multimedia material by students may not lead to significant gains in test and examination scores over the more traditional lecture approach, but it may be a more cost-effective solution than laboratory sessions. Gains in flexibility may be evident from the times of day that students use the material; accident and safety records may be improved; student experience may be enhanced because of the reality of the material presented; or efficiencies in learning time may be evident because students can cover the material in a shorter time. In developing the effectiveness evaluation plan for the multimedia material consider broadening the evaluation to include some of the parameters mentioned above.

6.5   Evaluating long-term impact

'What longer-term impact did using the IMM learning material have upon the students?' This question is the most difficult to answer and yet provides the strongest evidence to support the continued and enhanced development of the multimedia material. If it can be shown that it has had a longer-term impact that has influenced the way the student approaches similar learning situations or solves problems in the area then it can be argued that the material is truly effective in achieving its core goals.

6.5.1   Evaluating impact

Reeves and Hedberg (1997) suggest a number of techniques that can be used to provide data on the longer-term impact of the multimedia material.

Anecdotal records
Collect the human story of what happened after the event by talking to the students and teachers who have been involved with using the multimedia material. Look for evidence of changes in behaviour or learning patterns of the students which can be attributed to using the multimedia material. Revisit the groups over a period of time to validate your initial findings.

Observations
If possible observe the students in environments which would require the use of the skill or knowledge acquired by using the multimedia material. Clearly, single observations of one group would not support the hypothesis that the change in behaviour is attributable only to the material but it can provide data which can be correlated with other observations, taken over a longer period.

Interviews
Prepare a high quality interview schedule with a range of questions that probe for evidence of longer-term impact that can be attributed to the new skill; for example, questions about how the new skill is being used, situations where problems have been solved using this new skill, examples of how the skill has changed the approach to problem solving or work patterns. Be sure to include all of those who might be affected by the change, for example, lecturers, students, tutors, laboratory supervisors, support staff, etc.

Indirect measures
Evidence of longer-term impact may well be available through measures of other variables not necessarily directly associated with the newly acquired skill or knowledge. For example, a change in the borrowing pattern of physics books in the library may well be an indication of the impact of a new multimedia physics course just implemented. Reduction in student drop-out rate for a course, or time taken to complete a course, may be an indication of changing student attitudes as a consequence of the introduction of a multi-

media course. Some thought should be given to the sorts of things that may be indirect indicators or unobtrusive measures of longer-term impact that can be associated with the multimedia material.

In summary, look on evaluation as a vital part of the whole IMM development process. Used in an appropriate and effective manner, it will act as the catalyst to enhance the quality of the final and future products.

Notes

1. Most of the content of this Chapter is based on the work of an acknowledged authority on interactive multimedia evaluation, Professor Tom Reeves of the University of Georgia, USA, and his colleague, Assoc. Prof. John Hedberg from the University of Wollongong, Australia. The theoretical points from their book *Evaluating interactive learning* (Reeves and Hedberg, 1997) are backed up by practical examples from the projects with which we have been involved.
2. See also Chapter 2.
3. Focus groups – a tightly structured group discussion which follows a predefined thread or line of questioning – are commonly used in qualitative research.

Chapter 7

Implementation and Maintenance

Nick Jenkins

7.1   Introduction

If evaluation is often forgotten in multimedia production then maintenance is more or less ignored. The amount of time needed to maintain a multimedia title can often be severely underestimated. As was noted in section 3.1.5, there is an inversely proportional relationship between the time taken on design and the time spent on maintenance.

> The Dosage Calculation program was mostly developed before we had adopted the current design methodology. Some aspects of the design were not comprehensive enough to define clearly how the program would behave, particularly in respect of the testing modules, which should have been designed at the same time as the rest of the program, instead of being added at a later date. In addition, too little attention was paid to the laboratory environment in which the program would run. Consequently, more than 50% of the total development time was spent on unfunded maintenance and debugging of the program.
>
> The Carbohydrates program, on the other hand, went through a comprehensive design process. In this case, debugging and maintenance comprised five hours out of approximately 300 hours total development time.

Also neglected by developers is the process of implementation. Far too often developers concentrate on finishing the project without any real idea of how it is to be implemented for the user. The first part of this chapter is devoted to 'implementation', that is, delivering the finished project to the customer, while the second part focuses on maintenance. Many issues raised in this chapter have also been discussed under 'Feasibility studies' in section 3.3.

7.2   Implementation

How a project is delivered can be as important as its construction. If the project is difficult to install or will not run on a particular type of computer, then much of the effort that went into building it might be wasted. Just as packaging is crucial in the commercial world, implementation is crucial in the world of computer software.

7.2.1   Version numbers

In any large project, one of the most difficult tasks can be keeping track of where each part of the program is and what stage of development it has reached. The method most commonly used by programmers is to use 'version numbers'. (See also section 7.3.5.)

Each segment of a program should be assigned a version number, and the version numbers should be updated as changes are made. A log, or version history, should also be kept of the revisions and of each version. The version history lets the development team 'roll back' to previous versions, and provides an outline of progress made on the project over time.

There are various systems for using version numbers, but the simplest is to divide version numbers into minor and major revisions. When the version number is quoted, it should be read as a decimal number, with the 'major revision number' being the integer and the 'minor revision number' being the decimal fraction. For example a project might start at 0.1 and progress through to 1.5 before reaching 2.3. (Zero usually denotes 'pre-release' versions of software.)

A more complicated system uses three digits indicating release version, beta version and alpha version respectively. Alpha and beta refer to different stages in testing of software, with alpha usually being internal and beta being the first version that is shown to outside testers. Thus, a project that is in the early stages of testing might be 0.0.3, while a project nearing completion might be 0.9.5, and a project that has been on the market for some time might be 3.5.5.

Following is a sample version list from the 'Interactive Multimedia Toolkit' discussed in section 5.3.2:

0.1 Files, string manipulation
0.2 Syntax checking, Database commands
0.3 All objects/positions, links implemented, Inline commands
0.4 Code split, modular revision
0.5 Major syntax changes, removal of quotations
0.6 Major revision, removal of chunklist, Item build moved off screen
0.7 Save as function

0.8 New look control panel
1.0 First release !

7.2.2 Platform

The first factor to be considered when implementing a program is how the program will run on the end-user's computer. If the program is written and designed to run on this year's latest and greatest computer, it is hardly going to impress your users if all they have to run it on is a ten-year-old black and white model. Although it is critical to consider this at the design phase, there are some solutions which can be offered in the implementation phase.

Considerations like disk space, memory requirements and processor speed affect the implementation of a program on a particular platform. The program should be able to adjust to the differing requirements of different machines. At the very least, where possible, users should be offered a number of different configurations of the program to give the best results on their platform. These configurations can be offered either by allowing the user to set 'preferences' after the program has been installed, or by allowing them to install one of a number of configurations.

> The Japanese Videodisc project has a relatively complex preferences screen. This project was designed to be used in a number of modes by a number of users on a number of different hardware setups, as shown in Figure 7.1. Individual floppy disks are used to record users' preferences and allow them to carry these settings from machine to machine. Note the settings for the videodisc player which enable the program to be used with a range of different videodisc players.

7.2.3 Delivery and installation

Another important issue is how the product is transferred from the developer's computer to the user's computer. Will the developer install the program, or will it be delivered in a format which the user can install themselves? Another consideration is whether or not manuals or other information will be included with the project. Finally, a decision needs to be made on how the project is going to be distributed. Will it be distributed on floppy disks, via a CD-ROM, or possibly via the Internet?

Different environments have different requirements. For example because a CD is a 'read-only' medium, the program won't be able to save any files to it. If a project needs to record information, like user preferences for example, it will have to record them somewhere other than the CD. A networked environment can cause similar problems since many people may be accessing the same files at the same time.

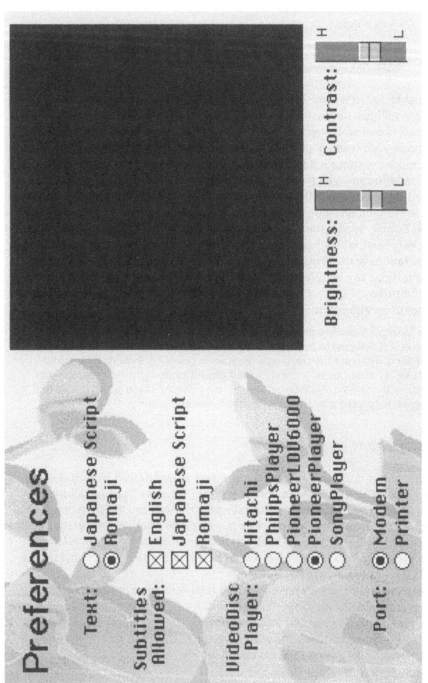

Figure 7.1   *The preferences screen for the Japanese Videodisc project*

A colour version may be viewed at http://www.curtin.edu.au/curtin/multimedia/devhandbook/toc.html

In the Dosage Calculations project we encountered problems with transferring the project from the stand-alone machines on which it was developed to the network server where it was to run. For the program to work successfully from the server it had to be 'locked' to prevent multiple users trying to change the document at the same time.

The Dosage program was developed in *SuperCard*, which automatically saves its configuration every time it goes from screen to screen. Since the file was locked this meant that the program reverted to its original state every time the user changed screens. In a test section of the program this caused mayhem, because the program gave the students the same question over and over again.

This problem was initially circumvented by a quick patch-up job, but a comprehensive rewrite and redesign were necessary to completely solve the problem. The solution was quite simple but, because the issues of use on a server had never cropped up before, it had not been considered during the initial design.

Like any part of a project, the delivery should be tested in the widest set of circumstances possible. Make up a dummy installation of the project and try installing it on a number of different machines before committing to that form of delivery. Implementation is often the last gasp of the project and testing in this area can be neglected. Implementation is, however, an essential link in the chain which takes the software from concept to the user's computer.

An example of a tiny error that caused a lot of trouble comes from the Interactive Design & Development company in the United States. A major project for the Dole food group had reached implementation stage and a batch of CDs were pressed to distribute the product. The files on the CD were laid out so that a user need only double click a single icon to run the program. Unfortunately a mistake with the CD meant that the icon pointed not to the files on the CD but to the hard disk on a computer within the company. This meant that when people tried to run the program using the icon the program searched for files on a computer located some hundreds or thousands of miles away! Consequently the company has been giving away the CDs since the defect makes them unsaleable.

7.2.4   Distribution

Distribution is a slightly different issue to delivery. Distribution deals not so much with the medium that is used but with the *way* in which it is distributed. For example, some IMM products are sold, others may be given away, while others may use techniques such as shareware.

If you choose to sell a product, you can either do so yourself, or you can seek the help of a software publisher. Like traditional book publishers, software publishers take commercially viable software and organize its widespread distribution. Smaller publishers may only arrange to make the software available in quantity, with distribution being left up to you. Again like book publishers, software publishers can be picky and getting a software title to 'print' may be a difficult proposition.

Because software can be easily duplicated, an alternative is Shareware. Shareware is a system by which a product is distributed free of charge, but anyone who keeps a copy is required to pay for it. This means that people can take a copy of a software package and see if it suits them. If they keep it longer than 15 days, however, they are required to pay for it. There are many forms of shareware, the simplest being a simple legal document distributed with the software which relies upon the honesty of users. More complicated forms of shareware include distributing cut down, demonstration versions of a project and requiring people to buy the full version, or distributing software which automatically expires after the 15 day limit if a serial number is not entered.

The final alternative is to distribute the software for free. With the spread of the global network, many people are writing and distributing software at no cost to the user. This brings no financial reward but is not necessarily as altruistic as it sounds. Distributing free, quality software can build a reputation on which further commercial products can be based.

Peter Lewis, who originally worked at Curtin University, developed a suite of network programs for the Macintosh. Programs like *Anarchie* and *FTPd* were distributed freely and made the process of connecting to the global Internet much easier for Macintosh users. Consequently, Peter is nearly a household name amongst Macintosh network users and has started his own company writing network software.

7.3   Maintenance

Just as people often neglect to allow for the cost of maintaining a new car in the purchase price, developers often neglect to account for the cost of maintaining a project in their budget. Inexperienced developers expect their responsibility to end when the program is handed over to the client. This can be a costly mistake. An example of the costs involved in such a project is a software program written for the US Air Force which cost $30 per instruction to develop and $4000 per instruction to maintain over its lifetime (Sommerville, 1989). Although this is an extreme example, it illustrates that if maintenance is ten times more costly than development, the price of maintaining such a system would soon become unsustainable.

7.3.1   Design and maintenance

Some time ago, traditional programmers identified what has become known as the 'software crisis'. As computers became more powerful and more and more software was written to utilize this power, the problems involved in maintaining the software became exponentially more difficult. Costs skyrocketed and projects were delivered late, were unable to cope with requirements and were unstable (Sommerville, 1989).

The major solution to the problems of the software crisis revolves around the design of programs. If a program is properly designed, the costs of maintaining it can be reduced significantly. Conversely, if a project is poorly designed, it can inflate, by orders of magnitude, the costs involved with maintaining it.

IMM is no different to traditional programming in this respect. A multimedia project which is badly designed will be difficult to maintain and will probably result in a much reduced life-span for the product. By following appropriate design principles such as those discussed in this book, developers can ease the process of maintaining a multimedia project.

Most of the design principles have been covered already, but some programming issues will be emphasized here. Foremost among these principles is the use of modular and reusable code. A project which is divided into individual sections or modules can be easily upgraded since each section can be taken off-line and modified without changing the other sections. A project which centralizes code resources within each module also reduces the effort involved in maintaining the program, because it eliminates the need to change those resources in all of the different areas.

Also important is the documentation and layout of a program. It is entirely possible that the person who maintains a project may not be the same as the one who wrote it. If this is the case then it can be very difficult indeed to track down bugs and discover where the program is at fault. Similarly, it is more than likely that a programmer will forget how he or she actually coded a particular project over a period of time. As a programmer's skill evolves, so does the way in which they develop projects. In order to ensure that projects are understandable when they are returned for maintenance six months or even six years later, all aspects of the project should be carefully documented.

One approach to ensure the quality of documentation is to require code reviews or walkthroughs of the program to a group of peers.

7.3.2 Debugging

Very few developers are lucky enough to have their projects run flawlessly the first time. Most have to go through a process of testing and debugging in order to achieve a finished project. A finished project is not necessarily bug-free either, as Bruce Sterling points out in his book *The Hacker Crackdown* (http://www.yahoo.com/Society_and_Culture/Cyberculture/Books/Hacker _Crackdown_The/):

> Some software is bad and buggy. Some is 'robust', even 'bulletproof'. The best software is that which has been tested by thousands of users under thousands of

different conditions, over years. It is then known as 'stable'. This does *not* mean that the software is now flawless, free of bugs. It generally means that there are plenty of bugs in it, but the bugs are well identified and fairly well understood.

The standard method of finding and recording bugs is through the use of 'bug sheets'. When testing a program it should be given to both experienced and novice users so feedback is received from a broad audience. Each person testing the program should be given a form (either paper or electronic) on which they can note bugs, problems and errors as they progress through the project.

On a typical bug sheet the project, the date and the members of the team involved (usually the person reporting the error and the programmer) are recorded at the top. Further down the sheet, bugs are listed individually with each bug being given a location and a detailed description. A sample bug sheet from the Dosage Calculations project is included in Figure 7.2.

It is important for the programmer to prioritize bugs. Most programs contain a number of bugs, ranging from fairly serious programming bugs to small problems with content or punctuation. The programmer can spend all his or her time fixing spelling mistakes unaware that a serious programming error lies in wait on the last page of the bug sheets. At the very least there should be a system for highlighting serious bugs which stop the program functioning correctly.

7.3.3 Debugging by the content expert

In a team environment there is something to be said for allowing content experts to debug their own copies of a project. In a typical project a lot of bugs are introduced in the process of translating the content into computerized formats. It is costly to have a content expert hunt down spelling, punctuation or logical errors in the content, and then give them to the programmer to fix. It makes more sense for these errors to be fixed on the spot by the people who uncover and understand them.

Having said this, however, this process raises many problems. Content experts are usually not conversant with the format and commands of a development environment and can cause serious damage while trying to fix an inconsequential bug. Another problem occurs when many people are working on many copies of the project. In this situation, it is difficult to know which is the master copy of the project and the question of version control (see below) becomes essential.

An alternative way to handle this process is to have the programmer sit down with the content expert and go through the program step by step, fixing bugs as they are found. This is more time-consuming and more complicated to organize, but is a useful technique for the final tests of an almost-finished project.

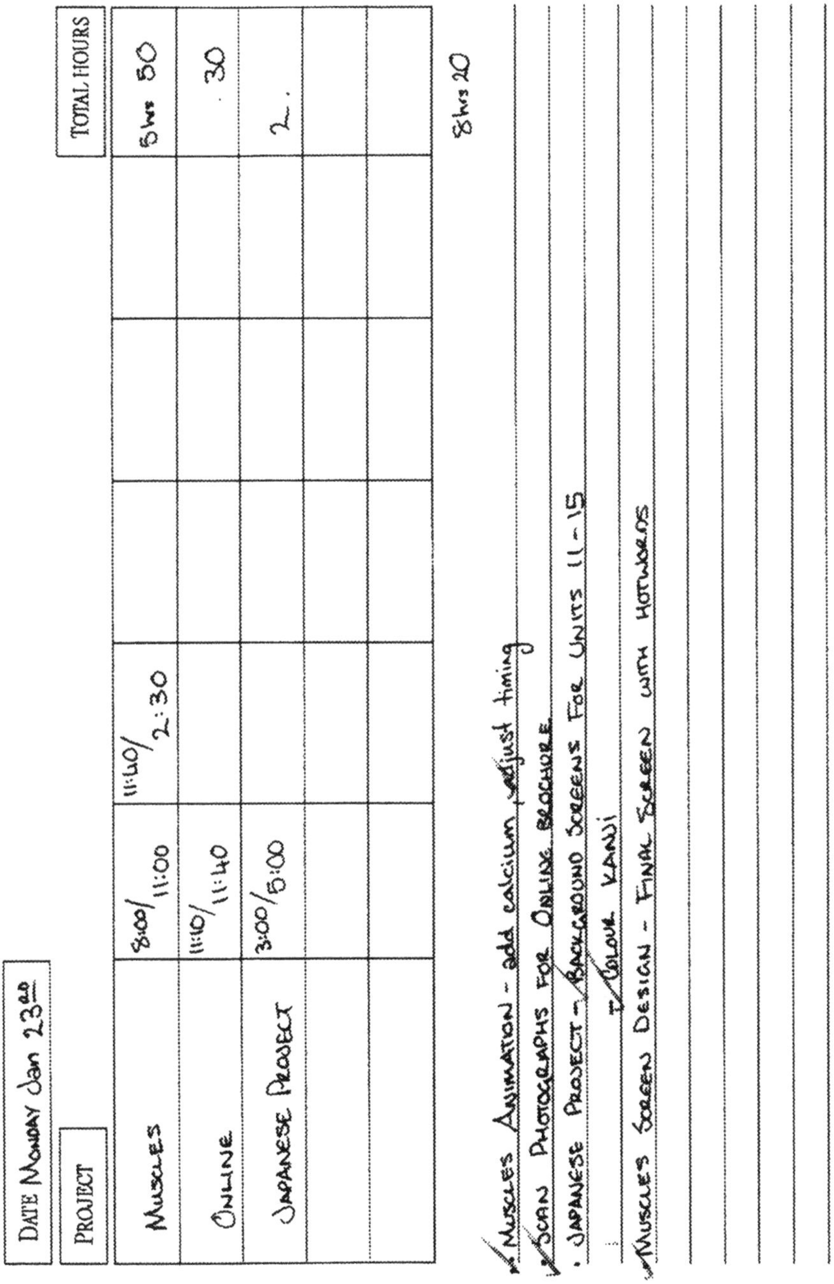

DATE Monday Jan 23rd							TOTAL HOURS
PROJECT							
Muscles	8:00/11:00	11:40/2:30					5 hrs 50
Online	11:40/11:40						.30
Japanese Project	3:00/5:00						2.
							8 hrs 20

✓ Muscles Animation - add calcium - adjust timing
✓ Scan Photographs for Online Brochure
• Japanese Project - Background Screens for Units 11 - 15
        - Colour Kanji

✓ Muscles Screen Design - Final Screen with Hotwords

Figure 7.2   *A representative bug report sheet*

7.3.4   Ongoing maintenance

In 'off-the-shelf ' packages, ongoing maintenance can be very low but the requirements for testing and quality are very high. Conversely, software purpose-built for a specific client can have very high ongoing maintenance, but may not need to be as robust a product. The reason for this is that, in an ongoing relationship with a client, problems can be revised and corrected as they come to light. With off-the-shelf packages, the contact with end-users is much lower and there is much less opportunity to make corrections after the product's release.

Ongoing maintenance is a mixed blessing. Although it provides a chance to polish a project, it also presents the possibility that the project may never be finished. Clients are, understandably, concerned with value for money and in getting the best possible project. If a specific date for delivery has been assigned, and the project is reviewed to everyone's satisfaction, then it should be considered finished. This process should be formalized by signing off the project, when the client agrees they are sastisfied with the product. Any further modifications made to the structure of the project should be charged for at an appropriate rate since this is, in effect, a redesign of the project.

Determining what constitutes a 'bug fix' and what constitutes a fundamental change to the structure of the project can be very tricky. While the client may view a change as a simple modification, there can be some severe ramifications of such a change. Modifying one button may not seem like much to the client, but when that button is spread across 2000 different screens of a particular project, the change can be enormous, and the potential for introducing consequential bugs even greater!

7.3.5   Version control

In a project of any reasonable scale it must be made clear who is responsible for each area of the project. If the work is being done by more than one person, then there exists a possibility that the project can be damaged or work lost.

Typically, a shared computer file opened at the same time by two people will contain *only* the changes of the person who saved it last. Some systems will warn users of this problem, and others will prohibit more than one user from opening the document simultaneously, but the danger still remains. If, for example, one person in a team copies a file from a central file server onto their own computer, works on it, and then copies it back, any changes made to the server version in the meantime will have been lost.

A solution to this problem is to formalize who holds the responsibility for each section of the project. Each section should be assigned to an individual who is responsible for any changes that are to be made to it. A master copy of the project should also be kept by the project coordinator in case of corruption or accidental erasure of the working copy.

> With the Japanese Videodisc project we had a large team of programmers and a large number of sections to cover. Towards the end of the project, when many people were working for short periods on many parts of it, we used a whiteboard with each unit of the program on it. Against each unit was the name of one of the project team. That person had control of that unit and if another person wanted to make changes they would have to formally assume control from the previous owner. Anyone who modified a unit without having control of it was opening themselves up to the possibility of having their work overwritten.

7.3.6   Backups

An important factor to consider with any software is how and how often it is backed up. Computers are notoriously unstable, with disk crashes and file corruptions a common occurrence. With any sizable project, steps should be taken to ensure that copies of the files are kept in a safe place. If the computer which contains the only copy of a project were to crash, you could be left with nothing. With really important projects it is a good idea to keep more than one backup.

> The author keeps up to four backups of the project. He keeps the original copy on his machine, and makes one backup on a nearby desktop computer and another on a file server (which is in turn backed up). He also makes a periodic backup to a set of floppies which is filed away. 'This way I can be sure that unless the building gets hit by a meteorite, one of my copies is going to survive.'

It is also sensible to keep one backup at an offsite location, to minimize the risk of meteorites. It is essential to keep backups up-to-date. There is no point in having a copy of a project that is four weeks old if the majority of the work has been done in the past four weeks. It is often a good idea to backup a project to a nearby computer *every time it is modified*. In addition to this, longer-term backups or master versions can be made to a file server or a tape drive. This way if something goes wrong you don't lose more than a couple of days' work.

> In the Microbiology project, delays in testing caused a real problem. The programming on one module was completed in October, but it was not tested for bugs until March. It was then found that the installed module was corrupt. In the meantime, the programmer's hard disk had crashed, but he was not worried, because there were any number of backups! Unfortunately, each of the backups was also corrupt, because the regular cycling of tapes over the monthly cycle had overwritten the uncorrupt version. If a master copy had been made when the module was completed, this problem would not have occurred.

Chapter 8

Microbiology Project Case Study

Peta Edwards, Robert Fox and Rob Phillips

8.1   Background to the project

8.1.1   Teaching context

Microbiology is a highly visual subject requiring opportunities to view and experiment with living micro-organisms. Practical experience is essential for the understanding of concepts and application of knowledge to the medical laboratory setting.

Many laboratory sessions involve considerable repetitive practical work and difficulty is experienced in the provision of clinical material essential for these practical classes. This difficulty is especially evident with increased hazard to students from diseases such as HIV/AIDS and Hepatitis B. The problems are even more pronounced when microbiology courses are taught as external programmes.

In a bid to overcome some of these problems, the first tertiary accredited broadcast telecourse in Australia was developed in 1990. This was produced to teach microbiology externally to registered nurses who were upgrading their qualifications from diploma to degree (Fox and Edwards, 1990). In addition to the telecourse, assessment by computer-managed learning (CML) and a series of IMM CBL tutorials were developed to provide a completely self-paced package for use by all students of nursing microbiology (Edwards, 1992; Edwards and Fox, 1992, 1993).

The incentive for the development of the IMM tutorials was that students completing their nursing diploma were bored with large-group tutorial sessions. We found that this was in part caused by the lack of obvious relevance of microbiology to nursing practice. There were a number of reasons for this, two major ones being that microbiology is introduced very early into the nursing course, before the student has had any contact with patients with infectious diseases; and we could well have concentrated too much on giving students opportunities to acquire information rather than opportunities to apply it. We were also conscious of the fact that our students often had their classes at the end of a long day and were tired, and that the class contact time for nursing students can be as high as 30 hours per week.

We felt that providing students with opportunities to experience situations they might encounter in their professional life would help. Providing students with case studies of real problems would make the subject more relevant to their nursing studies. Moreover, by giving students opportunities to solve problems, we felt we would be encouraging them to apply their knowledge and acquire new knowledge as they needed it (Fox and Edwards, 1990).

Clinical case studies were developed as a hypertext program, linked to a database of relevant background information, a self-assessment quiz and a short tutorial. After four years of development the program consists of eight modules on the microbiology of urinary tract infections, respiratory tract infections, gastrointestinal infections, infections of the blood, infections of the cerebrospinal fluid, sexually transmitted diseases, antimicrobials, and viral infections. The program now comprises nearly 2000 screens of information.

8.1.2 Objectives

The aim of this work was to develop a computer-assisted learning program that would give medical science and nursing students opportunities to independently problem-solve microbiological case studies. Students use the program by applying their skills to simulated real-life situations and by following a consequential pathway on the decisions they make. A series of videos were also produced.

Through these developments we aimed to provide students with greater independence and control over their learning within an environment that was attractive and interesting to the student. These factors are thought to be important in encouraging a deep approach to learning (Kember and Gow, 1989). Kozma (1991) has also indicated that the use of IMM can enhance student interest in a subject while developing cognitive skills beyond those obtained with standard teaching procedures. We aimed to achieve similar results through the types of materials we developed and a need to use higher levels of learning in problem solving.

The multimedia developments would also encourage small-group discussion within practical sessions, increase student control over hazardous organisms in the laboratory, increase the role of academics as facilitators in the classroom, standardize curriculum content, practical techniques and assessment and provide a reference source for other institutions, industry and retraining programmes.

8.1.3   Feasibility

When the project was first discussed we planned to incorporate the CML test banks and selected video clips from the telecourse into the CBL program. The use of *SuperCard* and *QuickTime* would allow us to import and compress colour moving visuals, stills and sound as well as to present the material in colour.

In practice however, we found that the use of the higher-end computer software programs took up huge amounts of memory and disk space and had much slower operational responses than black and white programs like *HyperCard*. As most students would only have access to basic Mac computers, we felt therefore that our initial CBL materials should be mostly text-based with limited line drawn graphics and the occasional black and white photograph (Edwards and Fox, 1992a).

Once the decision to use *HyperCard* had been made, we considered how the development of the proposed program should evolve. We began with a question-and-answer program but have since developed a database, tests and case study scenarios linked to contents and records stacks. The database can be used as a stand-alone information bank or can be accessed by moving in and out of the other stacks. Students can access information and exercises related to the case studies in a sequential or random order.

Most of 1992 was spent in developing a prototype version of the module on urinary tract infections. Several user interfaces and structures of information were trialled and the final prototype was tested by a limited number of staff and students as part of the formative evaluation process.

As a result, in 1993, the user interface was revised. Content was then developed and programmed for the next five modules. The next year was spent in testing and debugging the first six modules and developing the final two modules. In 1995, final touches were added to the program and the testing and debugging were completed.

8.1.4   Funding

Funding for this project began in 1992 with a Curtin University Minifellowship and a proportion of a large Government National Priority Reserve Fund received by the Computing Centre to seed IMM development. Funding continued in 1993 and 1994 with substantial grants from the Government-funded Committee for the Advancement of University Teaching (CAUT), although some of this funding was for production of video resources and CML test banks.

To date the project has been funded to the tune of approximately $Aus110,000.

8.1.5   Team

Peta Edwards, from the Curtin School of Biomedical Sciences, has been the leader of the combined computer and video project, as well as providing, with Martin Finn and Eleanor Shapiro, much of the CBL content expertise. She worked very closely, especially in the early stages, with Bob Fox, instructional designer from the Teaching Learning Group, who has also been a valued adviser on the two CAUT grants.

Subsequently, most of the microbiology academic staff from the School of Biomedical Sciences became involved with this part of the project, either as content providers or testers. These include Judy Sampson, Dianne Courtney, Martin Finn, Lynn O'Reilly and Eleanor Shapiro.

Programming was done at various stages by Onno Benschop, Martin Hill, Justin Maynard and Nick Jenkins from the Computing Centre. Other Computing Centre staff involved were graphic designers Susan Perry and Angela DiGiorgio, as well as Dr Rob Phillips, who provided project management and advice at the Computing Centre end.

In 1993, graphic design assistance was provided by the School of Design, through a student, Jodie Burgess, supervised by George Borzyskowski.

8.2   Description of the project

8.2.1   The development model

The history of the Microbiology project is very informative, because it has extended over four years, throughout the evolution of the development process described in this book.

Developing such a large project is difficult. There have been heated disagreements, frosty memos, dissatisfaction at other team members, quite a number of belly laughs and eventually feelings of satisfaction as the project neared completion. In short, the project has engendered the whole gamut of emotions. Most of the problems can be attributed to the large number of people involved and their other time commitments, the whole team's initial inexperience and the difficulties in managing such a large project.

In 1992, the project was driven mainly by Peta Edwards and Bob Fox, as content expert and instructional designer. The Computing Centre acted in an advisory and coordinating role, providing assistance where required, but was unable to actually *work* on the project because there was no funding allocated to this and all Computing Centre staff were needed for other duties.

Neither Bob nor Peta had the skills or time to do the programming work required. This severely restricted progress until funding was reallocated to allow a Computing Centre programmer to finalize the prototype. Progress was then faster.

In 1993, funding from CAUT explicitly included components for programming and graphic design. The team of content providers was increased; the Computing Centre was to provide programming; and graphic design was to be provided by students of the School of Design, because design staff from the Computing Centre were fully occupied on other projects; and Bob Fox continued in his role of support and mentor. Thus, there were four areas of the university involved, each with different requirements and demands on their time.

Peta Edwards was on study leave in the latter half of 1993. A program outlining content development for three further modules was left with the team but, due to other commitments, progress was very slow. The Computing Centre staff were trying to cope with six projects and a vastly increased training load, and were not able to coordinate the development and meet programming deadlines. The design student had little experience in IMM graphic design and the artwork took a long time to produce. Most of the modifications to the user interface were initiated by the programmer. Because there were no clear deadlines set, work from all four parties tended to meander along.

Lack of communication was also a problem. The programming on one module was completed in October, but the content team were not informed of this. It had also not been made clear that the program needed to be debugged by the end of the year. By the time bug testing was started in March, it was found that the installed module was corrupt, with consequences discussed in Chapter 7. Better coordination could have avoided this problem.

At the beginning of 1994, it was clear that there were three lessons to be learnt:

- large teams made up from several different units of the University were difficult to meld into one cohesive group;
- there must be clear timelines and deadlines for when work must be completed;
- there must be better and clearer communication between all members of the group.

Progress in 1994 and 1995 was improved considerably due to better communication and better management. Regular meetings were minuted and action items noted. Clear deadlines were set, and the dependencies between tasks were identified, so it was obvious that a delay in content preparation would delay programming, which would delay testing, etc. Most importantly, the timeline identified the delivery date, when the material had to be ready for use by students, and allocated sufficient slack time to account for delays.

In between meetings, urgent matters were resolved by e-mail. E-mail was also used to distribute a status report of each module and sub-module. With debugging and testing proceeding in parallel, it was also necessary to assign and transfer ownership of modules, so two people did not work on them at once.

There have been some missed deadlines, but this is expected in any project, and adjustments have been made to the timeline without difficulty. Certainly at Curtin University, and probably in all academic institutions, staff have so many demands put on their time through their normal duties that it is difficult to devote sufficient time to 'extra' activities such as CBL development.

8.2.2 Content

The completed program has eight modules:

- Urinary tract infections
- Respiratory tract infections
- Gastrointestinal tract infections
- Infections of the blood
- Infections of the cerebrospinal fluid
- Sexually transmitted diseases
- Antimicrobials
- Viral infections.

Each module consists of an Introduction, a Reference section, Tutorial, Quiz and Case Study Scenarios, as shown on the left of Figure 4.23.

The student can enter the program through any of the four areas of interest, depending on their needs. One student might want background information from the reference section, another might want to test factual knowledge or application of knowledge through the tutorials, another might want to use the quiz as a test to see whether the material is already known and understood. The Case Study Scenarios can be used at any stage to test understanding and application of knowledge to hypothetical real-life situations the student could meet.

Reference

The Reference section is a small electronic book, consisting of a hierarchical series of screens of information about relevant topics and subtopics. Essentially, the student chooses a topic from a menu, and then follows a linear sequence of screens. There is little branching, but there are more diagrams in this section than in others.

Tutorial

The Tutorial section contains a series of multiple-choice questions on topics referred to in the Reference section. Student answers elicit feedback, but there is no assessment. A button links the tutorial question to the relevant section of the Reference, so the student can reinforce their knowledge if they are having difficulty with answering a question.

Quiz

The Quiz provides a series of multiple-choice questions which pertain to a mini case history. Once an answer is selected the test card informs the student of the correct response and their score.

Case Study Scenarios

When a particular Case Study Scenario is selected, a case history of the patient is provided, followed by a multiple-choice question with up to four options. After making a choice, the student is taken down a consequential pathway which can branch in many directions. Through feedback on the choices made, the student can eventually find the best solution to the problem. The student is able to use different pathways resulting from different choices and answers. The multi-directional nature of the case studies can potentially lead to total confusion as the user finds it difficult to remember which path has been taken as well as the original facts of the case study. Therefore, a 'history list' system of navigation has been incorporated, which provides a record of the user's movement through the scenario maze. At any time the user can backtrack through one or more of the decisions they had previously made.

8.2.3   User interface

The user interface of the Microbiology program has been discussed from the graphic design point of view in section 4.3.3. Recapping here, navigation is achieved through the consistent button bar at the bottom of the screen, as shown in Figure 8.1. The only navigational function not described in Figure 8.1 is the Return button, which is superimposed on the Exit button when within any of the sections of content. The Return button takes the user back to the nearest menu level in all sections except the Case Studies, where it returns the user to the previous screen.

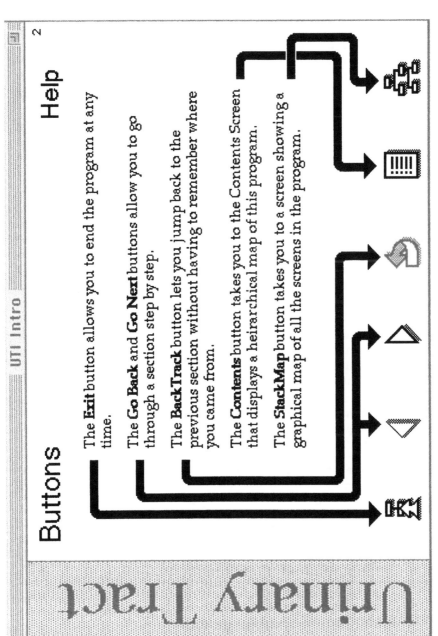

Figure 8.1   *The navigational functions of the Microbiology project*

8.2.4 Evaluation

Both qualitative and quantitative data were collected from students, staff at Curtin and other multimedia users and developers. Thirteen staff members (ten academics of whom five were involved in the project and three technical staff) and 35 students from the School of Biomedical Sciences were interviewed. Questionnaires were completed by 55 students from the School of Nursing and 50 from Biomedical Sciences.

The interview method was used to generate a more open-ended discussion on the perceived role and effectiveness of the project outcomes. Personal and small-group interviews were carried out face-to-face and by phone, during and after laboratory sessions and tutorials.

An interview guide with five open-ended questions was used. The semi-structured nature of the interviews allowed interviewees to pursue any area of inquiry about which they felt strongly. The open-ended approach encouraged respondents to draw their own conclusions about their experiences and/or opinions. The guide addressed usage of project materials, their perceived effectiveness, access to various technologies, the interrelationships between material developed and other components of the course, and possible future developments in other areas of the curriculum.

The questionnaire for the CBL evaluation (summarized in Tables 8.1 to 8.4) contained six general questions, 22 questions using a five-point Likert scale ranging from strongly disagree to strongly agree, and three open-ended questions. Fifty-five nursing students from a cohort of 92 completed this questionnaire. There were two invalid returns.

Table 8.1 *Attitude questionnaire from the microbiology project. Responses were recorded on a five point Likert scale, ranging from 1 (strongly disagree) to 5 (strongly agree)*

1.	The purpose of the computer program was clearly stated	4.35
2.	I consider the program to be relevant to my course and future employment	4.19
3.	The computer instructions were clear to me	4.29
4.	The written text on the screens was easy to read	4.59
5.	The graphics were clear	4.55
6.	I would have preferred the program in colour	3.4
7.	I would have preferred the graphics in colour	3.39

8.	The black and white program provided adequate information for my needs	3.98
9.	I was able to select what I wanted to look at	4.2
10.	The computer feedback guided my learning	4.22
11.	I was able to progress at a comfortable speed	4.3
12.	I kept getting lost in the program	2.08
13.	I don't like working with computers	2.0
14.	I found computer-based learning of this content stimulating	4.02
15.	I found the computer program user-friendly	4.27
16.	I would like to spend more time using the program or similar programs	4.4
17.	I would like to spend more time using similar programs and less time in lectures	3.63
18.	I would like to spend more time using similar programs and less time in practicals	3.27
19.	Compared to normal face-to-face lectures, I learnt more using the program	4.02
20	Compared to normal face-to-face practicals, I learnt more using the program	3.71
21.	I found the clinical case studies helped me understand more about microbiology and the areas under study	4.41
22.	I found the clinical case studies helped me apply my knowledge of the microbiology and the areas under study	4.45

Table 8.2 *Most popular aspects of the program from a total of 55 returned questionnaires*

Descriptor	No. of responses	% of responses
user-friendly	21	14.9
done at own pace/in own time	21	14.9
quizzes, case studies good for reviewing/liked/helpful	18	12.8

information given was sufficient for needs/relevant/variety	16	11.3
logical/systematic format/well planned/easy to understand guide to progress	12	8.5
feedback/helped address problems/clarify information, guide to progress	12	8.5
could go over materials many times until understood	4	2.8
provided opportunities for self-assessment/tested knowledge	4	2.8
provided more information than the text or lecture	3	2.1
challenging/stimulating	3	2.1

Table 8.3   *Least popular aspects of the program from a total of 55 returned questionnaires*

Least liked aspects of the program	No. of responses	% of responses
bugs in system/information errors/areas incomplete	21	14.9
available for use on only one day per week	21	14.9
too much information/too detailed for nurses/expected to learn too much	18	12.8
some information not covered in class/? examinable	16	11.3
time required to do programs	12	8.5
slowness of the computer	12	8.5
no printer so have to take notes	4	2.8
getting into the program is difficult	4	2.8
length of some programs	3	2.1
black and white	3	2.1

Table 8.4   *Most popular suggestions for improving the program, from 55 questionnaires returned.*

Suggestions for improving the program	No. of responses	% of responses
increase availability to students	9	24.3
get rid of bugs	3	8.1

have print-outs available	3	8.1
make programs for other units in nursing	3	8.1
design for nurses only	3	8.1
use colour/better graphics	2	5.4
increase information	2	5.4
give us more of the same	2	5.4
program works well as is	2	5.4

Students were enthusiastic about the CBL programs. They found the pathways that helped them navigate through the program easy to use. As one student said: 'The options and pathways are a really smart way of using this technology. I'm really impressed by the whole idea of the program.'

All students felt that the content of the programs was relevant and useful, particularly the more interactive components of the Quiz and Case Studies. All students felt the CBL programs went beyond the lecture, follow-up readings and laboratory sessions.

> 'I reckon the Case Studies are a good follow-on from the lecture – you can go at your own pace... There's the ability to go back and check the responses you made earlier... and to see alternative responses you could have chosen... or didn't even know about... By seeing all the options – it became a lot clearer to me what real options I have.'
>
> 'Sitting in a lecture – I often turn off – I don't intend to – it just happens... So to have this [program]... which I can use – going at my own pace – I'm really happy for a few hours. I really feel I've learnt something – the explanations are very clear.'
>
> 'I've learnt much more than I expected I would.'
>
> 'If you get something wrong, you can do it again and again. Things are explained as you work through them.'
>
> '[The CBL program has] sorted out certain issues the lecturers and practical sessions hadn't clarified for me.'

Students liked the scoring in the Quiz and the instant feedback from the questions in the Tutorial and Case Studies. They felt that their knowledge had greatly increased. Students felt that the program had enhanced and enriched their learning and that they would like to see greater use of the programs on their course. However, students did not want these materials, or any other, to replace face-to-face teaching or conventional laboratory sessions even though the CBL questionnaires results (Table 8.1, items 19–22 with Likert values of 4.02, 3.71, 4.41 and 4.45 respectively) suggest the CBL is a very effective way of learning microbiology. The latter comments support the following data from the questionnaires (Table 8.2) where students found the programs easy to follow and user friendly (12.8%; 18/141 responses). They also commented positively (8.5%; 12/141 responses) on the logical and well planned format which provided clear explanations and was easy to understand. They found the feedback helpful and this also provided valuable information and progress, (8.5%; 12/141 responses). The Quiz and the Case Studies were helpful for reviewing and self-testing (15.6%: 22/141 responses). Approximately, 14% (20/141 responses) commented on the fact that the program could be used as self-directed, self-paced study.

Interview data revealed that the main concern students had about the CBL programs was the lack of technical quality control. Students found the programs were 'riddled with programming errors'. The following students' comments summarize this point:

> The program is 'easy to use but frustrating in parts as some connections don't work – or worse – they take you to the wrong place', and 'Some sections in the Quiz don't keep a correct score... it marks me incorrect when I was right. I find this very confusing.'
>
> 'I've got limited time to burn... this is a demanding course. When I go out of my way to go down to the lab to use the computer programs, I expect them to work. When they don't... well, you won't catch me down there [Computer Lab] again until things work the way they should.'
>
> 'At this time of year it feels a bit frivolous to be playing with the computer... especially with all the bugs.'

A common comment made by students was their wish to have 'more convenient' access to the programs. They'd like to take the programs home. However, most students who said this had access to PCs and not Macs and saw this as a major problem. A few students asked whether the material could be put on the World-Wide Web. As one student said:

> 'It's a pity its only available in the computer lab, I'd like to use it from home – that is, once I get a modem... But will it work on PC?... Could it be put on the Web?

Similar comments were received to the open-ended question regarding what nursing students liked least about the CBL (Table 8.3). These students also commented on the heavy time commitment (5/66 responses) and the fact that too much detail or information for their needs was in the programs. In regard to the latter comment, one must bear in mind that the program was developed for multi-level use by students in different disciplines. Some nursing students (3/37 comments, Table 8.4) wanted the program designed for nursing only.

8.2.5 Implementation

Student use
All modules of the program are currently in use as part of the normal curriculum. The program is available to students in the Health Sciences

computer laboratory and on other computers throughout the university. The latter can be used after hours. Students will soon be able to purchase the program on floppy disk for home use.

Obstacles

This project was a perfect example of the problems involved in coordinating and organizing a large team which also changed considerably over time with different people being involved at different stages. This was characterized by the programming which was undertaken by four different programmers at different points in the project.

Having four different programmers involved in a project need not be a bad thing of course, but it does make the need for documentation and communication all the more apparent. In this project each successive programmer interpreted the project in a different way and made changes which, although they might have seemed the simplest solution to a specific problem, had a huge impact on the reliability of the program as a whole.

The project lacked formal definition of how it worked, both at a programming level and overall. Although these issues had been agreed between the content expert team and the first programmer in early meetings, there was no actual formal documentation of these. Because of this, some aspects of the program were not implemented as originally planned. If such documentation had existed then each successive programmer could have been given it as a guide to the structure of the project. Instead they were left to work it out in isolation and to try and interpret the structure and to build upon it themselves.

As an example: programmer No.3 detects a bug in unit 4 of the program and tracks it down to a central code resource; he fixes the bug there and tests the program again which apparently works; unfortunately programmer No.2 has over-ridden the central code resource for units 6, 7 and 8 which means that the bug might still exist in those units. Had programmer No.2 documented what he had done then programmer No.3 could have tracked down all the instances of the bug and fixed them.

8.3 Team review and opinion

8.3.1 Content expert

My congratulations and thanks must go to all who have participated in this huge project. I sometimes wonder that we might never have started had we envisaged how big it would become after two CAUT grants.

The sheer size of the program was the major stumbling block – eight modules, each module being the equivalent of one of the other multimedia productions described in this book. Another problem for the content team was that the multimedia development was only part of a larger project involving extensive video production and CML assessment modules. These sub-projects also required coordination with associated people in the Teaching Learning Group and the Computing Centre.

In addition, each content expert was teaching, with contact hours averaging 16 hours per week and some were coordinating loads of up to 300 students per semester. I won't talk about the postgraduate study we were all trying to complete as well! It is sufficient to say that everyone was pushed for time and often timelines became difficult to meet because of uncontrollable factors which cropped up from other areas of our working lives.

One other major problem from our perspective was the seeming isolation of the Computing Centre team from the subject expert team and, until 1994, the miscommunication between the two teams. It seemed that each team had its own objectives, which were described to the other team and agreement made as to fulfilment of those objectives. However, each team's perceptions of the other's objectives were different. These perceptual differences created some problems, ie, the subject experts trying to fulfil sound educational criteria for learning, and the programmers programming from their perspective, for example creating clear screens, where necessary instruction to the student might have been deleted. So, even though we thought we were all communicating, each of us was coming away with different messages as to what was required.

The annual programmer changes (two in 1995) also created a bit of a headache (for the programmers, it must have been like a banishment to Alcatraz), as we had to get used to new styles and personalities. The programmer had to get up to speed pretty rapidly on a program he had not designed, and had to work with people who not only had little idea of what programming was about, but spoke a wierd microbiological language to boot.

Within my own team of subject experts, the majority worked around the clock on the project for a number of years. However, there were occasions when getting material written and proofed and to the computing centre was like getting blood out of a stone. I found having to grouse on colleagues quite difficult and frustrating, especially when also trying to coordinate the other areas of the project. I would get e-mails from the Computing Centre requesting certain material for modules as soon as possible and similar messages from the Teaching Learning Group (Media Centre) asking for proofing of scripts, editing of film and voiceovers, also as soon as possible.

Over the four years that the project has taken to complete, we have all learnt much about working within a large team. All members were novices in the beginning. It took a long time to work out methods that would allow a large number of people from very different areas of the University and with very heavy workloads to work cohesively together. The methods evolved and the experience can now be put to good use in future developments.

In hindsight, we could have done it better; with less people we could have done it better, with more money and time we could have done it better, but we did eventually complete a massive project. I hope every member of the team can feel proud of this achievement and look back on the experience as one that created a huge learning curve for all.

8.3.2   Programmer

The amount of work in any project increases with the size of the project, and this was borne out in the Microbiology project. We have learnt many lessons through this project about project design, development and management. The complexity of the development reached epic proportions, because the project was so large, requiring a large development team over a number of years.

One aspect of a project that should not be underestimated is the importance of continuity! Four programmers worked on this project at separate times. Each new programmer felt daunted by the prospect of working with the program. They had to try and get the best out of the program while not really understanding how it worked or where it was going. What was worse was that when a problem arose, it had to be fixed without blaming it on any of the previous programmers (which was the first instinct!)

No one person can be blamed for any of the problems we had with the project. All aspects of communication could have been improved. A lesson we have learned is that when you even think that there might be a problem, you need to tell other team members so that it can be sorted out. As a programmer the need for this is even greater and the programmer has a responsibility to be firm and let people know what they can and cannot do. There is a temptation to give the 'client' what they want and promise what can't be delivered.

Another issue to beware of is the temptation to let other people do the work for you. In this project we attempted to reduce the debugging time by letting some of the content experts correct textual errors themselves. Although this worked 95% of the time, occasionally they introduced more bugs than they fixed because some aspects of the program were technically quite difficult to construct.

8.3.3   Project manager

At the beginning of this project in 1992, my role was purely that of coordinator, assisting the content experts wherever possible to the extent that resources in the Computing Centre permitted. In 1993, a programmer was allocated to the project, but total project management still resided with the content experts. Subsequently, it became clear that the CBL project was progressing too slowly, and this area needed a dedicated project manager. There was a need for milestones to be set for all team members, and timelines had to be established, showing how different tasks from different team members depended on each other.

A particular aspect of this was in the testing and debugging cycle. It appears that it was assumed there would be no errors in either the content or the programming. Given the lack of quality control in earlier stages, this was clearly not the case, and the content was riddled with typographical and other errors and the programming had many bugs. With such a large project, errors are hard to find, so a specific debugging cycle had to be established.

One of the key issues in managing a project such as this one, with a large team of busy people involved with other tasks as well, is communication. Most of the problems that arose could possibly have been solved very quickly by a phone call or an e-mail message. On some occasions, the programmers identified a design problem in the program, but did not raise it as an issue, because they believed the content experts did not want to change this. (The root cause of this attitude was that the programmers felt that they had no intellectual ownership in the project, while the content experts felt similarly when meeting with the programmers.) At other times, members of the content team doing testing identified inconsistencies with the navigation, and reported these to the programmer. The programmer noted on the bug report sheet that the navigation was according to the original design (despite the problem), and requested that the content team resolve the issue. However, this message did not filter back to the appropriate people in the content team. One of my key roles was to keep this day-to-day communication going.

On other occasions, phrases like 'This is what we decided last year' and 'I just assumed that this would be done' were used. Both of these phrases imply that one person's perception of the situation was not shared by another. The only reliable way to avoid these problems is by documenting all design decisions at all stages of the project.

I adopted the procedure of producing minutes of all meetings held. These documented decisions, set out timelines, identified action items and the people responsible for them, and gave resolutions for action items from previous minutes. In this way, last year's design decisions could be verified against the minutes.

A trap that I fell into at times in managing this project was that I would manage a crisis situation, get everyone communicating again, and then leave the project to its own devices. This was often caused by pressures of other work, or because the workload of other team members meant that progress halted for a period. However, the trouble was that the project would carry on until eventually another crisis would arise which demanded my attention. If I had been able to devote more time more consistently to the project it would have proceeded more smoothly.

Chapter 9

Dosage Calculations Case Study

Karen Glaister and Nick Jenkins

9.1   Background to the project

9.1.1   Teaching context

James is lying in bed six hours after surgery to remove his appendix. He is crying and distressed because of the pain. The nurse reassures him before going to check his medication chart. He is prescribed 35mg of Pethidine, PRN Q6h, the ward stock is 2 mL ampoules of 100mg of Pethidine. How much should the nurse give? The nurse needs to decide quickly – James is in discomfort! The nurse must also be accurate: too little and the pain may not be relieved; too much and the consequences could be fatal.

In the Bachelor of Science (Nursing) programme, the subject 'Dosage calculations' represents only a small component of the curriculum, yet it is vitally important. Important not only in terms of the patient's well-being and safety but also in respect to the students' welfare and academic progress.

Prior to this project, the teaching of dosage calculations used a lecture format with worksheets for practice, both of which were devoid of clinical contextual reality. Students had three opportunities to demonstrate competency, with a performance level set at 100%. This approach was problematic, mainly in terms of its administration and educational validity. Organizing worksheets and assessments for student groups of 80 to 120 presented a logistical nightmare. The teaching and assessment matrix was inflexible to the needs of large student groups with diverse mathematical backgrounds.

The subject persistently presents numerous difficulties to the student.

Observations from 1989 to date suggest that not only is the problem a conceptual one but also a mathematical one. A recent survey of first-year Curtin Nursing students revealed that 77% attained university entry Maths subjects, with 83% rating their ability to perform basic computational skills as average or higher. However, on analysis of the test papers, basic errors in addition, subtraction, multiplication and division of decimals and fractions exist when calculators are not permitted. Coupled with administrative and educational deficiencies, these problems contributed to an average pass rate of 52% for the first attempt at the test in the period 1989–1993.

9.1.2   Objectives

The overall aim of the project was to produce a more effective teaching, learning and assessment strategy that would:

- promote student competency in dosage calculations;
- present an opportunity for student-centred learning;
- facilitate the transfer of knowledge to the clinical areas.

With previous teaching and assessment practices placing inordinate demands on staff, there was an expectation that development of the program would decrease these demands, freeing staff to assist less adept students, without impeding the progress of other students.

Specific educational objectives are detailed at the beginning of each module of the computer program.

9.1.3   Place in the curriculum

The curriculum document requires that all third-semester Nursing students attain competency in drug dosage calculations and that fourth-semester students attain competency in both drug and intravenous therapy dosage calculations. Although the program was to be used by both semester three and four students, it was initially introduced only to semester three students.

It was decided that, following a large group presentation of related conceptual issues, all students would receive a one hour introductory session on the computer program. Students would then be free to book further laboratory practice and their own computerized testing time.

9.1.4   Feasibility

Prior to the commencement of the project in 1992, a needs assessment highlighted the problematic nature of current teaching and assessment practices.

There certainly existed scope for improvement. A literature search revealed the universality of the problem and hinted that the search for the 'holy grail' could be circumvented with computers. 'Oh boy, and didn't the literature make it all sound *so easy*!'

Unfortunately, at that time current software was invariably produced in America and failed to incorporate Australian drug names and labels. The one Australian piece of software located did not fully meet our teaching and assessment needs, and recent technological advances made the program seem outdated.

A decision was made to develop the program in *Allegiant SuperCard* on the Macintosh. This was the most appropriate authoring package at the time to achieve the sort of functionality we had designed.

At the time, there were neither Macintosh nor IBM compatible computer laboratories available to run IMM software in the university. However, a range of similar developments in IMM foreshadowed the expansion of 'Mac Labs' into the university structure. Indeed, in 1993, an Apple Macintosh Computing Laboratory was established for the Health Sciences.

9.1.5 Funding

The project commenced with funding through the 1992 University Mini-fellowship scheme. The scheme was coordinated by the Teaching Learning Group at Curtin University with financial backing from the Commonwealth Government Academic Staff Development Fund. The funding gained was sufficient to complete a prototype for module 1 of the program.

The Committee for the Advancement of University Teaching (CAUT) provided additional support for the continuation of the program. The funding was granted in the 1993 National Teaching and Development Grants organized by CAUT.

In total, this project received $Aus8832. Subsequently, a large amount of unfunded work was performed to complete the program to the satisfaction of staff and students using the program.

9.1.6 Team

The project team was initially made up of only two participants. Programming was done by Nick Jenkins from the computing centre, and Karen Glaister from the School of Nursing assumed the dual role of content expert and team leader. With the second round of funding, Michelle Robert-Libia from the media services section of the university's Teaching Learning Group was taken on board to produce artwork.

Other staff from the three departments involved were used as 'sounding boards' and were invited to make further contributions at various times.

9.2   Description of the project

9.2.1   The development model

As with all of the projects started in 1992, this one proceeded very informally. A small grant had been received to start development, and a series of meetings held between Computing Centre and School of Nursing staff. The meetings focused on an overview of the intended content, programming needs, feasibility and the production process. None of the team members had any real experience in designing IMM. No advice was available on how best to produce content for the computer screen.

After several meetings had decided the general structure of the program, a schematic outline of the entire program was drawn on large sheets of paper. Funding was available to employ a programmer but no other staff, so most of the development was to be handled by a team of two: Karen as content expert, and a programmer who was to be employed. Graphic design and educational advice was available from other computing centre staff when required, but only on an advisory basis, because these aspects had not been considered in original quotes from the centre.

Karen's first task was to produce a storyboard of the program, with one screen per page of A4 paper. The storyboard was produced before Nick was employed, so he had little say in the overall structure of the program. However, he was required to design and implement individual interactive aspects with which Karen had little experience.

Eventually, the prototype of module 1 was completed and tested with students, but by then the funding had run out, as a result of inadequacies in the computing centre budget predictions.

In 1993, more funding was obtained, and Michelle joined the team as graphic artist. The prototype was revised in response to student feedback, and programming started on module 2 and the testing facilities. The development model was still very informal, but seemed largely effective because of the small number of people involved and the effective communication between them.

Deficiencies in the development model only became apparent after some modules of the program were completed and in use with students. There were some severe problems, detailed elsewhere in this chapter, in the student use of the program, which stemmed from deficiencies in the paper design process. Had a more formal and thorough design process been carried out, the debugging and redesign that was eventually required would not have taken so long. In particular, when the testing facilities were added, the entire program should have been redesigned from scratch, instead of attempting to add complex new functions to an existing program.

9.2.2   Content

The Dosage Calculation program comprises two instructional modules with practice facilities, two related testing modules and a module to administer test results. The various modules in the program are shown in Figure 4.24. The two instructional modules are Drug Dosage Calculations, and Intravenous Therapy Dosage Calculations.

Both modules make extensive use of graphics and animation to enhance the teaching and learning process. The practice facilities use sophisticated drill and practice, supplying informative and corrective feedback.

The testing modules utilize the same format as the instructional modules with the addition of a mechanism to provide a time limit for the test. The test has the advantage of being computer generated and marked, providing immediate feedback to the student.

9.2.3   User interface

The user interface of the program was discussed from a graphic design point of view in section 4.4.3. Navigation controls are at the right bottom corner of screen, while the left bottom corner houses an animation of a drug capsule. The animation provides written instruction and feedback to the user. Sound was kept to a minimum following suggestions from students that, although noises were amusing, they were also distracting.

Animation and interaction played an important part in the whole design. While the nature of the content dictated that the overall structure of the program be based on an objectivist paradigm, resulting in a mixed hierarchical structure of information (see section 4.2.3), efforts were made to engage the student through animations. The program attempted to situate the learning in an approximation of the environment in which it would be applied.

9.2.4   Implementation

The Dosage Calculations program was included in the 1993–94 curriculum. The intention was to trial the program's instructional and assessment qualities on all students enrolled in the relevant unit. A one-hour introductory session with the computer program was followed by unlimited laboratory time for practice and assessment. It was the intention that these later sessions were unsupervised and organized entirely at the discretion of the student. However, on its first introduction into the curriculum, supervision was increased in response to some programming errors.

The placement of the clinical nursing component of the course meant that the program was in heavy demand at the start of the semester.

Student use

Students were given free rein to use the program on a self-determined needs basis. Unfortunately, due to competing demands by other Health Science students and the opening hours of the computing laboratory, together with an already busy timetable, access was somewhat restricted.

Most students used the program for one to two hours. Given the obstacles that some students encountered, it must have seemed like a very long time!

The practice and assessment laboratories were unsupervised, and as the evaluation showed, although 75% felt confident in using the program, 53% felt the need for a tutor to be present at all times.

Obstacles

The implementation period certainly had its share of hiccups – veritable eruptions in fact! These were chiefly attributable to the novel nature of the project and the constraints of time and budget.

Network problems

This program was one of the first developed at Curtin and it broke new ground in a lot of areas. One of the first problems encountered involved transferring the program from the stand-alone machines on which it was developed to the network server where it was to run. In order for the program to work successfully from the server it had to be 'locked' to prevent multiple users trying to change it at the same time.

Since the file was locked, the program reverted to its original state every time the user changed screens. When users of the test section clicked to go on to the next question, the program would flip to the next card, revert to its saved form and present them with the original question!

Communication between the server administrator, the programmer responsible for bug fixes and the tutors running the program was poor at some times. Many communication problems were exacerbated by the project leader's maternity leave. This caused the chain of communication to become stretched. Quite often a tutor would attempt to report a bug to the programmer, who wasn't available. The tutor would then contact the project leader at home with a verbal bug report, which she would subsequently pass on to the programmer, who then had similar problems in communicating that the bug was fixed, and requesting that the server administrator update the production version on the server.

With the project leader's return to work, and a concerted effort to improve the communication processes, subsequent testing proceeded satisfactorily.

Interface problems

A more fundamental problem with the design of the interface was identified with student use of the program. In some sections users are expected to enter a drug dosage calculation and have the program check its answer.

At first it was considered that only the figures in the calculation were important and the units could be discarded. It was soon realized that this would result in calculations which would resemble this:

$$\frac{1}{500} \times 1 = 2$$

This calculation appears to defy the principles of mathematics. However, if units are incorporated into this equation it becomes much clearer:

$$\frac{1\,\text{mg}}{500\,\text{mcg}} \times 1 \text{ tablets} = 2 \text{ tablets}$$

If you allow the user to insert their own units considerable programming problems arise. For the user to be able to use units the computer must understand the possible units and their variations. For example, the program must understand that there are a thousand micrograms (mcg) in a milligram (mg) and that the notation 'mg' is correct, but 'MG' is incorrect.

Although not insoluble, this problem would have required a fairly major change to the software. Given the finances and timelines it was impossible to accommodate the diversity of measuring units possible in each calculation. Instead, the measuring units were given when the calculation was being set up, but disappeared as the user entered the numerical values. As an interim solution this was successful, with the drawback that the final calculation seen is incorrect because the units disappeared as soon as the user started entering figures.

In the final version, the students are presented with the formula with the units pre-filled, and these units remain throughout the calculation. The students are then prompted to choose the units of the final dosages from a pop-up menu, as shown in Figure 9.1.

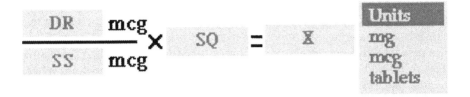

Figure 9.1 *Formula entry screen from the Dosage Calculation program*

A colour version may be viewed at http://www.curtin.edu.au/curtin/multimedia/
devhandbook/toc.html

This example again demonstrates the necessity for an exhaustive design and evaluation process, because the complexity of a project can make even the smallest of problems difficult to correct. The 'units problem' should have been raised and considered at design time and prototypes tested with a few students or tutors. The issue could have been resolved before the entire program was complete and in use with students. Instead, since the formula entry screen pervades all parts of the program, lengthy revisions were required to modify it in a number of locations.

Speed problems

Hardware limitations are always a consideration in the design and implementation of computer programs, and multimedia projects are no exception. They are, however, the easiest of problems to solve. They just cost money! Even the meagre graphics of the Dosage Calculations program (no live video, no complex animations) put a considerable drain on a computer's resources. As it turned out the computers on which the program was to be presented lacked sufficient memory to run the program properly. The lack of 'real memory' meant that 'virtual memory' had to be used, considerably compromising the performance of the program.

This drop in performance had an unforeseen side effect. The computers were sluggish to respond and users, in an effort to prod the computer into action, would often repeatedly click the mouse. Unfortunately they usually chose to click the mouse on the 'Next' button. The computer, busily loading the next screen would queue up these clicks (known as 'buffering'), pass them to the 'Next' button and skip through several screens.

This, at best, was a mere nuisance as students would miss screens and might lose valuable information. In the test, however, it proved disastrous as the student skipped from the first question through to the sixth without ever seeing the other four (missing a question counted as a wrong answer). The solution to this problem was simply to have the test bank refuse to go to the next screen without some kind of answer being provided by the user.

The authoring environment itself (*Allegiant SuperCard*) created a number of speed problems. The project made a major use of text files for storing test questions and user results. *SuperCard* made access to these text files easy, but also inordinately slow. When more than a hundred students had sat exams, their combined tests slowed the administration program to the point where it could take hours to simply record the results of their tests. This was solved in the latest version by the use of a custom 'XCMD' or external command to handle the file processing. By handing file access off to the external command and redesigning the administration program, the administration process was greatly simplified.

9.2.5 Evaluation

In 1992, a prototype of module 1 was presented to all semester-three Nursing students in conjunction with the usual teaching methods. A one-hour computing laboratory session introduced the student to Macintosh computers and the Dosage Calculation program. At least one member of the Nursing staff and the programmer were present throughout the trial period. Each student ($N = 68$) completed an evaluation tool composed of 19 Likert scale responses and open-ended questions. The questionnaire gathered formative feedback pertaining to the instructional design, user interface, content presentation and the student's satisfaction with the delivery medium. The prototype was extremely well received by the students; an average 97.5% of students answered favourably to all the criteria.

Given this exciting response we were motivated to continue, commencing with the expansion and modification of module 1. Amendments resulted from the student feedback, staff observations and staff-student interactions during the prototype trial. In fact the staff-student interactions proved to be an invaluable evaluation method. While using the program, students freely offered constructive criticism to the staff member in attendance. Each problem could then be investigated on an individual basis.

The Dosage Calculations program was deemed ready for a further trial a year later, after the problems discussed above had been resolved. This time, students were asked to complete a more extensive evaluation form, which addressed demographic characteristics (including computer and mathematical experience), as well as the student's response to the program design, content material and the learning opportunity.

Results were computer analysed using SPSS (Statistical Package for the Social Sciences). Overall, the students were supportive of the program, although not as convincingly as they were of the prototype. Twenty-four per cent indicated that they probably learnt less using the computer as opposed to other teaching strategies. Given the obstacles encountered, together with the fact the students had little experience with computers, this is perhaps not a surprising result. What was rewarding was the response given to the learning opportunity with:

- 95% supporting the self-paced mode;
- 99% preferring to decide their own practice needs;
- 96% preferring to select their own testing time;
- 82% considering it useful for learning dosage calculations;
- 92% considering it useful for practising dosage calculations;
- 64% enjoying the experience in preference to other teaching strategies.

Certainly student learning (measured by test results) was not compromised by using the computer program. A mean first time pass rate of 58% was obtained with the program compared to 52% prior to computer usage.

9.3   Team review and opinion

9.3.1   Content expert

My involvement with this project has certainly had its share of 'highs and lows'. Perhaps the two most rewarding aspects were witnessing the transformation of rather 'flat' instructional content into a visually stimulating format that accommodated the adult learner's needs. Second, seeing students using the program and, despite the obstacles encountered, still considering it a valuable learning tool.

While I do not necessarily see the program as the 'be all and end all', it certainly can add a new dimension to the learning and assessment of dosage calculations. It has the potential to advance instruction by offering conceptually based learning, that is both interactive and individualized. Together with the assessment module, it allows the student a greater freedom with their learning and assessment.

The production process was hampered (to some extent) by my computer illiterate nature. That's not to say I cannot use a wordprocessor, etc, but this was a whole new ball game! To prepare content when you're not quite sure how it can best be presented by the computer is difficult. To visualize content non-linearly requires lateral exertion of the grey matter. However, the programmer was able to take the stack of screen presentations and together with the creative juices of the team produce an exciting package. There is no question that the addition of a graphic artist to our team enhanced the content, and could have resolved some design flaws if time and money had permitted.

At the start I felt the instructional content was more than suitable material for CBL and it has proved to be just so, although a module was shelved when the complexity of the graphics required could not be legibly represented on the computer screen. The instructional content is discrete and relatively brief, accommodating those students who do not favour computer use by keeping 'hands on' time to an acceptable level. However, using the computer for assessment purposes presented more of a challenge – not only in terms of the technical aspects, but also with students' comfort levels. In hindsight, supervision of practice and assessment opportunities may have been preferable, but this would probably have negated students' independence.

Any future projects undertaken will see the development model altered to accommodate frequent trials of prototypes of the program. Although this would slow the production process, I feel that it is a necessary addition to achieve an educationally sound end-product, that is acceptable to students and staff alike.

9.3.2 Programmer

This was my first 'real' multimedia project and it showed. I succumbed to all the usual temptations of software development and this made the whole process of developing the project more complicated.

Chief among my errors was short-circuiting the design process by agreeing to fix bugs on the spot. When a bug is discovered, the usual process is to return to your design and to search for a solution. If you fix the bug on the spot, there is a risk of introducing a new set of bugs and complicating the process even further. The proper solution is to return to the design and find a *solution* to the problem, instead of a temporary fix.

Having said that, I must point out that (with a large investment of time) the original project has been greatly simplified and the bugs resolved. It takes a little faith to believe that the investment of time in a major rewrite will return worthwhile dividends, but it will always be far more effective than ad hoc solutions.

Working with the team that developed this project was easy and the synergy provided by the team kept the project moving even during difficult periods. Perhaps an important positive factor in this was the lack of 'ownership' by any one member of the team. All the team members were happy to hear suggestions on any part of the project from any of the other team members. This contrasts with other projects where members of the team place personal claims on certain aspects of the project and view suggestions as invasions of their personal territory. The relationship of all the aspects of the project means that the input of all team members was not only valued but actively sought.

The project was also rewarding for me professionally. It taught me a number of things about the development environment and some about generic multimedia development. One purpose of this book is to save other programmers and IMM developers from that steep learning curve which I encountered with this project.

9.3.3   Project leader

As project leader I was very much a novice, with at that stage a novice team. If that was not enough, the role became somewhat complicated by maternity-related absence. This in part no doubt accounts for some of the obstacles the team and users encountered. Certainly there were periods when the development model took on the threatening appearance of a whirlpool and I could see us being pulled down forever into its swirling mass!

A significant issue seriously impinging on the success of the project was the budget, or more correctly, the budget shortfall. Due to 'learning on the job', all three departments were short on their budget predictions. The largest cost overrun occurred with the programming predictions, which eventually consumed 66.5% of the total budget of $Aus8,832. Developers of CBT projects estimate that it costs $Aus10–20,000 to produce one hour of course work (Brown, 1991). More recently Canale and Wills (1993) have shown that these figures can be much higher, their own project ratio standing at $Aus35,000 : 1. The ratio for this project was $Aus2,208 : 1. However, this figure is low as a result of in-house fees and it certainly does not account for the unpaid hours. Officially, 470 hours were spent in developing four hours of learning material, but in reality the ratio is much higher. Programming difficulties and creative ideas easily expanded the time frame. I can still recall the lengthy discussions and experiments with background colour, text colour, etc. Stemming the flow of ideas and halting the desire to improve upon what was already on the screen was a necessary constraint to get the program running.

At times the program became a test of endurance. The project was started in 1992 and was completed in 1995. Even so, given the comparatively low budget, we have managed to produce a usable educational tool. Budget predictions for future projects would be much more accurate given our experience with programming and project management time needs. I consider the degree of success with such a project to be a reflection of the cohesiveness and commitment of the team. Certainly this project benefited from a motivated crew and while we all were relatively active in our team roles, at times, lack of communication was our downfall, adding to the frustration and delays with developing the program.

Unfortunately the programming delays and 'bugs' had repercussions on some Nursing staff members' acceptance (or rather, non-acceptance) of the program. It became increasingly difficult to deal with the ensuing negativity from computer-nervous staff. Currently, this response is more favourable, with staff accepting its value as a viable teaching and learning alternative.

Would I do it again? Well um, er, oh – of course I would! Given the learning curve that all team members scaled, one could only be more confident and capable next time. Of course, that is without a pregnant pause to fetter the proceedings! Given the student feedback one is encouraged to explore this medium more. Again, as I have already said, one should not consider computers as a replacement for other instructional and assessment modes (or indeed the teacher), but rather as an invaluable tool in the teacher's repertoire.

In a future project, I would recommend particular attention to the following:

- preparation of a more extensive outline of the content before requesting budget submission from the relevant departments;
- exploration of alternative content presentations in the design planning phase;
- incorporation of more frequent student evaluations throughout the production process.

9.3.4   Graphic artist

Working on the project required the use of still graphics and computer animation. As my experience with animation was limited, I had to familiarize myself with a new animation program in order to complete the sequences. It was a frustrating process, as time was not on our side, but after much help and countless hours I feel a satisfactory result was obtained.

As with all new projects, it had its fair share of teething problems. At times team communication was deficient, resulting in project hold-ups, which could have been avoided. However, I would say overall that the project worked well.

Another problem faced while working on the project was associated with the difference in the amount of memory capacity between development and delivery machines. I worked on a computer with a large amount of memory, but more often than not the completed animation sequences would not work in the student lab due to the limitation of memory capacity of the lab computers. As a result many of these sequences had to be modified to run under less memory.

As with most projects there were the usual budget and deadline restrictions. With regard to deadlines, at times it proved to be somewhat difficult to meet these within the time limitations given. This was partly due to communication problems and partly due to more pressing deadlines on other projects.

From my point of view the graphics appeared to provide an element of friendliness and humour to a large percentage of otherwise computer-phobic students.

As a result of this project a great deal of knowledge and understanding have been gained by all members of the team, providing a solid basis for future projects. I would definitely become involved in a similar project given the opportunity.

If I were to repeat the project I would involve a team member from each relevant area from the conception of the project. I feel this would eliminate many small problems from the beginning that could become major problems resulting in budget and deadline difficulties.

Chapter 10

Mitochondria Case Study

Rob Phillips and Linda Slack-Smith

10.1 Background to the project

10.1.1 Teaching context

> Biochemistry is often a difficult subject for nursing students, particularly those with a weak chemistry background. In addition, students are normally only newly acquainted with the fine structure of the cell, also necessary for understanding the biochemical processes discussed in the unit. Introductory biochemistry in the Curtin Nursing course involves 90 to 130 students per semester and is taught in the second semester of first year. In the past, Nursing biochemistry was taught by lectures and tutorials, and much time was used transferring simple factual material. (Slack-Smith and Fox, 1993)

Previous developments in this introductory Biochemistry unit have included the production of a study guide with the unit divided into modules with clear objectives, some notes and figures and review questions; the development of guided self-study modules; and the use of computerized multiple-choice assessment during semester by CML. Around 30% of lectures have been replaced by guided self-study modules, and tutorials and practicals have been combined as 'interactive sessions'. These developments have been designed to promote active learning and the responsibility of the individual student in the learning process. The use of guided self-study modules and computerized testing have allowed more flexible time management for both students and the lecturer (Slack-Smith and Fox, 1993).

The Mitochondria program and the related Carbohydrates program (Chapter 11) were developed as part of ongoing development of the unit to meet particular needs not covered by the other teaching techniques.

10.1.2 Objectives

The role of the components of the cell called 'mitochondria' in the production of energy molecules (Adenosine Triphosphate or ATP) is a seemingly complex area that would be aided with clear visualization of the processes. The aim in producing this program was to improve student understanding of the basic process of ATP production in the mitochondria.

The educational objectives were defined as clearly as possible, in that the student should be able to:

- describe the structure of a mitochondrion;
- describe the structure and function of ATP;
- explain the role of the mitochondria in the production of ATP including the details of the electron transport chain and oxidative phosphorylation;
- explain the meaning of 'respiratory control';
- compare the processes of uncoupling and inhibition.

Other, broader objectives were to:

- encourage inquisitiveness;
- discourage dependence;
- encourage active learning;
- encourage responsibility for time management.

10.1.3 Place in the curriculum

The material in the Mitochondria program was previously available as a guided self-study module (replacing a one-hour lecture supported by a one-hour tutorial). It was decided to make this self-study module available to students in their unit study guide, to refer to while using the software program and studying the topic. It was also decided to introduce the Mitochondria program into a timetabled interactive session with the support of tutors and additional staff as required. The program could, at a later date, be available in a self-study fashion either as a tutorial or to replace lectures (Slack-Smith et al., 1993).

10.1.4 Feasibility

A search for existing material of this type revealed that few resources were available in the area of introductory Biochemistry, with most available materials aimed at a higher level than required for this unit.

Other developments in the Health Sciences had led to the establishment of a Macintosh computer laboratory, and this determined the choice of computing platform for the development. At the same time, the choice of authoring language was determined by the computing centre's expertise in developing IMM programs on the Macintosh using *Allegiant SuperCard*. It was decided to develop the program in full colour, using graphics and animations where appropriate.

10.1.5 Funding

The mitochondria program is one of a series of IMM programs funded by the Committee for the Advancement of University Education (CAUT), through the Commonwealth Government Department of Employment Education and Training.

10.1.6 Team

Linda Slack-Smith from the School of Biomedical Sciences was the content expert for this project as well as being responsible for the budget and overall control. Susan Perry from the computing centre was the graphic designer, assisted by Cheu Yen Diong, then a student in the School of Design, who produced the drawings. Other team members were computing centre staff Onno Benschop (programmer) and Rob Phillips (project coordinator).

Support for the project came from Associate Professor John Wetherall, Dr Susan Jordan and Paul Sparrow of the School of Biomedical Sciences. Other contributions came from Robert Fox of the teaching learning group, George Borzyskowski and Associate Professor Patricia Stevenson. The enthusiasm and honesty of the Nursing students at Curtin also contributed greatly to the success of the project.

10.2 Description of the project

10.2.1 The development model

Unlike the Microbiology and Nursing projects (Chapters 8 and 9 respectively), which were part of the first year of development, the Mitochondria project started in 1993, which gave us an opportunity to improve on the development processes of 1992.

In this project, we attempted to tighten the design phase of the development. In previous projects, there had been a tendency to develop too many components before evaluating the educational and navigational aspects of the project, which was wasteful of time and money. There had also been a tendency for programmers and designers to direct energies into areas which did not necessarily suit the content or educational objectives.

In the Mitochondria project, we recognized that the content and design should be well established before programming was commenced, and we put together a more formal design team to achieve this aim. However, the teamwork component of the design phase was not always successful, because other work commitments often meant that the entire team could rarely meet. The result was a sequential division of activities. First, the content expert prepared the content, then the graphic designer developed the look and feel, then the programmer implemented it. It was difficult to maintain adequate communication between team members, particularly due to time constraints.

The entire development team took part in the initial planning. Linda lectured the content material to the team, and ideas for implementing the material were contributed by all team members. A written plan was produced by Linda, and revised regularly with the other participants. It was found to be essential to write as much on paper as possible. A paper-based storyboard was used, as was a list of 'cards' and a list of graphics. It took some time to get the language right so that all team members understood what was meant by terms such as cards, menus, etc. This component of the design process took several months.

After this effort, the actual programming development took only a few weeks.

10.2.2 Content

The program consists of five sections, as shown below and in Figure 4.28:

- Introduction
- Mitochondria
- ATP
- Mitochondrial Processes
- Review and Applications.

The content commences with a description of the individual components of the mitochondrion and ATP, and progresses to describe the processes in which they are involved. The program concludes with some applications of the function of the cell mitochondrion.

10.2.3 User interface

The structure of the program is essentially linear. However, the five sections provide 'entry points' to the linear sequence. The structure follows closely the format of the lecture, with topics being logically built up from previous information. An effort was made to reduce the amount of text presented, with an emphasis on providing a graphical view as an alternative to the text. This gave a valuable change in perspective for the academic content expert. However, in some cases where there were no appropriate graphics, this resulted in screens which were almost empty, containing just one or two lines of text.

On several screens students were expected to interact with diagrams, but not all graphics were interactive.

10.2.4 Implementation

The Mitochondria program was first used in the second semester of 1993. It has now been used over five semesters and in a separate Medical Technology unit and is an important resource in the teaching program in the School of Biomedical Sciences.

Students received it well and were supportive of the time spent on it by their lecturer. Many students used their own initiative to obtain access to the computer laboratory out of normal class times to repeat the program. The students were not required to do this, but apparently *wanted* to use the program. This also included students from other units.

Students were initially concerned that the program ran too slowly on the hardware available. The computing hardware has since been upgraded and students are now satisfied with the performance of the program.

10.2.5 Evaluation

In the early stages of design, a prototype was used to assist students who had queries about this topic. This provided extremely useful formative evaluation during early development of the program. The associated graphics were also found to be very valuable for explaining the topic.

The second part of the formative evaluation was to demonstrate an early prototype to one class for comment. The graphic designer and programmer attended one or two of these early trial sessions, which was valuable for them in refining the design. After revisions, the program ran smoothly and few changes needed to be made.

Several weeks later a further-developed version of the program was introduced in one of the normal two hour 'interactive sessions'. Students were given a sheet of questions relating to the program and left with the program, being able to ask for help as required. This trial ran smoothly, and after one week's testing, the use of the program was reviewed and it was decided to use it with the classes conducted in the following week (ie a different group of students). Informal interviews were held with staff and students to determine the worth of the package.

The student questionnaire gave consistently positive responses for three student groups. Qualitative observation by the lecturer indicated that the difficult concepts which the Mitochondria program was designed to convey were understood better and earlier by students. A side benefit was that the content expert learned more about the visual aspects of learning.

10.3 Team review and opinion

10.3.1 Content expert

The most difficult aspect of the project was balancing the completion of the product within a budget and limited time period against the desire to evaluate and alter the program based on a continual flow of new ideas. With more detailed planning undertaken prior to any work on screen, the final product was produced quite quickly once drawings were completed. The project was commenced in the middle of February 1993 and implemented by September 1993. The final product closely represents the original plan on paper.

Major problems were in underestimating the ongoing need for teaching release and restricting the more artistic developers to agreed budget figures.

The introduction of the program in classes was relatively easy and the program required only minor modifications. The Mitochondria program could also be adapted for higher level classes. The program was written with distribution to other institutions in mind, and the content is not specific to any particular discipline.

The primary aim in the development of this software program was to help students improve their understanding of a process they normally find difficult, and this was seen to have been achieved. Our experiment with multimedia has proved successful in this quest. The program, although currently being used in a tutorial setting of around 12 to 20 students at any time, could also be used as an alternative to lectures with students able to access it in their own time.

In addition, there is a long-term benefit in working as a team with team members having different skills. The completion of the project has definitely been of educational value to myself, and this gain in expertise will assist in future projects.

The support of our institution has allowed an environment where such projects can be completed successfully.

10.3.2 Programmer

On the whole the project was a productive one. The content expert was willing to listen to feedback from experts outside her field, and comments were listened to and taken in. Generally, the interaction within the group was effective and people got things done.

The graphics within the project were superbly done, but it was difficult to obtain them on schedule. Problems arose when the graphic designer attempted to program some aspects of the prototype. Pieces of script were scattered throughout the program and had to be located and removed. Subsequently, version control became a problem, because amendments by the graphic designer to some sections had inadvertently deleted the scripts from some objects.

We chose to use a stereotypical way of navigating through the content (using arrows), and icons at the left of the screen allowed users to select chapters within the contents (see section 4.2.3). Although the design looked attractive, users tended to only use the navigation controls at the bottom right, and to use the program as a book.

10.3.3 Project coordinator

This project commenced in early 1993, at a time when the first round of the government-funded Committee for the Advancement of University Teaching grants were awarded. Curtin had been successful in obtaining a number of these grants, and six of them were technology-based and involved the computing centre. I therefore had six projects to manage at the same time, with one graphic designer and several programmers who all had additional duties in user support.

My management tasks involved juggling people and resources in an attempt to find enough people to do all the tasks required. With individual projects, my role was necessarily one of coordination instead of management. I had to make sure that people were communicating and that progress was made, but had to largely leave the day-to-day details to individuals on the team. In some cases, especially with smaller teams, this model worked effectively. With larger projects it was less successful, because more coordination was essential.

The project was planned at a time when we thought that it would take 150 hours to develop an hour of IMM. The grant made allowances for overruns and budgeted for 200 hours at $Aus20 per hour. The total grant was for three tutorials, totalling just less than $Aus12,000. In reality, the Mitochondria project cost $Aus6000, mainly due to cost overruns in the graphic design. In a properly managed project these would have been detected and measures could have been taken. It turned out that Carbohydrates also cost approximately $Aus6000, which meant that the third project on liver function was very small. Essentially it was a shell into which multiple-choice questions could be entered.

The development of the Mitochondria program was largely successful, and the team worked well together most of the time. However, it was not without its moments, with two excitable team members openly exchanging verbal abuse on one occasion!

The lessons learnt from this project had a considerable impact on the development of the project design methodology which is discussed in this book.

Chapter 11

Carbohydrates Case Study

Rob Phillips and Linda Slack-Smith

11.1 Background to the project

The Carbohydrates program was the second of a series of three IMM programs funded by the government Committee for the Advancement of University Teaching (CAUT). Carbohydrates followed from the development of the first program, Mitochondria, described in Chapter 10.

Each project takes a different educational approach. Mitochondria has a 'traditional' menus and buttons approach, the graphic design is very attractive, the material is structured in a very linear fashion, and while it has some interactivity, this is not extensive. A more exploratory approach is taken in the Carbohydrates program, allowing the students to discover the structure of the program and construct their own knowledge.

The educational context in which the Carbohydrates program was to be used is similar to that described in Chapter 10 for the Mitochondria project.

After completion, the Carbohydrates program was introduced into a timetabled interactive session with the support of tutors and additional staff as required. The intention was that the program could be available at a later date in a self-study fashion, either as a tutorial or to replace lectures.

11.1.1 Team

Content knowledge and expertise for this project was provided by Linda Slack-Smith from the School of Biomedical Sciences. Graphic design was provided by Cheu Yen Diong, who had worked on the Mitochondria project as a student, and who had since graduated. Computing centre staff Onno Benschop and Rob Phillips continued their contributions, as programmer and project manager, respectively.

11.2 Description of the project

11.2.1 The development model

The Carbohydrates program started in late 1993, when the pressure of other projects had diminished, and some soul-searching had been done about the way to best approach such projects. In earlier projects, the development group had been viewed merely as service providers, with little input into the overall design of the material. By this we mean that project managers, programmers and graphic designers had had limited involvement in the formative stages of a project. While they had provided advice on individual aspects of a project, they had not been involved in the overall design of the content. From some points of view this can be seen as natural, because programmers, designers and project managers may not have content expertise. However, the development group had amassed a wide range of experience in developing IMM projects, and were capable of adapting ideas from other projects to the project at hand.

We therefore sought to become more proactive in project design at all levels. To help prepare the material in a way best suited to both IMM and the learner, all team members were closely involved with content preparation.

The development of the Carbohydrates project initiated the development model presented in Chapter 3, and led to subsequent revisions of the model. The planning was extensive and exhaustive, and we were mainly successful at avoiding moving into coding and implementation until the project aims and content were finalized. A weakness was that documentation of meetings and goals was not thorough enough.

11.2.2 Content

The Carbohydrates program was the first in which we used a brainstorming session to start to design the structure of the program. Linda gave her Carbohydrates lecture to a group of about 15 computing centre staff, who were involved, however tenuously, with IMM.

The lecture followed the progress of carbohydrates from the mouth to the small intestine, where they are converted to glucose, and then through the blood supply to the liver and finally to an individual cell. At each point, the processes involved are explained. The material becomes more complex at the cell level, where the glucose can be involved in a variety of processes.

It would have been very easy to directly convert the well-organized lecture into a book-like page-turning IMM application. There may even have been some interactivity on individual screens, but there would have been very little learner control and it would have been a very teacher-centred project.

11.2.3 User interface

Use of the brainstorming session allowed the group to throw around different ideas about how the content could be presented, while trying to avoid imposing rigid structure at this stage.

The outcome of this meeting was a decision to use a graphic of the body as the starting point, so that students could explore what happens to carbohydrates in different parts of the body by clicking on body parts. There is an implicit logical flow in this idea, in that food starts at the mouth, and there is a hint to start there, but this flow is not imposed on the student. Essentially the same information is accessed by using this interface as would be by using a series of menus. However, in this case the student has additional control over their progress.

The resultant design was very different from the initial idea of a sequential presentation with a menu providing entry points at different stages. Buttons and menus were discarded, and the learner interface is by means of a graphic of the human torso, which is explored with the mouse, as shown in Figure 4.12. The student is free to explore this material in any order they wish. The very graphical approach attempted to address the different learning styles of the target audience (first-year students with little science background), while introducing technical language at appropriate places.

A second design decision was to eliminate 'buttons' wherever possible. Students move between screens by using hotwords instead of clicking on an arrow at the bottom of the screen (see Figure 4.32). The first sentence on any screen is a summary of the previous screen, and it contains a hotword to take you back to that screen. Other hotwords take you deeper into the material. The material was organized hierarchically, and there was only a limited ability to move between branches of the hierarchy.

The third design decision was to have graphics behave consistently, wherever possible. Moving the mouse into any graphic will bring up a brief explanation in a help balloon. Clicking on a graphic will always cause something to happen. This may be to bring up more information on this screen or, sometimes, it may take you to another screen.

11.2.4 Production process

In previous projects, much programming and graphic design time (and money) had been wasted by continual changes in content and design. This time, a conscious decision was made to prepare everything on paper before starting programming.

The initial meeting was held in November 1993. Work had to be completed by the deadline set by CAUT that funding was to be committed by 30 April.

The written plan was produced by the academics (LSS and RP) and revised almost weekly with the other participants. It was found essential to write as much on paper as possible and to make sure that everybody understood what was envisaged. The storyboard was written in a wordprocessing program with hotwords shown in bold, and instructions for the production team in italics. These could then be easily transferred to the screens of the Carbohydrate program.

The material was also reviewed by an educational designer and academics experienced in the content area. The paper design phase continued from November to March. Some innovative ideas could not be included because they would not be achievable within time and budget constraints.

Some preliminary graphics were produced on paper early in the process, but the majority of graphics were only produced when the paper design was close to completion. Programming started late in March. While there were some modifications made as a result of actually viewing our designs on screen, and because not all team members understood the same thing from the design, the overall number of changes was minimal. The project was finished on 22 April, with minor revisions being carried out in May.

11.3 Team review and opinion

Many comments that could be made here have already been made in Chapter 10, so they won't be repeated. The comments made here are additional to those made in Chapter 10.

11.3.1 Content expert

The Carbohydrates program came from a lecture that was based on investigating the metabolism of carbohydrates in the body. The lecture had limitations which could be overcome by the use of multimedia.

The project generally progressed well, and the team functioned effectively, although there was a tendency for there to be too many bosses, and even agreed budgets were overrun.

Despite the concerns of fellow developers that the program was too complex, it worked well with students, who tended to find it easier to use than fellow academics and other IMM developers. This highlights the need to evaluate the use of IMM software in the environment for which it is intended, with students.

11.3.2 Programmer

At the initial meeting, the brainstorming session was very well attended and much positive input came from the group. I thought that the lecture given by the content expert was very useful to see where the project was supposed to go.

While the project was comparable in size to the Mitochondria project, we chose a different approach for navigation. Replacing arrows with hotwords worked for most students, who seemed to be able to find the content without trouble and could interact with it. There was initial resistance from some members of the group to implement the user interface in the way we did, but having implemented it, all team members began to see its merits. Students were encouraged not to thumb through the book page by page, but had to make associations in their own minds.

Many good ideas were generated in the design phase, but many of these were dropped because of budget constraints, as discussed in section 4.3.3. The idea of using a hotword in the first sentence to return to content higher in the hierarchy worked. However, other team members had some problems conceptualizing this process.

In my opinion, a shortcoming of this project is that when you come to the end of a branch, you have to go back up, and cannot go forward or around. It would have been desirable to be able to continue on a forward journey through the whole content, but because of budget and time constraints, this could not be included.

I felt that a lot of time was wasted going over ground again and again. We spent quite a bit of time in meetings continually going over the storyboards. I think that this was because the storyboards were not clearly structured and decisions were not written down properly. Both academics in the project wanted to discuss aspects of teaching well into the project design. It was valuable discussion, but the project was not progressing rapidly enough. I felt that this aspect should have been finalized before I even started coding.

11.3.3 Project manager

The Carbohydrates project was very satisfying to manage. It was clear before starting that a more effective project development model was needed than had been operating in the past, and all team members had a commitment to work towards evolving that model.

The process of designing thorough storyboards on paper was most effective, even though it must have seemed interminable to some team members at times. It took five months to design the project on paper, and four weeks to implement it on the computer. A more telling factor of the success of the model is that only five hours of debugging were needed. In part this is due to the excellent work of the programmer, but working with finalized storyboards certainly helped.

The progress of the project was not without difficulties, though. The fixed final deadline meant that some programming had to occur before all resources were available. It was quite challenging to juggle the timeline so that work could continue without effort being wasted. There were also some challenging people management issues as the deadline approached, with staff who tended to panic and make unilateral decisions about priorities.

Towards the end of the project, resource audit sheets proved useful (see Chapter 6). These indicated which graphics were not completed, and the parts of the program which were dependent on them. This enabled the programmer to identify which resources he needed first, so the graphic designer could produce them according to the programmer's priorities.

A lesson to be learnt from this project was the need to carefully write down all details of the design, and to minute all meetings with action items. Several times towards the end of this project it became clear that different team members had different conceptions of what was intended, and when it was needed. Thorough documentation can assist in alleviating misunderstandings and provide some guidance on progress.

Appendix 1

IMM Authoring Environments

Martin Hill

A1.1 Introduction

For various reasons, most of the projects we have worked on have been produced on the Apple Macintosh platform. Historically speaking, Apple's *HyperCard* was the first major 'hypermedia' type of package to garner wide support. *HyperCard*, along with other packages like *Macromind VideoWorks* (the predecessor of *Macromedia Director*), *SoundEdit* and in later years *Adobe Photoshop* and *Premiere* and of course Apple's *QuickTime* have all been based on the Macintosh platform. Only in recent years have these products been available on other platforms.

Apple Computer's hardware has also always had multimedia capabilities as standard, with the first Mac 128K back in 1984 having digital sound playback capability, and recent AV models incorporating video-in and -out capability on the motherboard. The major areas impacting on IMM, namely desktop publishing, graphics, multimedia and education have also traditionally been market strongholds for Apple Computer.

The IMM authoring packages described below are by no means an exhaustive listing, but they provide some indication as to the capabilities of some of the more popular IMM development environments currently available.

A1.2 *Apple HyperCard*

HyperCard was the first publicly available multimedia authoring package. It has suffered the depredations of time with Apple having neglected it for many years. At the time of writing, it is portrayed by Apple as a user programming environment for controlling other programs using *AppleScript* rather than a multimedia development environment. For a large portion of *HyperCard*'s life, Apple has bundled either the full environment, or a 'player' with new Macintoshes, making it a cheap and pervasive environment. We still use it for the odd project.

HyperCard introduced the 'stack of cards' metaphor where each screen is a separate card in a stack. *Hypertalk*, a natural-language like scripting language, provided the programming environment that enabled the revolution in user-friendly programming that *HyperCard* still represents. Individual objects on screen, including buttons, fields and menus as well as the cards and backgrounds making up each 'stack', could contain *Hypertalk* commands. This broke up the traditional, monolithic program listing into bite-size chunks that could be copied from object to object. *HyperCard* is also effectively always in 'runtime mode', in which scripts keep running in the background even while you are editing the stack. This does have the advantage of allowing you to try out scripts literally on the run but can cause problems when you get a 'runaway' script that will not stop.

This 'object-based' programming metaphor has proven to be extremely powerful, with a very short learning curve which significantly shortened development times. Commands like 'go next card' and 'play beep' illustrate the simplicity of many *Hypertalk* commands. *HyperCard* supports an extensible architecture allowing external commands and functions (XCMDs and XFCNs respectively) written in compiled environments like C and Pascal to be added to stacks. In the years since *HyperCard* was first introduced literally thousands of XCMDs and XFCNs have been written and are generally available, allowing stacks to control video discs, interface with scientific equipment, play animations and so on. A large range of tools, stacks and resources are available both commercially and in the public domain. *HyperCard* is now also fully OSA compliant, meaning *AppleScript* or other open scripting environments may be substituted for *Hypertalk* as the scripting language underlying *HyperCard*.

HyperCard does, however, have many shortcomings. Like most of the multimedia authoring environments available, the programming engine is only an interpreter, not a full compiler. This results in significantly lower performance compared with programs written and compiled in C or Pascal. Recent versions have added the capability of runtime compilation of scripts. This only helps where a script is being executed multiple times, but it is a step in the right direction. *HyperCard* is not truly an 'object-oriented programming' (OOP) language as it does not support inheritance and other OOP characteristics. If the built-in functionality of *HyperCard* is not sufficient, then creating XCMDs or XFCNs is not a trivial task.

Graphics is an area where *HyperCard* has lagged significantly behind competitors. The 'Colour tools' XCMDs built into recent versions of *HyperCard* illustrate that colour is still very much an added extra, not a built-in capability. Apart from having the feel of a hack, performance with colour suffers. *HyperCard* still lacks object-graphics[1] as opposed to bitmaps,[2] also limiting it severely. Buttons and fields cannot even be selected and moved, or copied as a group!

Standard buttons that follow Apple Human Interface Guidelines are now featured in *HyperCard*, although all buttons are still restricted to rectangular shapes. Try to make the countries on a map of Europe into buttons! At the time of writing, no cross-platform support was available although there are murmurings of a Windows version on the horizon. Heizer's *Convert-It!* does allow parts of *HyperCard* stacks to be converted to *Asymetrix Toolbook* on the PC.

Further reading

Complete HyperCard 2.2 Handbook, Danny Goodman, Random House
      Reference and Electronic Publishing, USA.
HyperCard 2.2 in a Hurry, Beekman, Addison-Wesley Publishing, USA.
Hands-On HyperCard, John Wiley & Sons, UK.

A1.3 *Allegiant SuperCard*

SuperCard is in many ways a superset of *HyperCard*. After a few years of stagnation under the ownership of Aldus, it has now undergone something of a renaissance following its purchase by Allegiant, a new company formed by the original authors. Version 2.0, with native PowerPC support, is now available with a Windows player on its way and a full Windows authoring environment on the horizon. Allegiant demands no licensing fee for products created with *SuperCard* and only charges a modest price for the environment itself.

SuperCard shares many features with *HyperCard*. It is fully compatible, allowing *HyperCard* stacks to be imported and run under *SuperCard* with minimal changes. It shares the stack of cards metaphor, but adds the extra feature of multiple windows within a single project, each window boasting varied sizes, different styles (dialog, floating palette, scrolling, resizable, etc), and its own stack of cards. *Supertalk*, a superset of *Hypertalk*, incorporates many extra commands and capabilities, including extremely useful animation functions. With the many window options available, creating complex dialog boxes and floating palettes is a relatively easy task, unlike *HyperCard*, which requires add-ons for such features.

In addition to the runtime editing environment called *SuperCard*, a separate editing environment named *SuperEdit* allows considerably more flexibility when authoring a project. It displays all the windows, menus, cards, sounds and other resources of a project as lists within scrolling windows, allowing the developer to rapidly navigate within large projects, moving and editing any of these objects and resources without the performance penalty of the runtime environment. It incorporates a variety of tools to assist the creation process, such as import and conversion functions and other editing tools not available in the runtime environment.

Script windows feature pop-down lists of all the *Supertalk* commands, functions and properties available, which, when selected, automatically insert formatted code for the programmer. An integrated script-tracer and variable-watcher facilitates the debugging process. A wealth of different button styles are provided, including irregular polygon and auto-traced outlines.

The graphics capabilities of *SuperCard* are a considerable improvement over *HyperCard*. Object-based draw graphics such as irregular polygons and freeform multi-point objects are supported along with auto-trace tools that turn bitmaps into draw objects or buttons. Separate drawing tools and a fairly comprehensive 8-bit colour painting environment are integral parts of *Super-Card*, not tacked on as in *HyperCard*. Both bitmap colour paint objects and draw graphics may have scripts attached to them, unlike *HyperCard* which limits scripts to buttons and fields. Both *SuperCard* and *HyperCard* allow scripts to be attached to cards, backgrounds and stacks (projects in *SuperCard*), while *SuperCard* also allows individual windows to contain scripts as well. All objects (including buttons and fields) may have particular colours, patterns, borders, transparencies and drop shadows attached to them, increasing the range of possible interface styles. Selecting, editing, grouping and moving multiple objects is fully supported, as are most other standard Macintosh editing features.

Animation options include PICs, STEP and Filmstrip animations as well as flexible path-based animations, where one can give commands of the form: 'move graphic "car" to the points of graphic "path"'. *QuickTime* digital video is also fully supported.

SuperCard, like all the authoring packages mentioned here, has its fair share of problems and limitations. While standalone double-clickable applications can be created without having to resort to a separate 'player', these are still not compiled binaries. *SuperCard* requires large amounts of memory and is not enormously quick. We have found it to be faster than *HyperCard* and *Authorware*, but slower than *Director* for common tasks like travelling from screen to screen and displaying graphics. The recent PowerPC native *Super-Card* 2.0 has upped the ante, although both *HyperCard* and *Director* now also boast native versions.

Like *HyperCard*, it is not a trivial task creating XCMDs, and *SuperCard* is not a true OOP language. The Windows player has been announced but it has not yet been released, and a full Windows authoring environment is still only being talked about. We have found quite a number of irritations with author-ing in *SuperCard*:

- Some actions (eg importing graphics and resources) are performed in convoluted ways with many modal dialogs getting in the way.
- The interface and keyboard shortcuts for editing in *SuperEdit* vary considerably from those presented by the runtime editor in *SuperCard*.
- The handling of resources (particularly sounds) can be frustrating.
- 24-bit colour bitmap handling is poor.

Despite its problems, of all the environments used, *SuperCard* has proved to be the best for our needs. The card/stack metaphor combined with the powerful but user-friendly *Supertalk* language, powerful multimedia capabili-ties, and the up-coming Windows player currently keeps it in its position as our tool of choice.

Further reading

Inside SuperCard, Microsoft Press, UK.
Steve Michel's SuperCard Handbook, S Michel, Osborne McGraw-Hill,
    Berkeley, USA.

A1.4 *Macromedia Authorware Professional*

Authorware boasts a user-friendly icon flowchart and screen metaphor rather than cards and stacks. It is mainly aimed at the CBT market. Unlike its competitors, the iconic programming metaphor used delivers multimedia titles without writing any scripts or code. This is both its greatest strength and greatest weakness. Doing anything beyond the built-in functions of the program can be difficult, making it an inflexible environment to work with.

A major advantage of this package is the availability of both Windows and Macintosh authoring environments. Apart from problems with palette shifts and different fonts, translating from one platform to the other is relatively straightforward.

The authoring environment itself presents a range of icons in a tool palette floating above the flowchart-like programming window. The icons represent various functions, including actions, interactions, timers, erasers, etc.

To create a project, the developer clicks these icons onto the programming window where they are joined by lines representing the flow of the project. For example, there may be an initial title screen represented by the display icon, followed by an interaction icon where the user chooses one of several options, thus branching off to an appropriate set of responses.

Double-clicking on any of the display icons brings up a window showing the graphics represented by that icon. Each individual graphic object may be made up of one or more bitmaps or draw graphics imported from elsewhere. Thus, a final screen may be composed of several separate graphics, buttons and fields, but can only be viewed in its entirety by running the project up to that point, to allow the separate elements to build up the resulting screen.

Double-clicking any of the interaction icons brings up a series of dialogues allowing the developer to set all the possible options for the interactions, including branching criteria, timer controls, number of iterations, etc. However, navigating the sheer number of dialog boxes to find the particular option one might need in a particular interaction can often put the lie to *Authorware*'s 'friendly' tag.

It can look all very non-threatening and understandable, but when a project reaches dozens or hundreds of screens, the iconic flowchart metaphor becomes sorely stretched. Fortunately, it is possible to group collections of icons into a single icon which when double-clicked displays a new window containing all these interactions. However, complex projects end up as awkward, massively deep hierarchies of group icons requiring considerable burrowing to navigate.

The flowchart metaphor has also proved to be very restrictive, forcing the developer to work in a very linear direction. Even implementing simple 'go previous screen' types of button or common background elements requires complex perpetual loops and the like.

Authorware relies virtually entirely on other programs for creating graphics, lacking any decent drawing or painting tools. It does, however, boast very capable path-based and animated sprite animations, although for creating the sprite primitives, you still have to rely on an external animation package such as *Director*.

The area where *Authorware* really shines is in its implementation of multiple-choice type queries. It very easily allows the developer to set up multiple-choice questions with all sorts of permutations, including random selection of questions, timed responses, scoring, limited number of retrys, and so on.

In general, we have found the built-in functions relatively competent, but very difficult to extend. Without the flexible scripting languages built into its competitors, *Authorware* rapidly frustrates advanced programmers and even non-programmers find themselves hitting the limits of the package quite quickly.

Authorware has always been positioned at the high-end of the market with high fees for the authoring environments and runtime licenses for commercial distribution. Educational discounts bring the price down closer to its competitors, but any hint of developing products for sale and the commercial price and runtime fees rear their ugly heads.

Further reading

Authorware Professional Training Manuals, Adelaide Institute Centre for
  Applied Learning Systems, Australia.
Authorware with Style, Sims, R, Sydney, NSW, Knowledgecraft.

A1.5 *Macromedia Director*

Director started life purely as an animation program, with interactive features
being added in later years. As a result, it inherits a filmstrip or frame-based
metaphor, which can be both an advantage and a disadvantage. We have
found the card-based metaphor generally to be superior to the filmstrip in the
educational realm in which we operate. However, the speed, cross-platform
capabilities and tools built-into *Director* offset the basic disadvantage of an at
times awkward metaphor.

The full authoring environment is available on both the 68K and Power
Macintosh as well as the Windows platform, with players available for the
3DO games machine. With the advent of 'shockwave', the new format from
Macromedia that allows *Director* movies to be integrated into Web pages,
Director is now moving into the vast realm of the World-Wide Web. This
potentially means delivery on just about any platform capable of browsing
Web pages, including Unix boxes, consumer set-top devices, etc.

Having started life as an animation program, *Director* is, not surprisingly,
well endowed with animation functions (sprites, tweening commands, accel-
eration and deceleration options, fades and wipes). It boasts automatic generation of all sorts of text animations including flying, scrolling, zooming and
'typewriter' text. It can also be used to animate graphs and has integrated
QuickTime support.

In the graphics department, it features a capable colour painting environment with quite flexible graduated fills. However, its separate drawing tools
palette is quite basic, limited to simple ovals, rectangles and lines. *Director*
supports anti-aliased text and a range of transfer modes allowing object
transparencies and the like. However, it does not easily support multiple
windows or floating palettes, or other standard interface elements like pop-
up or pull-down menus.

Director supports two channels for sound playback, allowing, for instance,
simultaneous background music and voiceovers. *Director*'s built-in programming language, 'Lingo', is a feature-rich and flexible language that allows
scripts to be attached to individual cells, frames or sprites. Like many of the
other environments, *Director* is also extensible through the use of 'XObjects',
but again, creating such extensions is not a trivial task, requiring programming in Pascal or C. *Director* is also not an OOP environment, nor does it

produce compiled code. It does, however, allow the creation of protected standalone players, allowing developers to protect their intellectual property and distribute their results widely.

The linear multi-track filmstrip can get very complex and difficult to manage, particularly when many elements appear on one screen, but it does have the advantage of allowing the developer to see every object listed in the 'score' window and its level and movements. The package is generally regarded as having a steep learning curve and it has a steep price as well. It may be less expensive than *Authorware*, but it is still two to four times the cost of much of its competition. At the time of writing, *Director* is the undisputed world leader when it comes to IMM titles.

Further reading

Director 4 for Mac: VQSG, Kobler, Addison-Wesley Publishing, USA.

A1.6 *Apple Media Tool*

The *Apple Media Tool* (AMT) is an interesting example of an IMM authoring environment composed of two separate packages at opposite ends of the programming spectrum. The user-friendly AMT is a non-programmer's delight, requiring no scripting or programming to put together multiple screens linked in all sorts of different ways, with hot areas and buttons taking the user from screen to screen. Beyond simple navigation and triggering of movie or sound playback, however, the *Apple Media Tool* is very limited. It has no in-built capabilities to perform conditional branching, as needed in testing or tutorial-type packages. Another important omission is the ability to have common background elements.

This is where the other half of the dual environment comes in. The *Apple Media Tool Programming Environment* (PE) is a fully fledged programmer's OOP workshop for creating code to be combined with a project created in the AMT for all those more complex interactions needed in most IMM projects. The strategy behind this package is eminently laudable, seeking as it does to provide a composition package for content-providers and graphic artists to create the structure and content of a project, while allowing the programmer to produce the extra code to include interactivity and other specific functionality. Unfortunately, the AMT suffers from the severe lack of many basic functions, making the presence of a skilled programmer absolutely essential for even elementary functionality.

The user-friendly authoring environment does however show much promise with its hybrid of card and flowchart metaphors. It allows the creation of an iconic map of the project in a much more freeform manner than *Authorware*, and with much less complexity. Unlike the latter's top-to-bottom flowchart with links between icons automatically and rigidly being created, the AMT allows the developer to grab icons representing each screen and drop them anywhere on the screen, and then link them in any fashion with directional lines. Double-clicking on any of the icons opens a window showing what is on that screen, allowing the developer to import graphics, movies, sounds, etc, and to select hot areas and buttons, as well as to determine what leads where and how.

AMT has no graphics or media creation tools of its own, relying entirely on other programs for media creation. Even text creation on-screen is very basic, encouraging the developer to create virtually everything in other packages and use AMT only as a composition tool. Treated in this fashion, it works well enough, particularly for kiosk-type applications, but for best productivity, it demands large amounts of RAM to allow the developer to be running copies of their favourite graphics, animation, sound and movie-editing packages simultaneously. AMT is intelligent enough to automatically switch to (or open) the appropriate editor when the developer double-clicks on a media object on screen. It also keeps all the media separate from the project file itself, allowing the developer to substitute media elements and other content without even having to go into the authoring environment. This strategy also eases cross-platform delivery, allowing one set of media elements to service both Mac and Windows versions of the package.

The programmers' environment is both a programming language and application framework, provided in Apple's MPW (*Macintosh Programmer's Workshop*). In the words of the advertising, it combines the power of OOP with the ease of a scripting language. In practice, knowledge of MPW-style programming is essential. A very large advantage of the programmers environment is that the custom code created and compiled in MPW is portable between both the Macintosh and the Windows platforms. It also provides access to both Macintosh and Windows toolboxes through a C language interface, for platform-specific applications.

A1.7 *Kaleida ScriptX*

ScriptX is not a multimedia authoring environment *per se*. Rather, it is a programming language, file format and delivery environment designed from the ground up for IMM. It was expected that IMM authoring environments would be created using *ScriptX* as their foundation, or at the very least allow import and/or export in *ScriptX* format. Kaleida Corporation was formed out of a major alliance between Apple and IBM in 1992. At that time, delivering IMM on the multiplicity of platforms available was a considerable task. The large amount of resources (RAM, hard disk space and processing power) required by most titles was also a problem, particularly for the many newly introduced media players like Philips' CD-I, the 3DO and the late Commodore's CD-32.

Kaleida aimed to address this problem by providing the programming language called *ScriptX*, programming environments for *ScriptX* for the major platforms, and *ScriptX* players for all the possible delivery platforms. In the case of the media player hardware, an optimized consumer operating system (COS) was planned.

Although there is definitely a need for a common IMM file format to ease the compatibility woes between divergent authoring environments, *ScriptX* largely seems to have lost its relevance, at least as far as industry acceptance is concerned. The increasing level of cross-platform support provided by environments such as *Director*, the meteoric rise of the World-Wide Web, and the up and coming interactive add-ons like *Java* and *Shockwave* have stolen much of *ScriptX*'s thunder.

The fact remains, however, that technically, *ScriptX* has large potential. It is a full OOP environment, which is geared specifically to the needs of IMM. It addresses such needs as placement of different media types at particular locations on CD-ROM disks for best access performance, and support for a multiplicity of metaphors including stack and card and linear frame-based. It is fully multi-threaded, sprite-based and is reasonably friendly in a programming sense. It is, however, definitely not as easy as the very English-language-like *Hypertalk* or its successors.

Time will tell if Kaleida is successful at promulgating this as the new *Postscript* of the IMM world or not. They have been working on it for long enough now for it to start becoming clear that the industry doesn't look like taking it on board – which is unfortunate considering its merits in particular areas.

A1.8 *Asymetrix Toolbook*

Asymetrix Multimedia Toolbook Version 3.0 is perhaps the leading software development environment for CBL materials under the Windows operating system. Applications developed using *Toolbook* consist of one or more 'books', which are composed of 'pages'. This is identical to the *HyperCard* 'stack' and 'card' metaphor. Pages are constructed using a wide selection of graphical objects like text fields and buttons. These objects are easily available to the developer from a range of floating toolbars which can be made visible at any time. Each object can have an associated script which will handle user events like mouseclicks. *Toolbook* scripts are written in 'OpenScript' (which is again very similar to *Hypertalk*).

Once the pages of a book are developed, they can be presented to the user through special windows which *Toolbook* calls 'viewers'. It is possible to have more than one viewer open at one time, making it very easy to construct toolbars and windows displaying video and animations

Toolbook is a useful development environment for producing hypermedia applications, interactive kiosks, and CBL material. *Toolbook* is easy to learn and the 'object-based' nature of its development environment makes construction quick and easy. Any object which is created can be copied and then pasted into another *Toolbook* application. All of the scripts which are associated with the object move with it.

Toolbook Version 3.0 comes with an extensive library of objects which you can cut and paste into applications. Another strong feature of *Toolbook* is the ability to assign user-defined properties to objects, a feature not available in environments like *HyperCard*.

While you are developing *Toolbook* applications, it is possible to switch freely between author and reader levels to see what the project will look like to the end user. The final version of the application can be compiled into an intermediate form which is viewed with a *Toolbook* runtime player. The *Toolbook* licence allows you to distribute applications and the *Toolbook* runtime player with no associated fee. A special version of *Toolbook* called the 'CBT version' contains an extensive range of CBT examples and 'Wizard' development tools. *Toolbook* enjoys wide popularity and support amongst CBL developers around the world.

Toolbook's drawbacks are similar to most of the card-stack/page-book metaphor development environments. It is not overly quick and even simple applications can occupy a large amount of disk space. One glaring omission in *Toolbook* is the apparent inability of the program to interrupt its own scripts. If you are confronted with a 'runaway' script in *Toolbook* which is stuck in an infinite loop, there is very little that you can do about it. *Toolbook* is also a single-platform solution, so you do not have the possibility of delivering titles on both Macintosh and PC-compatible computers.

Further reading

Using Asymmetrix Multimedia Toolbook 4, Natal, D and Reitan, E,
    Indianapolis, IN, Que Corporation.
Utilizing Multimedia Toolbook 3.0, Hall, T L, Danvers MA, Boyd & Fraser.

Notes

1. Object, or vector, graphics are generated by the computer as commands instructing the processor to draw a line from point a to point b. Each object graphic

behaves as if it is drawn on a sheet of transparent plastic, and the sheets can be layered and shuffled.

2.   Bitmapped or paint graphics are created by simply colouring different pixels (dots) on the screen. They function like an oil painting – once a section is recoloured, the old colours have been painted over and can't be retrieved.

A Representative
Requirements Specification

A2.1 Introduction

The use of a requirements specification was discussed in section 4.1. The requirements specification defines the scope of the project and how each aspect of the project will be treated; it specifies the *functionality* required of the project. Details of the user interface are described, as are guidelines about the graphic design. The requirements specification does not contain any content, other than perhaps the headings of the topics, or other details required to define the navigation.

In the incremental prototyping model described in this book, the requirements specification, along with the storyboard, documents the design cycle. Such a document evolves with time, as its details are analysed and evaluated.

In case the form of a requirements specification as advocated here is not clear to readers, this Appendix contains abstracts of a representative requirements specification. It is a snapshot taken at a particular stage in the design process. Readers will notice from the formatting and mistakes that this document is clearly a 'work in progress'. However, it serves the essential purposes of focusing the development team's attention on issues at hand, at the same time as documenting design decisions made.

A2.2 Muscles Project requirements specification

1. Parts of the program

There are two parts of the program, implemented as two stacks; the tutorial will be finished and the resource front-end will be modifiable [see Figure A2.1].

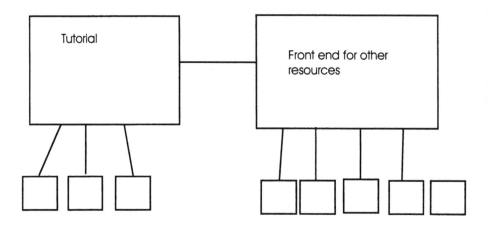

Figure A2.1   *The two parts of the program*

There are also three sets of functionality required of the program:

- Animation controls.
- Exploration functions – related to manipulating stopped frames of the animation.
- Non-exploration or context functions. Other Resources, Glossary, Where am I?, Where have I been?, Find, Quit(?) Test(??), Scale Monitor/Size Context. We are attempting to absorb the rest of these into the interface.

It is unclear where and how some other functions can be included. Some suggestions are below, but these need to be explored and discussed.

- The scale animation showing how actin and myosin zoom out to form actual muscles. Part of the Main Animation screen. As part of the video controls??
- General info on muscle types and skeletal muscle. In Supplementary Material.
- The Neuro-muscular Junction (NMJ). In Supplementary Material?

1.1   Animation parts

The central animation is the contraction process, swivel, attach, etc. It is almost finished.

There are five other subsidiary animations:

	Status
Thin filament formation	complete
Thick filament formation	complete
The process at the neuro-muscular junction NMJ	not defined
Relaxation – reverse of contraction	not defined
Micro-macro – sorcerer's apprentice	starting

It is not certain where all of these will be included, but some of them will certainly be accessible from the Content screens. These subsidiary animations will behave differently to the main animation. No exploration will be possible. Students can play them, or use a slider to move through at their own pace. It seems a good idea to associate descriptive subtitles to the animation, so a written commentary appears.

2. Animation user interface and definition

The contraction animation is the central core of the tutorial. It has two functions:

- the student observes and manipulates the contraction process;
- a user interface (main menu) to access other information in the tutorial.

2.1   Observe and manipulate

The student observes and manipulates the contraction process (play video, slide through video, change speed of playthrough). While the video plays, perhaps we should have a whirring sound like a film projector. Use other sound cues when animation is stopped. Angela has yet to design these controls. She is attempting to improve on the traditional 'video' metaphor.

The user starts the animation. When they see something they want to find out more about, they stop the animation, either by releasing the mouse button (dragging a slider) or by clicking. They may also click on the 'stop' button, but any click in the exploration area will do. Nick suggested doing away with the slider, using 'skip' controls instead. The problem with a slider is that the slider will move after mouseup to the nearest key frame. Perhaps the slider frame should have a sawtooth appearance, so the slider drops into a depression when it is stopped?

2.2   User interface (exploration)

After the animation has stopped, it acts as a user interface (main menu) to access other information in the tutorial. The user interface works like this [see Figure A2.2].

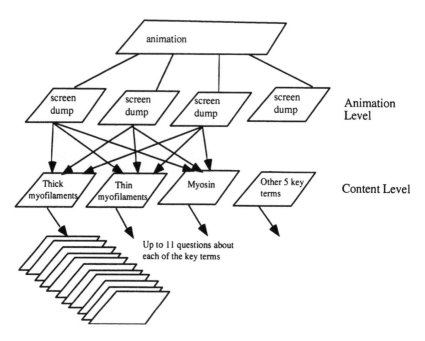

Figure A2.2   *Structure of the program*

The animation stops at the nearest key frame. This is how it looks to the user, but actually the program jumps to a card which contains a screen dump of that frame of the animation (framecopy). The animation will need to be carefully designed so that the key frames are not too far apart. When the animation has stopped, the cursor should change to indicate the user is in exploration mode.

This screen has hotspots that the user can investigate. Moving the mouse into a hotspot will bring up its name. Do we highlight the outline of the hotspot as the mouse is moved into it? Or do we change the cursor to indicate we are in a hotspot? Or both?

The eight types of hotspots are *Thick Myofilaments, Thin Myofilaments, Myosin, Actin, Tropomyosin, Troponin, Ca^{++}, ATP/ADP*. All hotspot descriptions appear in a field on screen. Each word has its own icon as well as name, to make it clearer that it has changed. It will be difficult to distinguish between individual Actins and the thin myofilament. *This needs to be investigated.*

In the third level of the diagram, the user can get to the same piece of information from several screen dumps, depending where that hotspot was at the time the animation was stopped. This is called the *content level*. The user interface is different at this level.

2.3   Content level

The content level is determined by the table contained in a separate file called 'Fyfe Contents Matrix'. It contains the following ten questions, most of which apply to each of the eight key terms:

- What is it made of?
- What does it do? Level (1)
- What does it interact with?
- What controls its activity?
- Where does it come from?
- Where is it made?
- Where does it work?
- How big is it?
- How does it work? Level (2)
- Why do you need it?

There is an implicit assumption in this that each of these 88 topics will fit on one screen. Do they? This is crucial.

The prototype interface contains a picture icon (picon) with the grey background of the animation containing an image of the hotspot chosen. This gives the context of where you are (as well as the label at the top), and gives you a cue to go back to the animation. Angela needs to produce separate graphics for each of the eight cases, which will be programmed to return to the animation screen.

The general description of the key term will appear on this screen, as will a series of questions, hidden in the quadrant picon under what, where, how, why. Clicking on one of the questions will pop up the series of specific questions for that pronoun. Clicking on the specific question will bring up appropriate information.

The quadrant picon will rotate so that the highlighted question is at the top. Use a sound cue while rotating.

The specific question responses may include text, pictures or animations. Text may contain hotwords to link to other sections. Pictures should behave consistently and allow exploration as in the main animation. Animations will be able to be explored, but will not lead to other content.

Each of the ten question answers should appear on ten different screens, which share the same basic appearance.

2.3.1   The interface

It was decided that the content screens could now be 640x480 pixels. The quadrant picon is at the bottom left with the pop up items just to its right. The *Return* picon is at the bottom right. On the main animation screens, this location is occupied by a *Quit* picon.

2.4   Hotwords and hyperlinks

The structure of the program is shown in the external document called 'Content structure'. Basically, the normal links go horizontally through this diagram, via the questions. Hyperlinks, whether from hotwords or graphics, go vertically.

There are two types of hotwords. The eight key terms form one type. Other glossary entries form the other. They need to be distinguished.

2.4.1   Key term hotword

If one of the key terms crops up anywhere, clicking on it will take the user to the first screen of the 'Content level'. This is the screen which contains a basic description of the key term. It should also highlight the appropriate question which was being asked before going here. The user can get back to the animation using the *Return* picon at the bottom right.

It seems that the user will not be able to return directly to where they came from. Instead they have to go back to the animation.

2.4.2   Glossary hotword

A glossary hotword is any other term which needs description. Clicking on one of these pops up a fairly large window. This contains a description of the term, with a picture if appropriate. No animation, we hope? It contains a context-sensitive button (a sack?) which takes the user to relevant 'Other Resources'. It may also have a *Find* function. Will it give a list of other terms in the glossary? It may have a *See Also* function, where a student can make a *quantum leap* to another part of the program.

Glossary of Graphic Design Terms

Angela DiGiorgio

The following glossary describes commonly used terms related to screen design. It should be read in conjunction with section 4.3.

Achromatic colour   A combination only of black and white, found anywhere along a grey scale.

Alignment   Usually referred to in terms of type alignment, but also refers to object alignment. Alignment for type can be either centred, aligned left (ragged right), aligned right (ragged left) or justified.

Anti-aliasing   The process of blending the outer edge pixels of objects or text so that they appear smoother when displayed on a monitor.

Baseline   An imaginary line on which text sits.

Bit   One pixel.

Bitmap   When an image or typeface is made from a collection of pixels.

Body text   The main information of text, not including headings or sub-headings.

Bold   Variant of a typeface with heavier than normal weight.

Character   Any letter, numeral or punctuation mark.

Colour resolution   The number of different colours or grey scale values a system can display.

Condensed type   A very narrow type style, where the characters appear squashed together.

Contrast   The difference between the dark and light values in an image. High contrast images contain very dark and very light values with minimal intermediate shades. Low contrast images contain predominantly medium grey values.

Cool colour   A colour which has a predominantly blue base.

Cropping   Cutting down or trimming an image or object.

Dithering   A technique for altering the values of adjacent pixels to create the effect of an intermediate value therefore providing a smoother appearance.

DPI   Dots per inch; indicates screen or printer resolution. For example: 72 dpi means there are 72 dots per linear inch.

Draw program   A graphics software package that creates images using vectors (line and curve segments) rather than individual dots.

Drop capital   (or drop cap) A capital letter that drops into the lines of text below, used to mark the beginning of a section in a block of body text.

Drop shadow   A tinted or solid area set to one side of an object to give a shadow effect.

EPS   Encapsulated PostScript. A file format commonly used for high resolution printing.

Export   To output an object from a program in a form suitable for use in another program.

Fill   A colour or pattern occupying a defined area.

Flatbed scanner   These work in a similar manner to a photocopier, where the image or artwork is placed face down onto a glass surface and converted into a digital form.

Focal point   The area of an image to which the eye is first drawn, or which holds the eye for the longest.

Font style   One style of typeface offering, in most cases, upper and lower case, numerals and punctuation marks.

Graphics   Refers to any illustration, photograph, animation or diagram.

Grey scale   Tints produced by mixing only black and white.

Grid   A positional plan used to place objects together in a layout and achieve balance.

Highlight   The lightest part of an image, usually white or a hue containing a large amount of white.

Intensity   Refers to the lightness of an image.

Italic   A type style which is slanted to the right.

JPEG   Joint Photographic Experts Group – an image compression standard.

Justified   Refers to the way type is formatted, when both the left and right hand edges are even or flush.

Kerning   Spacing between letters within a word.

Landscape mode   Refers to the orientation of a rectangular design or design area, with the shortest dimension being vertical and the longest horizontal.

Layout   The arrangement or 'map' relating to a design which determines where objects are to be placed.

Leading   Spacing between lines of text, measured in points.

Left alignment   Refers to formatting of type when it is placed flush against the left edge with a ragged right-hand edge. Also referred to as range left, ragged right.

MPEG   Motion Picture Experts Group – a digital video compression standard.

Negative space   Areas of a design or image which are not occupied by positive objects – the leftover space.

Oblique   (*see* italic).

Paint program   A graphics software package that creates images using individual dots (pixels) rather than a collection of shapes made up of lines.

Palette   The collection of colours available for use at the same time within a program.

PICT   Picture format, used for the exchange and storage of graphics.

Pixel   Picture element. The smallest dot you can draw on a screen.

Point size   The most common unit of measure for type. Sizing of fonts and leading is usually specified in point size (1 point, or pt, is 1/72 of an inch).

Portrait mode   Refers to the orientation of a rectangular design or design area, with the longest dimension being vertical and the shortest horizontal.

QuickTime   A Macintosh system extension that compresses and decompresses digitized video and animation.

Ragged   Margins of text which are not vertically aligned.

Render   To draw an image using colour and pattern as opposed to a skeletal representation.

Resolution   The amount of data available in which to represent graphic detail in a given area, generally described in terms of the number of pixels.

Reverse   To make the darker elements lighter and the lighter elements darker.

Right alignment   Refers to formatting of type when it is placed flush against the right edge with a ragged left-hand edge. Also referred to as range right, ragged left.

Roman   A type style which is set upright.

Sans serif   A font which does not have serifs (the small strokes at the top and bottom of a letter). An example is Helvetica.

Scan   To transform an image from a printed form to an electronic form.

Scanner   A graphic input device which converts printed matter into digital data.

Screen resolution   The number of line or dot positions in each dimension of a display.

Serif   A font which has serifs (the small strokes at the top and bottom of a letter) such as Times.

Shade   A colour with black added to it.

Solid   A filled area with a 100% tint.

Style   In terms of text, refers to the typographical attribute such as font, size, leading, etc.

Thumbnail   Miniature sketch of a layout design.

Tint   Any colour which has white added to it.

Tone   The variation of lightness and darkness in a colour.

Typeface   The full range of letters and other characters of a given type design. Sometimes includes all the weights and styles.

Visual   A mock-up of a design or layout, larger and more detailed than a thumbnail.

Warm colour   A colour which has a predominantly red or orange base.

Weight   Refers to the degree of thickness of fonts or lines.

Appendix 4

Technical Aspects of Digital Video

Martin Hill

A4.1 Introduction

The impact and utility of video sequences integrated into a multimedia package has been appreciated for some time. Implementing this media type, however, can be a complex issue.

For many years, computer-controlled videodiscs were common in areas where video imagery was an important aspect of a project. The video was stored as standard composite, analogue video on the videodisc and either viewed on a separate TV monitor or displayed on the computer screen using a video overlay card. This solution, although delivering random access, high quality, full screen, full motion video and CD-quality stereo audio, suffers from a number of disadvantages. Foremost among these drawbacks is the need for separate expensive peripherals, namely the videodisc player and either a video overlay card or a separate video monitor. Second, the production of the videodiscs themselves is an expensive task, requiring the services of a videodisc production house. Third, the several incompatible video standards common around the world, namely NTSC, PAL and SECAM, and the CLV vs CAV formatting of the disc itself, have contributed to the fragmentation of the videodisc market.

To overcome some of these disadvantages, a large amount of development has been directed towards making video available in digital format on the computer itself and playing it back directly from disk or CD-ROM. Intel's DVI digital video solution was one of the early attempts at achieving this aim. Although capable of playing compressed video directly from a hard disk at reasonable frame rates, it suffered from low quality video, the requirement of extra hardware (the DVI decompression card) and the necessity of using a bureau service to compress the video source to achieve reasonable quality video.

It was the introduction of Apple Computer's *QuickTime* Architecture for the Macintosh and Windows platforms and subsequently Microsoft's *Video for Windows* that brought digital video to the masses. These initial solutions, although only capable of low resolution video (initially 160x120 pixels in size) and low frame rates (12–15 frames per second [fps]), required no extra hardware to play back from a CD-ROM or hard disk and were able to be digitized by cards costing well under a thousand Australian dollars, Super-Mac's *VideoSpigot* and Creative Lab's *VideoBlaster* being prime examples.

Improvements in hardware and software performance are such that, at the time of writing, high quality quarter-screen playback (320x240 at 30fps) is readily achievable in software without hardware assistance. Full screen video is achieved by pixel doubling[1] to achieve 640x480 pixels at 15fps or more.

The prevalence of software-only digital video playback has not removed the need for hardware-assisted playback, however. On the contrary, the market for these higher quality video capture and playback solutions has been legitimized and is growing substantially. The rapidly emerging MPEG (Motion Pictures Expert Group) standard is a popular format for final delivery on multiple consumer platforms as well as desktop computers equipped with MPEG playback chips. MPEG capture and playback boards, such as the *Xing-it!* and *Reelmagic* are popular at the consumer end of the market with a number of CD-ROM titles available that take advantage of MPEG video. At the high end, Motion-JPEG boards such as the *Radius Videovision, Media 100* and *Avid* systems are taking the video editing world by storm. There is also the distinct possibility of MPEG chips being built onto the motherboards of personal computers with games consoles such as the ill-fated CD-32, the Philips CD-I and others featuring MPEG playback boards as either standard or low-cost add-ons.

Time will tell whether such hardware-assisted video playback will garner a significant proportion of the market. The increasing horsepower available with Pentium and PowerPC CPUs has already led to software MPEG decoders being demonstrated that will probably ensure software decompression will stay the most popular delivery vehicle for digital video in the future.

A4.1.1 Video compression

The major problem with video is the large data rates required; that is, the amount of data that has to be transmitted from the storage device to the processor, and hence the screen. Full screen, full motion video consumes around 20 megabytes per second (Mb/s) compared with CD-quality stereo sound which consumes a relatively minor 150 kilobytes per second (Kb/s). To make digital video viable, compression techniques (compression algorithms) are employed to reduce the storage size and data rates.

The two main current video compression schemes are MPEG and JPEG, produced respectively by the Motion Picture Experts Group and the Joint Photographic Experts Group. The characteristics of these two schemes are given in the following sections, together with an explanation of some of the important differences between them.

MPEG – Motion Picture Experts Group

MPEG is a popular format for final delivery on multiple consumer platforms as well as desktop computers equipped with MPEG playback chips. It is not appropriate for desktop video editing, or playing back video on computers not equipped with the extra MPEG playback hardware. However, the advent of software-only MPEG decoders such as *SoftPEG* will undoubtedly eliminate this last qualification.

The recent VideoCD (White book) format, which uses MPEG I, is supported by 'media players' from various companies including CD-I, 3DO, CD-32 as well as MPEG playback boards for Macs and PCs. It can store 72 minutes of 'full-screen' video and a stereo soundtrack on one CD-ROM disc.

It has very high compression ratios (around 200:1), thus resulting in relatively small file sizes.

MPEG I only supports video up to 352x240 (352x288 at 25fps for PAL) in size. For full screen MPEG, various implementations use interpolation to pixel-double the video to achieve 'full size' playback. This is limited to 150Kb/s data transfer rates (the rate of original single-speed CD-ROMs). MPEG II, which is only now starting to appear, is capable of larger sizes and higher transfer rates (750Kb/s to 5Mb/s) and is being implemented in many Video On Demand (VOD) systems.

MPEG uses inter-frame as well as intra-frame compression techniques with frames between key-frames only recording the changes from the previous frame. Thus MPEG is not appropriate for non-linear off-line video editing, or on-line video editing. Deletion of a key-frame leaves the following frames without a reference, and corrupts the file.

Encoding MPEG video is very processor-intensive. Only very expensive systems are capable of recording and compressing high quality MPEG video in real-time. There are a number of low-cost MPEG encoding solutions available, but these are only capable of producing low quality images, they do not follow the full MPEG standard and often only achieve quite low compression ratios.

JPEG – Joint Photographic Experts Group

'Motion-JPEG' is the most common compressor used for non-linear on-line and off-line video editing. It is also useful for the capture of high quality video at large sizes and frame rates direct to disk for recompression later using software-only compressors/decompressors (codecs), for play back on computers not equipped with extra hardware. It is, however, not an appropriate delivery format for video play back from CD-ROM or hard disk on other computers or media players.

Video boards using M-JPEG have been available for some time, and are typically capable of capturing and compressing digital video in real time, direct to disk at resolutions up to 640x480 at 30 frames per sec (576x768 and 25fps for PAL).

M-JPEG can achieve close to broadcast-quality images for professional video editing with compression set low for best quality. These capture and compression boards produce much higher quality video images than the MPEG standard, but at the cost of file size and transfer rates – Multi-gigabyte RAID arrays with SCSI-II disk controllers being the norm for this near broadcast-quality video.

By using the JPEG board only for the initial capture and compression, codecs like *CinePak* (see section A4.1.2) allow the video to be recompressed for playback on personal computers at frame rates and sizes similar to MPEG.

JPEG produces very large file sizes (3–5Mb/s and more) at its higher quality settings. Maximum compression rates are only of the order of 25:1 before image quality starts suffering inordinately. This is because M-JPEG only performs intra-frame or spatial compression, which gives much smaller compression ratios compared to MPEG.

M-JPEG playback-only boards are expensive compared to MPEG playback-only boards, and they are not supported by the many consumer media players coming onto the market.

A4.1.2 Compression schemes

There are four main characteristics by which image compression algorithms may be judged:

- compression ratio;
- image quality;
- compression/decompression speed;
- spatial/temporal compression.

Compression ratio and transfer rates

The compression ratio describes how small the compressed data is in relation to the uncompressed original. MPEG boasts compression ratios up to 200:1, while JPEG compression achieves acceptable image qualities around the 10:1 to 30:1 levels. These sorts of ratios bring video down to the much more manageable figure of between 1 and 5Mb/s using JPEG or 150Kb/s using MPEG I. The low data rate of the latter originated with the need to play back video from the first single-speed CD-ROMs which had a 150Kb/s limit. Since that time, however, the speed of CD-ROM drives has been doubling almost yearly, with quad-speed and greater drives capable of 6–800Kb/s or more becoming common. The number of double-speed drives already on the market does, however, mean that keeping below 300Kb/s is an eminently sensible aim in the near term.

Image quality
Compression schemes are either 'lossy' or 'lossless'. Lossless codecs typically use so-called RLE (run length encoding) compression algorithms to achieve around 2:1 compression ratios without losing any of the data or quality of the original video stream. Lossy codecs like JPEG use DCT (discrete cosine transform) routines to eliminate some extra information not recognized by the human eye, and in so doing achieve considerably higher compression ratios. Generally, the higher the compression ratio for a given lossy codec, the lower is the quality. Algorithms like JPEG and MPEG work best with large areas of similar shades of a colour and gentle transitions from one colour to another without hard and sharp edges. Therefore, the compression ratio can vary widely depending on the type of image being compressed.

Compression/decompression speed
Compression and decompression speeds vary widely from codec to codec and are important to take into account. Apple's original video compressor is an example of a fast symmetric codec. It compresses in real time as the video is captured to hard disk and plays back (decompresses) at the same rate. Its disadvantages are that the resulting video data files are fairly large on disk, and the image quality and frame rate is typically quite low. In contrast, Radius's *CinePak* codec is asymmetric. It takes 30 to 60 times longer to compress the original video data than it does to decompress it. However, it has the advantage of considerably higher quality images with much smaller file sizes and higher frame rates. One of the reasons for this is that like MPEG, *CinePak* performs temporal compression.

Spatial/temporal compression
Spatial or intra-frame compression is where compression occurs within each individual frame of a video stream. Temporal, or inter-frame compression is where there is also compression between frames. This is achieved by choosing key-frames every 15 frames or so which record all the data for that frame.

Every subsequent image records only the changes that make it different from the previous frame. As a result, talking-head shots and other fixed camera position shots compress very well using temporal compression, while any movement of the camera or fast changes in the video image are not as effectively compressed. However, temporal compression almost always results in considerably smaller file sizes and data transfer rates than spatial compression routines.

A4.2 Digital video capture tips and tricks

Digital video capture and playback on off-the-shelf personal computers has proved to be something of a minefield. Lured by the promises of this attractive technology, many users have experienced results well below expectations. Small, jerky, low quality video clips captured on typical base level computers have been quite common.

At the time of writing, video of quarter-screen size (320x240) running at 15–20fps with a data rate of 150–300Kb/s is typical of the quality levels accepted in many commercial IMM products. To achieve this level of quality, there are a number of important issues to take into account. These are:

- disk transfer rate;
- compression strategy;
- standalone operation;
- memory issues;
- video source quality.

Disk transfer rate

It is important to use the fastest possible hard disk as the place to capture the video. Sustained transfer rate is more important in this regard than access time. RAID (redundant arrays of inexpensive disks) arrays with SCSI-II controllers are essential for full-screen, full frame-rate M-JPEG cards, but they will also significantly improve the frame-rates of more basic AV-class Macintoshes and equivalents. Special 'AV drives' which reduce the impact of thermal recalibration of the drive head are available for top-end systems and can reduce drop-outs and 'glitches' during capture and playback of full-screen video.

In the absence of specialized disks (or even with them), it is advisable to defragment the hard disk being used as the capture volume, either by using a special utility, or by formatting the disk.

Compression strategy

Capture the video, if possible, using a high-quality full-screen, full frame rate capture board, and the fastest but cleanest codec available. In lieu of a JPEG compression accelerator card, the software-only YUV codec available under the *QuickTime* architecture is a good example of the former sort of codec. It only provides 2:1 compression, so plenty of disk space is essential, but it is very fast, thus maintaining good frame rates while giving a very high quality image.

Subsequently the video should be recompressed using the *CinePak* (or equivalent) asymmetric compressor to achieve the maximum possible compression.

Standalone operation

It is important that only the video capture program is running while video is being captured. Some tasks, such as network services, running on the computer in the background, can interfere with the smooth operation of the video capture. It is necessary to disable all non-essential background processes, leaving active only those necessary for video capture. The second step is to quit from any other applications.

Memory issues

If the video clip is short enough and the computer is well-enough endowed with random access memory (RAM), capture directly to RAM rather than disk. The speed of RAM compared with magnetic media is greater by several orders of magnitude.

Disabling background processes in the step above will also make more RAM available to the video capture application. It is important not to use virtual memory, which simulates RAM by using the hard disk. This can slow the capture process appreciably.

Video source quality

Use the cleanest possible video for the source material. Use of new video tapes and well-maintained cameras and players will assist in reducing noise. Lots of noise in the video signal considerably impacts the speed and compression ratios of most codecs. Component video sources (S/VHS and Betacam SP) are definitely preferable to consumer VHS in this regard.

If possible and viable, capture the sound tracks for the video clips separately and then overlay and resynchronize the sound track later in a video editing package like *Adobe Premiere*. This enables all the resources of the computer to be devoted to capturing and processing the video stream.

Aim for short, succinct video clips where possible, with minimal panning, zooming and rapidly changing imagery.

With the use of these guidelines, it is possible to achieve considerably better results from most video capture systems, from expensive M-JPEG cards right down to basic consumer systems lacking any codec hardware assistance.

Note

1. Pixel doubling is where each pixel in the original video is doubled in size in the horizontal and vertical directions. The video therefore looks 'blocky'.

References

Brown, M (1991) 'An investigation of the development process and costs of CBT in Australia', paper presented at ASCILITE 91, Launceston, Tasmania.

Budd, T (1990) *An Introduction to Object-Oriented Programming*, Addison-Wesley, Reading, MA.

Canale, R and Wills, S (1993) 'Producing professional interactive multimedia: Project management issues', paper presented at the Australian Society for Computers in Learning in Tertiary Education Conference, Lismore, NSW.

Candy, P C, Crebert, G and O'Leary, J (1994) *Developing Lifelong Learners through Undergraduate Education*, NBEET Commissioned Report #28, Australian Government Publishing Service.

Cosgrove, M and Alexander, S (1993) 'A multimedia-based tutoring system for introductory electricity', *Reaching Out With IT*, Proceedings of the 10th Annual Conference of the Australian Society for Computers in Learning in Tertiary Education, The University of New England-Northern Rivers, Lismore, NSW.

Cotton, R and Oliver, R (1993) *Understanding Hypermedia*, Phaidon Press, London.

Edwards, P and Fox, R (1992) 'Enhancing the quality of teaching and learning through alternative teaching methods? A computer-assisted learning case study', *Research and Development in Higher Education*, 15, 360–66.

Edwards, P (1992) 'Multimedia and microbiology: An Australian first', paper presented at the Interactive Multimedia Symposium, Perth, Western Australia.

Edwards, P and Fox, R (1993) 'Hyper infections: case studies in problem solving', paper presented at the Sharing Quality Practice, Teaching Learning Forum, Perth, Western Australia.

Ellis, H D (1994) 'Learning catalysis and other concepts in computer-based education', paper presented at the Asia Pacific Information Technology in Training and Education Conference, Brisbane, Australia, APITITE 94 Council.

Flagg, B N (1990) *Formative Evaluation of Educational Technologies*, Lawrence Erlbaum, Hillsdale, NJ.

Fox, R and Edwards, P (1990) 'Microbes and the media: a telecourse for nurses', *Open Learning and New Technology*, Australian Society for Educational Technology, Perth, Western Australia.

Gagné, R (1977) *The Conditions of Learning*, Holt Rinehart & Winston, New York.

Gillespie, L (1995) Constructivism/Behaviorism Discussion, *Instructional Technology Forum Electronic Discussion List* <*ITFORUM@ugaccugaedu*>.

Hedberg, J G and Harper, B (1995) 'Exploration and investigation in information landscapes', paper presented at the Apple University Consortium Conference, Perth, Western Australia.

Howell, G T (1992) *Building Hypermedia Applications: A software development guide*, McGraw Hill, Maidenhead.

Jonassen, D (1994) 'Technology as cognitive tools: learners as designers', *Instructional Technology Forum Electronic Discussion List* <*ITFORUM @uga.cc.uga.edu*>.

Kember, D and Gow, L (1989) 'Model of student approaches to learning encompassing ways to influence and change approaches', *Instructional Science*, 18, 163–228.

Kennedy, D and Taylor, P (1994) 'Hypermedia design for enriching conceptual understanding in chemistry', paper presented at the Second International Interactive Multimedia Symposium, Promaco Conventions, Perth, Western Australia.

Kozma, R B (1991) 'Learning with media', *Review of Educational Research*, **61**, 2, 179–211.

Laurillard, D M (1993) *Rethinking University Teaching: A framework for the effective use of educational technology*, Routledge, London.

Laurillard, D M (1994) 'Multimedia and the changing experience of the learner', paper presented at the Asia Pacific Information Technology in Training and Education Conference, Brisbane, Australia, APITITE 94 Council.

Lee, H B and Allison, G (1992) 'A comparative study of the presentation of anatomy by lectures versus ICAL packages to physiotherapy students', paper presented at the International Interactive Multimedia Symposium, Perth, Western Australia.

Maor, D and Taylor, P (1995) 'Teacher epistemology and scientific inquiry in computerised classroom environments', *Journal of Research in Science Teaching*, New York: John Wiley & Sons, **32**, 839–854.

Marra, R and Jonassen, D (1993) 'Whither constructivism?' *Educational Media and Technology Yearbook*, D Ely, B Minor and C I Englewood (eds), Libraries Unlimited Inc, published in cooperation with ERIC and AECT, pp.56–77.

Nott, M (1995) 'Costs of multimedia compared with other teaching', *Personal communication*, University of Melbourne, Australia.

Posna, G J and Rudnitski, A N (1994) *Course Design*, Longman, London.

Reeves, T C (1992a) 'The effective dimensions of interactive learning systems', paper presented at the Information Technology for Training and Education Conference (ITTE'92), The University of Queensland, Brisbane.

Reeves, T C (1992b) 'Evaluating interactive multimedia', *Educational Technology*, May, 47–52.

Reeves, T C (1992c) *Evaluating Interactive Multimedia: A Book* (Draft 10).

Reeves, T C and Hedberg, J G (1997) 'Evaluating interactive learning.' Unpublished manuscript, University of Georgia, USA, University of Wollongong, Australia.

Slack-Smith, L M and Fox, R (1993) 'Results of the introduction of guided self-study in first year biochemistry: A management perspective', paper presented at the Teaching Learning Forum, Perth, Western Australia, Curtin University of Technology.

Slack-Smith, L, Phillips, R, Benschop, O and Perry, S (1993) 'Making mitochondria meaningful', paper presented at the ASCILITE Conference, Lismore, NSW.

Smith, R M (1983) *Learning How to Learn: Applied theory for adults*, Open University Press, Buckingham.

Smith, W and Hahn, J (1989) 'Hypermedia or hyperchaos: Using hypercard to teach medical decision making', paper presented at the Thirteenth Annual Symposium on Computer Applications in Medical Care, Washington DC.

Sommerville, I (1989) *Software Engineering*, Addison-Wesley, Reading, MA.

Twite, M (1973) *The Age of Cars*, Hamblyn, London.

Wilson, J (1994) 'The CUPLE Physics Studio', *The Physics Teacher*, 32, 578–523.

Winship, J A (1986) *National Software Clearing House Feasibility Study*: Western Australian Institute of Technology.

Winship, J A (1994) *Computing Centre Annual Report*, Curtin University of Technology.

Index

Milton Keynes UK
Ingram Content Group UK Ltd.
UKHW031532071024
449327UK00005B/113